ÅBO ADDRESSES

SOUTH FLORIDA STUDIES IN THE HISTORY OF JUDAISM

Edited by
Jacob Neusner
William Scott Green, James Strange
Darrell J. Fasching, Sara Mandell

Number 22

ÅBO ADDRESSES
and Other Recent Essays on
Judaism in Time and Eternity

by
Jacob Neusner

ÅBO ADDRESSES

and Other Recent Essays on Judaism in Time and Eternity

by

Jacob Neusner

Scholars Press
Atlanta, Georgia

ÅBO ADDRESSES

and Other Recent Essays on Judaism in Time and Eternity

© 1993
University of South Florida

Publication of this book was made possible by a grant from the Tisch Family Foundation, New York City. The University of South Florida acknowledges with thanks this important support for its scholarly projects.

Library of Congress Cataloging in Publication Data

Neusner, Jacob, 1932—
    Åbo addresses : and other recent essays on Judaism in time and eternity / by Jacob Neusner.
        p. cm. — (South Florida studies in the history of Judaism ; no. 22)
    Includes index.
    ISBN 1-55540-933-4
    1. Rabbinical literature—History and criticism. 2. Judaism—History—Talmudic period, 10-425—Historiography. I. Title. II. Series.
BM496.5.N477 1994
296—dc20   93-39349
                                                  CIP

Printed in the United States of America
on acid-free paper

For My Colleagues at

INSTITUTUM JUDAICUM ÅBOENSE
ÅBO AKADEMI
ÅBO, FINLAND

A token of appreciation for five months of intellectual stimulation of
an exceptionally acute order
and also
cordial hospitality of an exemplary character

April through August, 1993

Table of Contents

Preface

Periodic research reports serve as guide posts, allowing me to situate my work and its direction for the benefit of a reading public that is unlikely to consult the monographs themselves. In these pages I spell out work accomplished in connection with my very happy term as Visiting Research Professor, Institutum Judaicum Åboense, Åbo Akademi. These addresses, prepared for students and colleagues in Åbo, Helsinki, Lund, and elsewhere, take up fundamental questions of method and substance. The stimulus for them came from my colleagues in Åbo, among the most sophisticated, and best informed, scholars of the study of Judaism I have found anywhere. The well-focused questions they assigned to me attest to their power to identify fundamental and urgent problems for study.

Specifically, my hosts asked me to set forth my views on some basic issues: how we date Rabbinic documents, what use we can make of attributions in those documents, how I see form-criticism or form-history in the context of Rabbinic compilations, and an overview of where I think we stand in learning on the formative age of the history of Judaism and its literature. The questions on form-criticism, attributions, and dating documents required me to take up issues I have tended to sidestep, and I found them unusually stimulating. I was further asked to speak for the wider public of Åbo, as well as for the Jewish community of Helsingfors, and the fifth and sixth papers served for that purpose. It struck me that, given the present interest in religions' treatment of matters of gender, I should explain in at least a preliminary way why I regard the Judaism of the Dual Torah as androgynous: feminine in the here and now, masculine in the age to come; feminine in its systemic center, masculine in its aspirations. Since I see the Jewish communities throughout the world as having reached a crossroads in their history, I further take up the fundamental question concerning the foundations of Jewish existence.

The occasions were various. The first four were for a seminar conducted in Åbo for the Theological Faculty of Helsinki University, the last two for a wider public both at home in Åbo and elsewhere. The first four questions were set by Dr. Nils Martola, and I responded to them in a systematic way, with the results set forth here; I was struck by the importance, indeed the urgency, of the questions he set for me, and I also was surprised that I had never before formulated a systematic reading of them. The lecture on the Feminization of Judaism was translated from American to Swedish by my Swedish teacher, Robert Paulsson, a student at the University of South Florida, and given by me in Swedish. I gave the same lecture at the Scandinavian Society for Judaic Studies meeting in Lund, also in Swedish. For the Theological Faculty of the University of Lund I also presented the opening lecture, on what I think we know, and what I think we do not yet know, in the study of formative Judaism. That same lecture, of course, outlines some of the research I now plan.

In the same season in which I was writing these lectures, I received an invitation to present the 1993 Bellarmine Lecture at St. Louis University. As is often the case, I wrote several lectures, finally choosing the one that seemed best suited for the occasion. In these pages I present both the one I gave and the one I set aside; the wisdom of the choice, which I owe to Professor William Scott Green's advice, is self-evident.

Since my research professorship at Åbo involved five months of sustained research on my own, I further spell out the work that I did there, outlining the issues and explaining what is at stake in the two projects begun in Florida and completed in Finland. This inquiry concerned, first, the premises and presuppositions of the documents of formative Judaism and is now coming into print in a planned six or seven volumes as *The Judaism Behind the Texts. The Generative Premises of Rabbinic Literature.* Chapter Nine explains the problem on which I worked, and Chapter Ten defines the context in which the problem takes on urgency. I pursued a second project right alongside, examining each text and document from two quite distinct perspectives; this was *From Text to Historical Context in Rabbinic Judaism: Historical Facts in Systemic Documents.* It, too, is now working its way through the press, in a projected five or six volumes. Chapter Eleven sets forth the character of that research. in Åbo I was able to complete both sets of research reports, and I expect that the general results will be spelled out in due course.

I conclude with two occasional papers, one for a magazine in Hong Kong, the other a book review.

No work of mine can omit reference to the exceptionally favorable circumstances in which I conduct my research as Distinguished Research Professor in the Florida State University System at the University of

South Florida. I wrote this book as part of my labor of research scholarship, expressed through both publication and teaching at the University of South Florida, which has afforded me an ideal situation in which to conduct a scholarly life. I express my thanks for not only the advantage of a Distinguished Research Professorship in the Florida State University System, which for a scholar must be the best job in the world, but also of a substantial research expense fund, ample research time, and some stimulating and cordial colleagues. In the prior chapters of my career, I never knew a university that prized professors' scholarship and publication and treated with respect those professors who actively and methodically pursue research.

The University of South Florida, among all ten universities that comprise the Florida State University System as a whole, exemplifies the high standards of professionalism that prevail in publicly sponsored higher education in the USA and provides the model that privately sponsored universities would do well to emulate. Here there are rules, achievement counts, and presidents, provosts, and deans honor and respect the University's principal mission: scholarship, scholarship alone – both in the classroom and in publication. Here at last I find integrity, governing in the lives of people true to their vocation and their mission.

As is clear, I defined the work at hand in conversation with Professor William Scott Green, who gave me substantial help in clearly formulating my problem in its own terms. As ever, I acknowledge my real debt to him for his scholarly acumen and perspicacity.

JACOB NEUSNER

Distinguished Research Professor of Religious Studies
UNIVERSITY OF SOUTH FLORIDA
Tampa, FL 33620-5550 USA

Part One

ÅBO ADDRESSES

1

What Do We Know,
What Don't We Know?
A Mid-Course Assessment

**This lecture was given for the Theological Faculty
of the University of Lund.**

My assignment here is to spell out what I think we now know, and what I think we do not yet know. So I turn to questions that, in my understanding of the state of learning, no longer demand attention, then turn to questions we cannot yet answer. What defines a settled question is the state of public debate. There are ideas that no longer come under serious analysis, debate has moved on to other questions. Then ideas that have fallen away attest to settled issues. That is not to suggest all the believers in a given proposition have taken leave; it is only to point out the simple fact that, in the generality of books, articles, published lectures, sessions at scholarly meetings, one set of premises has given way to another, and a once firm consensus has lost its hearing. Other people now are doing work on the foundation of other presuppositions altogether. In the nature of a subject pursued under diverse institutional auspices, that is a quite natural way in which minds change and agenda shift. The old really never dies; it only loses currency. And as to neglected questions, these are equally simple to identify. They are the ones that, when asked, produce confusion, not consensus. I find three of each classification worthy of attention when we ask about the state of learning in the formative age of Judaism. To give two examples pertinent to Gospels' research: people no longer write harmonies of the Gospels. But they also have reached no consensus about the historical Jesus. That defines settled issues and open questions for that field. How about the one in which I work?

3

I. Settled Issues

1. From Judaism to Judaisms

The generality of learning no longer takes seriously the proposition that there is now, or ever has been, a single Judaism, which defines the norm by which all allegations about what Judaism teaches or imagines are measured. Books on Judaism in the formative age that posit a single, normative Judaism, dismissing as heretical or sectarian evidences that do not conform to the law or theology or that official Judaism no longer gain a serious hearing; outside of the Jewish institutions, textbooks that purport to describe such a single unitary, incremental, official Judaism rarely are adopted; dissertations on such a foundation rarely are written and their authors seldom find positions; and, in all, the fabrication of "normative Judaism" or "Orthodox Judaism," for late antiquity nowadays meets with not so much incredulity as indifference. Efforts to respond to the multiplicity of Judaisms take the place of a single Judaism, and, whether these appeal to the lowest common denominator or allege what was essential to all Judaisms, they respond to the new episteme: not Judaism but Judaisms.

In the study of ancient Judaism, "Judaism" has nearly everywhere given way to "Judaisms," a brief way of stating a complex category. For antiquity, we can find no single Judaism practiced everywhere. We have diverse bodies of writings, which scarcely acknowledge anything in common beyond Scripture. We identify various social groups through archaeological evidence, so asking about the interplay of religion and the social order, and then discover that correlating archaeological and literary evidence presents enormous difficulties for those who wish to harmonize everything into a single Judaism. The conception of a unitary, continuous, incremental "Jewish law," with a beginning, a middle, and a conclusion (for example, in the Talmud of Babylonia) scarcely correlates with the consequences of not only archaeological challenge to some of the laws of documents, but literary evidence, for example, from Elephantine and from Qumran, harmonized only with difficulty with law found in later documents. Analytical questions addressed to diverse documents produce diverse and contradictory answers. If we ask any of the ·bodies of writing deemed to coalesce, apocalyptic, Rabbinic, Christians who identify themselves as Israel, that found in the Dead Sea library, Philo's, Josephus's, not to mention Jewish writing in Greek and Aramaic, the diverse translations of Scripture being only one, if enormous, body of evidence – if we ask the same question to all of these writings, each will give a well-formed answer that stands entirely on its own and contradicts all the others. Whether we ask about God, or Torah, or Israel, to identify the three generative categories of any Judaic religious system (standing for the system's ethos, ethics, and ethnos), what we find is everything and its opposite. Indeed, the real question now demanding attention, as I shall explain, has shifted. If Rabbinic Judaism constitutes a single, coherent Judaism, as is presently broadly taken as fact, then can we find a set of premises that animate all of its canonical writings, and, if so, where and how are we to locate them? The analytical program has now come to a problem of inductive synthesis.

The upshot is simple. The issue, how do we define Judaism, is now settled: we do not. We define Judaisms, and the first step in the work of definition requires identifying the particular Judaic community that stands behind a given set of writings or that values and lives by those writings. All analytical work in the academy proceeds from that premise, and books on Judaism that posit a single, unitary, incremental Judaism, deriving from Sinai through written and oral tradition, command slight attention these days. In that context, books that claim to define essential Judaism or common denominator Judaism simply ratify the change that has taken place; in the sectarian world, people did not find urgent the problem that such books propose to solve. Consequently, we find ourselves asking theological questions concerning the coherence of discrete truths, but we propose to answer those questions out of not doctrine but, for literary study, hermeneutics. Precisely where the Jewish sponsored centers of learning alleged to locate their greatest strengths – exegesis of texts, philology, even text criticism – the academy has now to carry its venture. For we cannot abdicate the most grave intellectual responsibility of all: the reading of the texts in the new, and sole right way.

2. From History to Religion

History and its agendum of identifying historical fact from religious fancy has now proved simply, monumentally irrelevant to the very sources that were supposed to contain it. History gave way to religion because of the recognition, a given in the study of religion, that the canonical writings of Judaism are fundamentally religious books, framing an account of a Judaic religious system. A further factor in the decline of interest in history as the study of what really happened lay in the fact that the study of religion encompassed history within a different definition. The academy's insistence that a religious system deals in a fundamental way with an urgent and ineluctable question that faces a social entity, and that that system provides an answer deemed self-evidently valid to the question people confront – these redefine the study of history. The Judaisms of late antiquity then have come to form a laboratory case for the examination of religion and society: religion as something people do together to solve their problems.

History asks about matters of origin and development, claiming to explain things when it can account for the order in which they took place and the connections among them. But by the time religions produce the documents that permit us to study them in historical context, they have long passed their point of origin. We describe systems mainly from their end products, the writings. But we have then to work our way back from canon to system, not to imagine either that the canon is the system, or that the canon creates the system. The canonical writings speak, in particular, to those who can hear, that is, to the members of the community, who, on account of that perspicacity of hearing, constitute the social entity or systemic community. The community then comprises that social group the system of which is recapitulated by the selected canon. The group's exegesis of the canon in terms of the everyday imparts to the system the power to sustain the community in a reciprocal and self-nourishing process. The community through its exegesis then imposes continuity and unity on whatever is in its canon. The writings then yield a different kind of information from that which conventional historians require. Most of the questions of origin and development that historians claim to answer cannot find answers in the evidence canonical writings provide, as historians of Christianity have found in their work on the Gospels and Church traditions. But the canonical evidence answers other, and in the view of many, more urgent and formidable questions of religious persistence: Why this, not that?

While, therefore, we cannot account for the origin of a successful religious-social system, we can explain its power to persist. It is a symbolic transaction in which social change comes to expression in symbol change. That symbolic transaction, specifically, takes place in its exegesis of the systemic canon, which, in literary terms, constitutes the social entity's statement of itself. So, once more, the texts recapitulate the system. The system does not recapitulate the texts. The system comes before the texts and defines the canon. The exegesis of the canon then forms that ongoing social action that sustains the whole. A system does not recapitulate its texts, it selects and orders them. A religious system imputes to them as a whole cogency, one to the next, that their original authorships have not expressed in and through the parts, and through them a religious system expresses its deepest logic, *and it also frames that just fit that joins system to circumstance.*

The whole works its way out through exegesis, and the history of any religious system – that is to say, the history of religion writ small – is the exegesis of its exegesis. And the first rule of the exegesis of systems is the simplest, and the one with which I conclude: *The system does not recapitulate the canon. The canon recapitulates the system.* The system forms a statement of a social entity, specifying its worldview and way of life in such a way that, to the participants in the system, the whole makes sound sense, beyond argument. So in the beginning are not words of inner and intrinsic affinity, but (as Philo would want us to say) the Word: the transitive logic, the system, all together, all at once, complete, whole, finished – the word awaiting only that labor of exposition and articulation that the faithful, for centuries to come, will lavish at the altar of the faith. A religious system therefore presents a fact not of history but of immediacy, of the social present.

3. From "The (Unitary, Indifferentiated) Tradition" to the Integrity of Singular Documents

"Judaism teaches," "The Talmud says," followed by a proposition alleged to characterize all of the writings – that trait characterizes the episteme of Judaism – seen as a single, unitary, harmonious, incremental "tradition" – as against that of Judaisms; it also governs how the documents are read. In the world of a single Judaism every document contains "Torah," and that "Torah," lacking all history or other differentiating traits, occurs everywhere and anywhere. Consequently, we have no reason to read any document from beginning to end and by itself. Our task is to collect whatever all documents say on a determinate subject and so define the Judaic position on said subject. The Judaic equivalent of "the harmony of the Gospels," which is, "The Talmudic and Midrashic View of...," defines the documentary hermeneutics of parochial scholarship, yielding a labor-saving device of hunting and gathering, collecting and arranging, topical sayings. That is the result of not sloth or even stupidity but a hermeneutics that commences with the unity, historical and theological, of all canonical writings.

A theological premise, serving the religious institutions, drew attention to the status, as Torah, of all writings; if each document finds its undifferentiated place within the (oral part of the) Torah, then little effort will go toward differentiating one document from another. A historical premise concerning the contents of documents serves equally well to account for the problems not ordinarily addressed in the same setting. If, as we have seen, we take as fact all statements (except those concerning miracles) in all writings of the canon, then our inquiry concerns the facts documents supply; we shall take a position of indifference to the venue, origin, auspices, and authority, as to historical fact, of a given document and to relationships of documents to one another. All are held to draw indifferently upon a corpus of "tradition," deemed to have circulated orally hither and yon before coming to rest in a particular compilation. Therefore, it was taken for granted, we open a document and come up with a fact, and which document yields what fact bears little meaning.

Not only so, but the paramount trait of all documents – their constant attribution of sayings to named authorities – afforded a distinct point of differentiation, namely, the names of authorities. Whatever is given to a specific name, whether in a document that reached closure ("only") two hundred years after he flourished or as long as five hundred or a thousand years later, serves equally well to tell us what said authority really thought and stated. Lives of Talmudic masters, along with histories of Talmudic times, therefore brought together, collected, and arranged in intelligible order, attributed sayings without a shred of interest in the time or place or circumstance of the documents that preserved them. The upshot, once more, was simple: considerations of time and circumstance do not register; every writing is equally useful; all may be assumed to wish to make the same, factual contribution to "the Torah," and, for the secular, history consists in opening a document, pointing to a sentence, paraphrasing the sense of that sentence, and speculating on its meaning: a labor of paraphrase and pure fabrication.

Today, by contrast, people understand that the documents viewed as free-standing and autonomous require description, analysis, and interpretation. Each exhibits its own differentiating traits. Not only do people grasp that the Mishnah is different from Leviticus Rabbah which is different from the Talmud of Babylonia. They also understand that each of those documents sets forth its own program in its own way. Systematic analyses of distinguishing traits of rhetoric, the logic of coherent discourse, and the topical programs of the various documents leave no ambiguity. Each writing exhibits its own formal traits, and each sets forth its own message. No document is readily confused with any other. Many, though not all, exhibit a cogency of program, working on the same few questions time and again. What that means for the received, sectarian episteme is simple. The point of origin of a given saying or story governs our reading and use of the item. True, some sayings and stories occur in more than a single document. The changes and developments of these items as they make their journey from here to there have to be traced, accounted for, if possible, in terms of the interests of the framers of the documents that make use of them. Among the parochial scholars, occurrence of the same sayings in the name of a single authority in two or more documents yielded "he often said." A different conception now prevails.

Scholars who take for granted that the Gospels yield not a single, harmonious life of Jesus but several distinct statements will hardly find surprising these simple rules of analysis. Each of the Rabbinic documents – the Mishnah, Tosefta, Midrash compilations, the two Talmuds – represents its own compilers, their taste and judgment in selecting from available compositions what they used and neglecting what they did not, their program in organizing and arranging and formulating matters in one way, rather than in some other. The collective statement and consensus of authorships (none is credibly assigned to a single author and all are preserved because they are deemed canonical and authoritative) and show us how those authorships proposed to make a statement to their situation.

II. Neglected Questions

1. Dating Documents

With documents bearing no named author, coming to us in an indeterminate and sparse textual tradition, we have yet to formulate a valid means for dating, or even a clear definition of what we might mean by assigning a date to a document. It is easier to explain what we do not now know than to define what we should want to find out.

The established protocol for dating a document rests on the premise that statements attributed to a given rabbi really were said by a historical figure, at a determinate time, and so permit us to date the document at the time or, or just after, that figure; if all the rabbis of a document occur in the Mishnah as well, then that document is assigned to the period of the Mishnah and given a date of ca. 200. If the last-named rabbi of a document is assumed to have lived in ca. 500, then the document gets the date of 501. In general, documents presently are dated by reference to the names of the authorities who occur in them, for example, if the last-named authority is a rabbi who flourished in the Mishnah's period, the document as a whole is assigned to "Tannaitic times," that is, the first and second centuries, when, it is generally supposed, the Mishnah came to closure. But that date then presupposes the reliability of attributions and does not take account of pseudepigraphy in the rabbinic manner. The same sayings may be assigned to two or more authorities; the Talmud of Babylonia, moreover, presents ample evidence that people played fast and loose with attributions, changing by reason of the requirements of logic what a given authority is alleged to have said, for instance. Since we have ample evidence that in later times, people made up sayings and put them into the mouths of earlier authorities (the Zohar is only the best known example!), we have no reason to assign a document solely by reference to the names of the authorities found therein. But no other basis for dating documents than gullibility about their contents has yet been devised, and, since language usages are dated (in the Judaic and Jewish institutions) in accord with the dates of sages to whom sayings are attributed, philology provides no help whatsoever.

Precisely what we date in dating a document proves less clear than once was supposed. Studies of the enormous variation in the formulation of writings given the same title, for example, some of the so-called mystical texts, make us wonder what, exactly, we date when we assign a date to a writing. Is it every word in the writing? Then what are we to make of the uncertain text tradition of every rabbinic compilation, beginning, after all, with the Mishnah itself? But if the date does not situate at a determinate time (and place) the entirety of the document, then what in fact is alleged?

A further problem arises in this context. If a document is assigned, for convenience's sake, to ca. 400 or ca. 600, people take for granted that the document accurately portrays the state of opinion not only at that specific time but for any time prior, the attributions of sayings to earlier authorities being taken at face value. It is commonly argued that merely because a saying occurs in a writing assigned the date of 200, that does not mean that the writing conveys no accurate information on opinions held prior to 200. If that view prevails, then we have to ask what else we know if we are supposed to know that the document was redacted (or reached closure) in 200? New Testament scholarship places a heavy burden on Rabbinic literature to portray the Judaism of the first century, the Judaism that Jesus and Paul knew. But nearly all New Testament scholars today rightly dismiss as uncritical the promiscuous citation, for that purpose, of Rabbinic writings dated many centuries after the first. Clearly, we have reached a negative consensus; it is time to frame a positive one, beginning with a clear formulation of what "dating a document" requires – and explains.

These and comparable problems on the dating of documents await rigorous reflection. Right now, we are working with the results of confused categories. The only fact now in hand is simple. We have a reasonably reliable order of writings, the Mishnah standing at the head of the line, the Talmud of Babylonia at the end, between 200 and 600. All histories of ideas formed on documentary lines then tell us what came first and what happened then, but we have no clear knowledge of when the "first" or the "then" took place. When a well-grounded consensus on what we mean by a date for a document, as well as how we may determine the date of the document's contents, has taken shape, all historical work, including the histories of ideas that provide such academic history of the formation of Judaism as we now have, will be redone, and, I think, even redefined.

2. Systemic Statement of Documents Read as a Whole

When we dismiss as wrong-headed the reading of documents all together and all at once, it is because that reading contradicts the material traits of the documents themselves. That explains why a rereading of the documents, one by one, has now taken place, and it also accounts for the necessity of others' rereading the same documents and examining the differentiating data from fresh perspectives. The work of documentary description confronts each generation of active scholars.

But reading the documents one by one certainly does not exempt us from the task of saying how things fit together, what they said when read whole as a coherent statement. Rather, the documentary composition of the canon redefines the task of description. Once we do not take for granted that all of the writings say the same thing about everything, then our task is to find out how the writings say some one thing about anything. The task of theological description, of systemic analysis of wholes, not only parts, proves still more formidable than before. It is the simple fact that all of the writings of a given Judaism cohere in the community of those who valued those writings and regarded them as authoritative. But then we must ask ourselves how that community knew what mattered and what did not matter all that much, what defined and what merely refined matters, above all, how diverse and implicitly contradictory legal or theological conceptions held together in a cogent and coherent way. For communities suffer contradictions because they perceive only their own coherence, so our task is to investigate the intellectual foundations of coherence in a diverse and complex canon. Christians will understand the issue perfectly well when they remind themselves of the familiar issue of whether there was a pattern of Christian truth or simply a mass of competing heresies. It follows that a question neglected until now is simple: What holds together the various writings deemed canonical by a given Judaism? Is there a Judaism behind these texts, to the task of the expression of some aspect of which each text is assigned? Or, viewing the authoritative writings as a whole, are we able to identify premises that govern throughout, presuppositions that characterize all these writings but no others?

Some things tell us what is necessary for any religious system to find a place as a Judaism (the "essential" or "lowest common denominator" Judaism of some recent studies). All Judaisms differ from all other religious systems of their time and place because they exhibit in common traits that nowhere else come to the fore. But what is necessary for all Judaisms does not suffice for the description, analysis, and interpretation of any one of them; for Judaisms cohere but also differ, and a sufficient description therefore explains not only cogency but also incoherence. Here therefore we revert to the distinction between what is necessary and what is sufficient. Some premises are necessary to any Judaism, but insufficient to account for the shape and structure of any particular Judaism. What makes a Judaic system important is what marks that system as entire and imparts to that system its integrity: what makes it different from other systems, what holds that system together. Defining that single, encompassing "Judaism" into which genus all species, all Judaisms, fit helps us understand nothing at all about the various Judaisms. But all we really have in hand are the artifacts of Judaisms. Efforts to find that one Judaism that holds together all Judaisms yields suffocating banalities and useless platitudes: we do not understand anything in particular any better than we did before we had thought up such generalities. So by "generative premises," I mean, the premises that counted: those that provoked the framers of a document's ideas to do their work, that made urgent the questions they address, that imparted self-evidence to the answers they set forth.

3.   Exegesis of the Talmud of Babylonia (the Bavli)

How can anyone maintain that the exegesis of the Talmud represents a neglected question, when, after all, the yeshivas and some of the rabbinical seminaries devote their best energies to the study of that Talmud, its commentaries and codes and the law based therein? They rightly maintain that the Talmud re-presents the law and theology of the entire Torah, oral and written, that the world calls "Judaism." Not only so, but the American and European rabbinical seminaries as well as the Hebrew colleges deservedly take pride in their studies of problems of philology and exegesis. While, to be sure, they have yet to produce a complete dictionary for Rabbinic literature, a complete corpus of critical texts for its main documents, and a reliable account of the meanings of words and phrases in context – the three tasks at which they claim to have succeeded – still, the parochials have centered their best energies on problems of exegesis and philology. It is the simple fact that, in the past half-century, marked by the growing prominence of the Talmud in public discourse, not a single sustained, ambitious, systematic exegetical enterprise has gotten underway; most of the work that has been done recapitulates received answers to conventional questions, forming a massive paraphrase, not an introduction in any provocative sense.

But exegesis of a text takes shape in response to the hermeneutics that defines how we wish to receive the document, and hermeneutics finds its definition in the intellectual framework of learning, whether theological, whether historical. Two bodies of received exegesis presently are deemed to suffice. The first is the paraphrastic and legal, given its definitive form in the yeshiva world by the exegetical genius, R. Solomon Isaac of Troyes ("Rashi"), 1040-1105. The simple meaning of words and phrases in context is conveyed by that exegetical mode, and the hermeneutics that comes to realization in that essential exegesis need not detain us; there is no reading of the Talmud without solutions to the problems of reconstruction into cogent statements of what are in fact notes on a conversation to be reconstituted by our own intellects. Rashi provides those solutions. The second exegesis indeed is the philological and text critical, and that, too, conforms to the rule that exegesis is the child of hermeneutics. The critical program of the world of the rabbinical seminaries and Israeli universities dictates the inquiry of philological and text critical exegesis. And, it must follow, the new setting for the study of ancient Judaism and its texts has also to generate a hermeneutics, and a consequent program of exegesis, the shape and structure of which are dictated by the intellectual forces in play where we are now working.

The exegesis that now is required takes shape in response to a simple fact: in the academy, we find our place within that same intellectual tradition that governed the intellectual lives of the framers of the Talmud itself. We understand the Talmud when it is properly mediated to us because we are the children of the great tradition of intellect in which the Talmud, too, took shape. The Talmud is itself a philosophical document in the conventional sense in which "philosophy" refers specifically to the Greco-Roman philosophical tradition. Formed in that same tradition, our minds therefore enter into the Talmud, requiring only a modest introduction to its particularities. That explains why we can join in the conversation, the spaces of silence leaving open to us a place even for our own active intellects.

That shared rationality explains the self-evidence of connections that are made, conclusions that are drawn. The matter of connection is prior. No document takes more for granted concerning relationships and connections, one thing to the next, than this one, and anyone reading this writing will find puzzling how one thing links to the last or the next. So a systematic exegesis in the setting of the academy must ask for an explanation of what was self-evident in the yeshiva and seminary: How do two matters (in the Talmud, meaning whole compositions set in sequence) relate, and what conclusions we are to draw from their deliberate juxtaposition by the Talmud itself? Since the Talmud's discipline requires us to follow the shifts and turnings of a protracted analytical argument, the very dialectics of the document to begin with requires us to ask the question: What has this to do with that? And if we do not ask that question, we know for certain we are not following the argument at all. The program at hand demands that we examine the very character of the Talmud as a work of critical reflection, writing, and redaction: What does it say about a fundamental question, how does it make the successive parts of its statement, and in what manner do the components of the statement link together to form a whole that exceeds the sum of the parts?

The principles of exegesis may involve identifying these data of one passage after another:

1. A Mishnaic rule is philosophical in its categorical structure;

2. The Talmud examines that rule within the received Mishnaic categories;

3. But there is a point at which the connection between one thing and something else requires elucidation, and that is the point at which, the Talmud (by definition) having fallen silent, we intervene.

4. The work of exegesis then responds to the issue of connection when we explain the connections and draw the conclusions.

When the Talmud arouses our curiosity, it also leaves space for our own inquiry. Where a new point is not continuous with the other, the exegesis within the academy is going to ask why. Indeed, the connection between the exposition of the received categories of the Mishnah and the introduction of an entirely new consideration has to be established, meaning, rationally explained. If we can draw a rational conclusion, a theological conclusion, from that odd juxtaposition, the adventitious intersection of two distinct compositions becomes a deliberate statement, and imposes upon us the task of reasoned inquiry into the substance of that statement. It is at the specific point of discontinuity – the boundary marked by the conclusion of the Mishnah exposition by the Talmud, followed by the turning toward what is jarring and discontinuous – that our particular entry point opens up. Then we ask, what has this got to do with that? And we answer the question for ourselves. And that is the particular point at which we join the conversation: we do so by making a connection, or by explaining the connection between what is merely juxtaposed but superficially discontinuous. Then we draw a conclusion from the connection we have explained; the discord now has been resolved, harmony restored: a single message formed out of two discrete statements.

The premise of all that has been said is that the Talmud is the way its framers wanted it to be. The document conforms to its teleology; then we may seek out the connections between this and that and draw rational conclusions from those connections. This we do by explaining how what is juxtaposed in fact interrelates. So if the compilation of the Talmud is deliberate and not simply the juxtaposition without purpose of thematically congruent materials, then the Talmud makes a powerful statement not only through the contents of its compositions (which really form the nouns of its sentences) nor the context defined by its composites (the verbs of the sentences) but through the selection, formulation, and presentation of the whole – which is what we mean by hermeneutics, the explication of a received texts, and the rules thereof.

Read from start to finish, meaning, from one Mishnah paragraph to the conclusion of its Talmud, the Talmud turns out to make a statement, not merely to collect relevant composites of compositions. So the hermeneutics of the Talmud consists in showing the connections between things; the theology of Judaism as re-presented by the Talmud, the formulation of the two Torahs, oral and written, as one, emerges from drawing conclusions on the strength of the making of connections. And, it is self-evident, these things being left implicit in the text, for us to discover, the hermeneutics dictates the asking of questions concerning what is not said or even suggested, meaning in this case what one thing has to do with something else. I could not find a better way of saying what the academy takes as a principal intellectual task than that – making connections, drawing conclusions, from things people have formerly thought unrelated.

The next important task in the study of formative Judaism calls for the rereading of the definitive document of that Judaism, which is the Talmud of Babylonia. In no language at this time do we find a reading of the whole, or of any of its parts, that sees the document in a coherent way, as a cogent statement. Talmudic exegesis goes forward with no articulated hermeneutics, and the meanings of words and phrases, on the one side, or the episodic and unsystematic search for the original wording and meaning of passages now in hand, on the other, define the current work of Talmud commentary. That work is ignored in the yeshiva world because it answers no questions important to that world. And it also contributes nothing to the humanistic reading of the document, since the exegetes have no grasp whatsoever of the entirety of the document they purpose to explain, only its bits and pieces. We may now say with some certainty that the greatest authorities of the Talmud in our century really did not understand Rabbinic literature, since they saw only the twigs, never the branch, never the tree, never the forest. It follows that, if the academy is to do its work, the next step leads to a rereading of, therefore a commentary to, the Talmud of Babylonia. It is not premature to announce the title of the one I now undertake: *Making Connections and Drawing Conclusions. An Academic Commentary to the Talmud.*

Combining the categories "academic" and "Talmud" forms the appropriate point of conclusion. For I can imagine no two things formerly thought unrelated but now formed into a close and constant union than the holy books of the Torah, on the one side, and the academy, on the other. What has Athens to do with Jerusalem? is a question now rephrased by circumstance, what has the Talmud – which stands for Judaism in its formative age – to do with the university? The last decade in this journal attests to the naturalization, into the academy, of a formerly alien tradition of learning. Quickly settled issues leave open the way for a long and leisurely encounter with neglected questions of considerable weight and acute relevance to the study of religion in the academic humanities. The editorship that now draws to a close marks, for what it published in this field and for what it did not publish, the turning.

2

Dating the Documents of Formative Judaism – and Their Contents

**This lecture was given for the Theological Faculty of
Helsinki University at a study day held in Åbo.**

My assignment is to deal with the following question: "The question
of attributions: On dating documents, are there any absolute dates?
What are the main criteria for relative dating?" To answer this question
directly: there are no absolute dates. The criteria for relative dating – one
document is prior to another in time because the (theoretically) later
document can be shown to cite the (theoretically) earlier one – serve
where they serve, which is to say, episodically. Let me spell out these
two points and then reformulate the question in a much different way.

We have no basis on which to assign a firm, specific, determinate
date to any document of the Judaism of the Dual Torah, not the Mishnah,
not Tosefta or Sifra, not the Talmud of the Land of Israel or the one of
Babylonia, not Genesis Rabbah or Leviticus Rabbah or The Fathers
According to Rabbi Nathan – not to a single compilation of any kind. We
have reasonable grounds on which to place some of the documents into
relationship with one another. Specifically, when a composition is
primary to one document but secondary to another, then the document
to which the composition is secondary may be assumed to have reached
closure later than the document to which said composition is primary.
Determinations of what is primary or secondary rest on quite formal,
therefore objective, criteria. If the formal traits of a composition shared
between two compilations are definitive in the one but found in the other
only in items shared with the one, then the composition is primary to the
one to the definitive traits of which it conforms, and secondary to the
other.

A concrete example comes to us from the Mishnah, which occurs also in the two Talmuds, Tosefta, and Sifra. That the Mishnah is prior to Sifra is shown very simply. The Mishnah is cited verbatim in Tosefta and Sifra. The formal traits dominant in Sifra involve citation of a verse of Scripture followed by a few words of paraphrase or extension, often with some secondary development; the formal traits dominant in the Mishnah involve simple declarative sentences, disputes, and other free-standing formulations, rarely including citation and paraphrase of a verse of Scripture. Where we find in Sifra free-standing propositional compositions, they ordinarily are shared with the Mishnah; materials particular to Sifra do not exhibit the formal traits of said compositions. So, it follows, the materials common to the Mishnah and Sifra are primary to the Mishnah and secondary to Sifra, which cites them for its own purposes; and, it further follows, Sifra is later than the Mishnah, which it cites. The same argument of course applies to the two Talmuds. But this mode of placing into an order of temporal priority a sequence of documents serves only where it serves, and the conception that Genesis Rabbah and Leviticus Rabbah are fifty years later than the Talmud of the Land of Israel rests on nothing so tangible as the type of evidence I have just now set forth.

My documentary history of ideas rests on the order of documents, in some instances demonstrable, as just noted, in others, a matter of conventional opinion at this time. People generally suppose that we have a reasonably reliable order of writings, the Mishnah standing at the head of the line, the Talmud of Babylonia at the end, between 200 and 600. Histories of ideas formed on documentary lines then tell us what came first and what happened then, as the sequence of documents permits us to trace the unfolding or the sequential treatments of a given idea. Still, we have no clear knowledge of when the "first" or the "then" took place. When a well-grounded consensus on what we mean by a date for a document, as well as how we may determine the date of the document's contents, has taken shape, all historical work, including the histories of ideas that provide such academic history of the formation of Judaism as we now have, will be redone, and, I think, even redefined. But the documentary history of ideas and the history of ideas obviously stand at some distance from one another. The one is relative to the order of writings, but does not permit us to localize a particular idea within a particular historical context or circumstance, let alone to relate such an idea to the events of a specific time and place.

Now to generalize: with documents such as those of Rabbinic Judaism, bearing no named author, coming to us in an indeterminate and sparse textual tradition, we have yet to formulate a valid means for dating, or even a clear definition of what we might mean by assigning a date to a document. It is easier to explain what we do not now know than to define what we should want to find out. This minimalist position of course contradicts the maximalist one that reigns in the standard accounts of Rabbinic documents and their dates.

That position assigns very specific dates to the various rabbinic documents; these assignments take for granted a position rejected by nearly the entire academic world, which is: believe everything unless you find reason to doubt something, the formulation regnant at last glance in the Jerusalem school, the Jewish seminaries of the USA, and other centers of the study of Judaism other than academic ones. Since all documents present numerous attributed statements, we date the various documents in accord with the assumed dates of the authorities that are cited in them. Now this conception, gullible and primitive and nearly universally rejected, yields groupings of documents, for example, before 200 are "Tannaite" in that all the authorities in said compilations are assumed to have flourished in the first and second centuries. Not only so, but attributions date sayings within documents, so the date of 200 signifies not only closure at that time but also the latest date for whatever is unattributed in the document; much that is in the document, in accord with this theory, is much earlier.

Most talmudic historians, and all of them in the State of Israel, accept as fact all attributions of sayings and therefore assume that if a document's authorship presents a saying in a given sage's name, that sage really made such a statement, which therefore tells us what he, and perhaps others, were thinking in the time and place in which he lived. A corollary to this position is that a saying that bears no attribution is "earlier than" a saying that has one. Hence what is anonymous is older than what is assigned (how much older depends on the requirement of the person who assumes that fact). If, for instance, we have a named saying and, in context, an anonymous one that bears a contrary view, the anonymous saying is not deemed contemporary with the named saying on the same topic but earlier than the assigned one. It goes without saying that much energy goes into restating these propositions, but not much has been invested in demonstrating them. That is, of course, because they lie far beyond the limits of the evidence. Still, these two complementary positions presuppose a literary process in which sayings circulated independently of the documents in which they (later on) are written down and took shape within the circle of the disciples of a master to whom they are attributed. That position on the literary process that yields the documents that now contain these sayings has not yet been squared with the literary traits of those same documents, and analysis of those traits scarcely sustains the hypothesis of inerrant attribution and its corollary. These results of course also dictate the dates of documents.

Tannaite documents contain only authorities who occur in the Mishnah, so they all are supposed to originate before ca. 200, even though, as a matter of fact, they ordinarily cite the Mishnah and therefore ought to be dated later than the Mishnah, after 200, and I think, much later.

I do not exaggerate. Consult any encyclopedia, and you will find that the Mishnah was redacted in 200, the Talmud of Babylonia in 500, and so on and so forth. One consideration makes improbable the certainty that presently prevails. The established protocol for dating a document rests on the premise that statements attributed to a given rabbi really were said by a historical figure, at a determinate time, and so permit us to date the document at the time, or just after, that figure; if all the rabbis of a document occur in the Mishnah as well, then that document is assigned to the period of the Mishnah and given a date of ca. 200. If the last-named rabbi of a document is assumed to have lived in ca. 500, then the document gets the date of 501. In general, documents presently are dated by reference to the names of the authorities who occur in them, for example, if the last-named authority is a rabbi who flourished in the Mishnah's period, the document as a whole is assigned to "Tannaitic times," that is, the first and second centuries, when, it is generally supposed, the Mishnah came to closure. But that date then presupposes the reliability of attributions and does not take account of pseudepigraphy in the rabbinic manner. The same sayings may be assigned to two or more authorities; the Talmud of Babylonia, moreover, presents ample evidence that people played fast and loose with attributions, changing by reason of the requirements of logic what a given authority is alleged to have said, for instance. Since we have ample evidence that in later times, people made up sayings and put them into the mouths of earlier authorities (the Zohar is only the best known example!), we have no reason to assign a document solely by reference to the names of the authorities found therein.

But no other basis for dating documents than gullibility about their contents has yet been devised, and, since language usages are dated (in the Judaic and Jewish institutions) in accord with the dates of sages to whom sayings are attributed, dates that derive from Gaonic historians who flourished half a millennium after the times of those to whom they assign precise dates, philology provides no help whatsoever. Not only so, but the so-called philological dating, based on language usages, rests on precisely the same premise. If a saying is attributed to Aqiba, that means the usage of language in that saying attests to first or early second century conventions, and, consequently, other such usages also place the documents that contain them in the first or early second century. What we have therefore is simply an extension, to the dating of documents and of their contents, of the familiar gullibility and credulity of Talmudic studies: our holy rabbis really made these statements, so the rest follows.

The problem of dating documents proves still more complicated by two further considerations. First, precisely what we date in dating a document proves less clear than once was supposed. Studies of the enormous variation in the formulation of writings given the same title, for example, some of the so-called mystical texts, make us wonder what, exactly, we date when we assign a date to a writing. Is it every word in the writing? Then what are we to make of the uncertain text tradition of every rabbinic compilation, beginning, after all, with the Mishnah itself? But if the date does not situate at a determinate time (and place) the entirety of the document, then what in fact is alleged?

Second, if a document is assigned, for convenience's sake, to ca. 400 or ca. 600, people take for granted that the document accurately portrays the state of opinion not only at that specific time but for any time prior, the attributions of sayings to earlier authorities being taken at face value. It is commonly argued that merely because a saying occurs in a writing assigned the date of 200, that does not mean that the writing conveys no accurate information on opinions held prior to 200. If that view prevails, then we have to ask what else we know if we are supposed to know that the document was redacted (or reached closure) in 200? New Testament scholarship places a heavy burden on Rabbinic literature to portray the Judaism of the first century, the Judaism that Jesus and Paul knew. But nearly all New Testament scholars today rightly dismiss as uncritical the promiscuous citation, for that purpose, of Rabbinic writings dated many centuries after the first. Clearly, we have reached a negative consensus; it is time to frame a positive one, beginning with a clear formulation of what "dating a document" requires – and explains.

Any account of dating documents, moreover, must take account of a very broadly held method of assigning dates to the contents of documents, that is, to the composition held together in large-scale compositions. That the method I shall set forth still serves will surprise colleagues who work in the more sophisticated fields of ancient studies, such as critical study of biblical history, for example, but in work in the Hebrew language that is set forth as exemplary, that of Gedaliahu Alon, reprinted only a few years ago by Harvard University Press without a line to suggest the forty-year-old work had been criticized and in fact superseded, this mode of analysis is routine. I therefore do not exaggerate the primitive state of thought on dating documents when I call attention to the method of dating documents by appeal to their contents. Specifically, a fixed trait of mind characteristic of the received, and uncritical, tradition in the use of talmudic tales for historical purposes instructs us to "date" stories by their contents. This works two ways, one positive, the other negative. If a story refers to the destruction of the Temple, for example, then that story was made up after A.D. 70, a reasonable, if trivial, supposition. That positive evidence is uncommon and therefore solves few problems. The negative side tells us that if a story does not "know" about a certain important event or fact, then said story was made up, or reflects conditions, prior to that event. The possibility that the storyteller may have chosen not to refer to that important event is not considered, and other explanations for the allegedly indicative negative trait of the story are not proposed.

Not only so, but in a given document, stories and sayings are treated as individual and autonomous units, without relationship to the larger document in which they are found. Consequently, if a given story or saying in a document omits reference to what is regarded as an emblematic event, then without any reference to the literary setting in which the saying occurs, that saying, raised up out of its context, is assigned to a provenience prior to the event at hand. In these two ways stories are not only dated through their silences, but they also are represented out of all relationship to the documents that now preserve said stories. There is yet a third trait of mind. If we have two or more versions of a given story, then both of them, of course, refer to things that really happened – but different events. Consequently, if a given story comes to us in diverse documents, and each document tells the tale in its own way, we may be asked to believe that each story describes its own event. These three principles of historical explanation derive from ancient times but go forward into the twenty-first century. And that is why it is important to review them, first, in their realization in the classical texts of Judaism. Only then shall we understand how, in the hands of contemporary, younger scholars, they live on.

Sages of ancient times recognized that sayings and stories appeared in diverse versions. They, too, proposed explanations of how a given saying or story could come down in more than a single statement. The principal approach to the question posited that each detail represented a different stage in the history of the story, or of the life of its hero in particular, with one version characteristic of one such stage, and another version attesting to a different, and later one. So the successive versions of a saying or story supply a kind of incremental history. How so? Each version tells something about concrete events and real lives (biographies) that earlier versions did not reveal. The classic Talmudic expression of the incremental theory takes up a passage of the Mishnah in which Rabban Yohanan ben Zakkai is called merely "Ben Zakkai":

The precedent is as follows:

Ben Zakkai examined a witness as to the character of the stalks of figs [under which an incident now subject to court procedure was alleged to have taken place] [Mishnah Sanhedrin 5:2B].

Exactly the same story is reported, on Tannaite authority. Now *Rabban Yohanan* ben Zakkai is alleged to have made exactly the same ruling, in exactly the same case. The item is worded in the same way except for the more fitting title. Then, at P-Q, the two versions are readily explained as facts of history. The one of Ben Zakkai was framed when he was a mere disciple. When, later on, he had become a recognized sage, the story was told to take account of that fact. So the theory I call "incremental history" is simple: each story related to, because it derives from, historical moments in a linear progression. The Talmudic passage, which appears at Babylonian Talmud Sanhedrin 41a-b, is as follows:

IX.   A.   Who is this "Ben Zakkai"?

        B.   If we should proposed that it is R. Yohanan ben Zakkai, did he ever sit in a sanhedrin [that tried a murder case]?

        C.   And has it not been taught on Tannaite authority:

        D.   The lifetime of R. Yohanan ben Zakkai was a hundred and twenty years. For forty years he engaged in trade, for forty years he studied [Torah], and for forty years he taught.

        E.   And it has been taught on Tannaite authority: Forty years before the destruction of the Temple the sanhedrin went into exile and conducted its sessions in Hanut.

        F.   And said R. Isaac bar Abodimi, "That is to say that the sanhedrin did not judge cases involving penalties."

        G.   Do you think it was cases involving penalties? [Such cases were not limited to the sanhedrin but could be tried anywhere in the Land of Israel!]

        H.   Rather, the sanhedrin did not try capital cases.

        I.   And we have learned in the Mishnah:

        J.   After the destruction of the house of the sanctuary, Rabban Yohanan b. Zakkai ordained... [M. R.H. 4:1]. [So the final forty years encompassed the period after the destruction of the Temple, and Yohanan could not, therefore, have served on a sanhedrin that tried capital cases.]

        K.   Accordingly, at hand is some other Ben Zakkai [than Yohanan b. Zakkai].

        L.   That conclusion, moreover, is reasonable, for if you think that it is Rabban Yohanan ben Zakkai, would Rabbi [in the Mishnah passage] have called him merely, "Ben Zakkai"? [Not very likely.]

        M.   And lo, it has been taught on Tannaite authority:

        N.   There is the precedent that Rabban Yohanan ben Zakkai conducted an interrogation about the stalks on the figs [so surely this is the same figure as at M. 5:2B].

The key language is as follows, given in italics:

O.   *But [at the time at which the incident took place, capital cases were tried by the sanhedrin and] he was a disciple in session before his master. He said something, and the others found his reasoning persuasive, [41B] so they adopted [the ruling] in his name.*

P.   *When he was studying Torah, therefore, he was called Ben Zakkai, as a disciple in session before his master, but when he [later on] taught, he was called Rabban Yohanan ben Zakkai.*

Q.   *When, therefore, he is referred to as Ben Zakkai, it is on account of his being a beginning [student] and when he is called Rabban Yohanan b. Zakkai, it is on account of his status later on.*

On the basis of this analysis, scholars of the life of Yohanan ben Zakkai present the two versions as formulations of his opinion at different stages in his career. We have here the model, out of antiquity, for modes of thought characteristic of contemporary scholarship of an order I regard as primitive and uncritical.

So much for the problem and the received solutions. Let me now frame the problem in my own way. I state at the outset I do not know how to date documents. But I can make a contribution to the formulation of the question. For that purpose we turn to the elementary issue, precisely what do we date when we date documents? My answer is, two distinct issues require attention. First, we have to define the document as a whole and propose a point at which that document came to closure, if it did come to closure. Second, we have to identify the several components of the document, and identify a point at which we think these reached the form in which we have them (controlling, of course, for variations in wording and phrasing, which may continue to evolve for many centuries after closure). Closure therefore stands for two distinct moments, the one, the document as a whole, the other, the document's principal parts.

By "the document as a whole," I mean, the document as we know it, defined by its governing traits of program and proposition, form and rhetoric, cogent argument and coherent, intelligent re-presentation of thought. Each of the score of documents that make up the canon of Judaism in late antiquity exhibits distinctive traits in logic, rhetoric, and topic, so that we may identify the purposes and traits of form and intellect of the authorship of that document. It follows that documents possess integrity and are not merely scrapbooks, compilations made with no clear purpose or aesthetic plan. When we date a document as a whole, we assign a determinate point in time at which, in our judgment, the definitive traits of the writing coalesced to govern whatever would enter that writing or to dictate the reshaping of candidates for inclusion. Now that point can have arrived earlier or later in the process of accumulation. That is to say, a document may reach its definitive form but continue to admit new materials, indeed, may make provision for their inclusion. The Siddur and the Mahzor, of course, represent likely candidates; the form of prayer was well established early on, but the documents kept expanding and contracting for many centuries to come. But, as a matter of theory (for reasons I shall suggest), other writings, too, can without losing this distinctive character have taken into their composites new compositions, aggregations of materials originally written for some other purpose all together. Later writers imitate earlier ones; heirs of a document may expand its limits while adhering to its protocol. It follows that a document reaches definition well before it comes to definitive closure, and we have to take account of that possibility. But that simple fact also calls into question what we mean by "redaction," "closure," and dating.

If, as a matter of fact, we mean the point at which the writing ceased to accommodate new candidates for admission, so that closure is definitive, then we have to rely upon manuscript evidence to show us the point at which the writing simply had jelled, with variations now limited to words and phrases. That is to say, we may know for certain that a document has come to closure – "redaction" in the conventional sense – when a population of manuscripts shows us pretty much the same version of the same writing: contents, character, wording. So, too, when external witnesses tell us that various people have access to a uniform version of the document, with variations only as to wording, a few lines here, a few lines there, we may say that, at that point, the writing had come to closure. For Rabbinic compilations, to be sure, manuscript evidence is so late that such definitive evidence proves difficult to amass. But when we speak of "redaction" meaning "closure," that is the sort of evidence required to validate our language.

And this brings me to a much more important question, which is, how do we date not only the compilation of a document but the compositions of which it is made up? For we may demonstrate, for most, though not all, Rabbinic compilations that a long process of writing produced some of the compositions collected in a given compilation, and that that process of writing produced completed compositions long before said compositions were selected for inclusion in the documents that now preserve them. I realize that, in making that statement, I shall be understood to be saying pretty much what those I criticize allege about the writing: the compositions reach us through a long process of tradition, so that we cannot assign to everything in a document the final date of the document overall. We have, rather – so it is claimed – to date each sentence, each paragraph, each completed unit of thought, in its own terms. And that leads directly to reliance upon attributions, on the one side, and to appeal to the very allegations or contents of the writing, on the other, that I insist we must set aside as not demonstrated. I have broadly argued, what we cannot show, we do not know. How then do I propose to show that not everything in a given document must be dated to the point at which the document as a whole is assigned?

Absent attributions, on the one side, and allegations as to facts, on the other, where do we turn? The answer requires that I specify material and concrete facts, facts that compel assent and that do not consist of unprovable allegations that Rabbi X said such and so. I have, too, to appeal to the possibility of others' reaching the same conclusions that I present, which is to say, I have to show how to conduct experiments through which others can test and replicate my results. In other words, for once, objective evidence must intervene, and the subjective pronouncements of "great authorities" must be dismissed as merely someone's opinion, buttressed by politics, not by well-crafted propositions, arguments, and evidence, such as, in ordinary, secular fields of learning, we expect to be given.

I have already adumbrated the main lines of my theory on how to identify components of a document that come prior to the compilation of the document as a whole. It rests on the allegation that a document exhibits definitive traits of rhetoric, logic of coherent discourse, and topical program, even proposition. Let me now spell this out and explain the consequences for the analysis of a piece of writing and the dating of its contents.

I identify – and I maintain anyone examining the same evidence also will discern – three stages in the formation of writing. Moving from the latest to the earliest, one stage is marked by the definition of a document, its topical program, its rhetorical medium, its logical message. The document as we know it in its basic structure and main lines therefore comes at the end. It follows that writings that clearly serve the program of that document and carry out the purposes of its authorship were made up in connection with the formation of *that* document. Another, and I think, prior stage is marked by the preparation of writings that do not serve the needs of a particular document now in our hands, but can have carried out the purposes of an authorship working on a document of a *type* we now have. The existing documents then form a model for defining other kinds of writings worked out to meet the program of a documentary authorship.

But there are other types of writings that in no way serve the needs or plans of any document we now have, and that, furthermore, also cannot find a place in any document of a type that we now have. These writings, as a matter of fact, very commonly prove peripatetic, traveling from one writing to another, equally at home in, or alien to, the program of the documents in which they end up. These writings therefore were carried out without regard to a documentary program of any kind exemplified by the canonical books of the Judaism of the Dual Torah. They form what I conceive to be the earliest in the three stages of the writing of the units of completed thought that in the aggregate form the canonical literature of the Judaism of the Dual Torah of late antiquity.

As a matter of fact, therefore, a given canonical document of the Judaism of the Dual Torah draws upon three classes of materials, and these – I propose as a mere hypothesis – were framed in temporal order. Last comes the final class, the one that the redactors themselves defined and wrote; prior is the penultimate class that can have served other redactors but did not serve these in particular; and earliest of all in the order of composition (at least, from the perspective of the ultimate redaction of the documents we now have) is the writing that circulated autonomously and served no redactional purpose we can now identify within the canonical documents.

We start from the whole, therefore, and work our way back toward the identification of the parts. In beginning the inquiry with the traits of documents seen whole, I reject the assumption that the building block of documents is the smallest whole unit of thought, the lemma, nor can we proceed in the premise that a lemma traverses the boundaries of various documents and is unaffected by the journey. The opposite premise is that we start our work with the traits of documents as a whole, rather than with the traits of the lemmas of which documents are (supposedly) composed. Having demonstrated beyond any doubt that a rabbinic text is a document, that is to say, a well-crafted text and not merely a compilation of this-and-that, and further specified in acute detail precisely the aesthetic, formal, and logical program followed by each of those texts, accordingly, I am able to move to the logical next step. That is to show that in the background of the documents that we have is writing that is *not* shaped by documentary requirements, writing that is not shaped by the documentary requirements of the compilations we now have, and also writing that is entirely formed within the rules of the documents that now present that writing. These then are the three kinds of writing that form, also, the three stages in the formation of the classics of Judaism.

My example of a document that is written down essentially in its penultimate and ultimate stages, that is, a document that takes shape within the redactional process and principally there, is, of course, the Mishnah. In that writing, the patterns of language, for example, syntactic structures, of the apodosis and protasis of the Mishnah's smallest whole units of discourse are framed in formal, mnemonic patterns. They follow a few simple rules. These rules, once known, apply nearly everywhere and form stunning evidence for the document's cogency. They permit anyone to reconstruct, out of a few key phrases, an entire cognitive unit, and even complete intermediate units of discourse. Working downward from the surface, therefore, anyone can penetrate into the deeper layers of meaning of the Mishnah. Then and at the same time, while discovering the principle behind the cases, one can easily memorize the whole by mastering the recurrent rhetorical pattern dictating the expression of the cogent set of cases. For it is easy to note the shift from one rhetorical pattern to another and to follow the repeated cases, articulated in the new pattern downward to its logical substrate. So syllogistic propositions, in the Mishnah's authors' hands, come to full expression not only in *what* people wish to state but also in *how* they choose to say it. The limits of rhetoric define the arena of topical articulation.

Now to state my main point in heavy emphasis: *The Mishnah's formal traits of rhetoric indicate that the document has been formulated all at once, and not in an incremental, linear process extending into a remote (mythic) past, (for example, to Sinai).* These traits, common to a series of distinct cognitive units, are redactional, because they are imposed at that point at which someone intended to join together discrete (finished) units on a given theme. The varieties of traits particular to the discrete units and the diversity of authorities cited therein, including masters of two or three or even four strata from the turn of the first century to the end of the second, make it highly improbable that the several units were formulated in a common pattern and then preserved, until, later on, still further units, on the same theme and in the same pattern, were worked out and added. The entire indifference, moreover, to historical order of authorities and concentration on the logical unfolding of a given theme or problem without reference to the sequence of authorities, confirm the supposition that the work of formulation and that of redaction go forward together.

The principal framework of formulation and formalization in the Mishnah is the intermediate division rather than the cognitive unit. The least-formalized formulary pattern, the simple declarative sentence, turns out to yield many examples of acute formalization, in which a single distinctive pattern is imposed upon two or more (very commonly, groups of three or groups of five) cognitive units. While an intermediate division of a tractate may be composed of several such conglomerates of cognitive units, it is rare indeed for cognitive units formally to stand wholly by themselves. Normally, cognitive units share formal or formulary traits with others to which they are juxtaposed and the theme of which they share. It follows that the principal unit of formulary formalization is the intermediate division and not the cognitive unit. And what that means for our inquiry, is simple: we can tell when it is that the ultimate or penultimate redactors of a document do the writing.

Now let us see that vast collection of writings that exhibit precisely the opposite trait: a literature in which, while doing some writing of their own, the redactors collected and arranged available materials.

Now to the other extreme. Can I point to a kind of writing that in no way defines a document now in our hands or even a type of document we can now imagine, that is, one that in its particulars we do not have but that conforms in its definitive traits to those that we do have? Indeed I can, and it is the writing of stories about sages and other exemplary figures. To show what might have been, I point to the simple fact that the final organizers of the Bavli, the Talmud of Babylonia, had in hand a tripartite corpus of inherited materials awaiting composition into a final, closed document. First, the first type of material, in various states and stages of completion, addressed the Mishnah or took up the principles of laws that the Mishnah had originally brought to articulation. These the framers of the Bavli organized in accord with the order of those Mishnah tractates that they selected for sustained attention. Second, they had in hand received materials, again in various conditions, pertinent to Scripture, both as Scripture related to the Mishnah and also as Scripture laid forth its own narratives. These they set forth as Scripture commentary. In this way, the penultimate and ultimate redactors of the Bavli laid out a systematic presentation of the two Torahs, the oral, represented by the Mishnah, and the written, represented by Scripture.

And, third, the framers of the Bavli also had in hand materials focused on sages. These, in the received form, attested in the Bavli's pages, were framed around twin biographical principles, either as strings of stories about great sages of the past or as collections of sayings and comments drawn together solely because the same name stands behind all the collected sayings. These can easily have been composed into biographies. In the context of Christianity and of Judaism, it is appropriate to call the biography of a holy man or woman, meant to convey the divine message, a gospel. This is writing that is utterly outside of the documentary framework in which it is now preserved; nearly all narratives in the rabbinic literature, not only the biographical ones, indeed prove remote from any documentary program exhibited by the canonical documents in which they now occur.

The Bavli as a whole lays itself out as a commentary to the Mishnah. So the framers wished us to think that whatever they wanted to tell us would take the form of Mishnah commentary. But a second glance indicates that the Bavli is made up of enormous composites, themselves closed prior to inclusion in the Bavli. Some of these composites – around 35 percent to 40 percent of Bavli's, if my sample is indicative – were selected and arranged along lines dictated by a logic other than that deriving from the requirements of Mishnah commentary. The components of the canon of the Judaism of the Dual Torah prior to the Bavli had encompassed amplifications of the Mishnah, in the Tosefta and in the Yerushalmi, as well as the same for Scripture, in such documents as Sifra to Leviticus, Sifré to Numbers, another Sifré, to Deuteronomy, Genesis Rabbah, Leviticus Rabbah, and the like. But there was no entire document, now extant, organized around the life and teachings of a particular sage. Even The Fathers According to Rabbi Nathan, which contains a good sample of stories about sages, is not so organized as to yield a life of a sage, or even a systematic biography of any kind. Where events in the lives of sages do occur, they are thematic and not biographical in organization, for example, stories about the origins, as to Torah study, of diverse sages; death scenes of various sages. The sage as such, whether Aqiba or Yohanan ben Zakkai or Eliezer b. Hyrcanus, never in that document defines the appropriate organizing principle for sequences of stories or sayings. And there is no other in which the sage forms an organizing category for any material purpose.

Accordingly, the decision that the framers of the Bavli reached was to adopt the two redactional principles inherited from the antecedent century or so and to reject the one already rejected by their predecessors, even while honoring it. [1] They organized the Bavli around the Mishnah. But [2] they adapted and included vast tracts of antecedent materials organized as scriptural commentary. These they inserted whole and complete, not at all in response to the Mishnah's program. But, finally, [3] while making provision for small-scale compositions built upon biographical principles, preserving both strings of sayings from a given master (and often a given tradent of a given master) as well as tales about authorities of the preceding half millennium, they *never* created redactional compositions, of a sizable order, that focused upon given authorities. But sufficient materials certainly lay at hand to allow doing so.

We have now seen that some writings carry out a redactional purpose. The Mishnah was our prime example. Some writings ignore all redactional considerations we can identify. The stories about sages in The Fathers According to Rabbi Nathan for instance show us kinds of writing that are wholly out of phase with the program of the document that collects and compiles them. We may therefore turn to Midrash compilations and find the traits of writing that clearly are imposed by the requirements of compilation. We further identify writings that clearly respond to a redactional program, but not the program of any compilation we now have in hand. There is little speculation about the identification of such writings. They will conform to the redactional patterns we discern in the known compilations, but presuppose a collection other than one now known to us. Finally, we turn to pieces of writing that respond to no redactional program known to us or susceptible to invention in accord with the principles of defining compilation known to us.

My analytical taxonomy of the writings now collected in various Midrash compilations points to not only three stages in the formation of the classics of Judaism. It also suggests that writing went on outside of the framework of the editing of documents, and also within the limits of the formation and framing of documents. Writing of the former kind then constituted a kind of literary work to which redactional planning proved irrelevant. But the second and the third kinds of writing respond to redactional considerations. So in the end we shall wish to distinguish between writing intended for the making of books – compositions of the first three kinds listed just now – and writing not in response to the requirements of the making of compilations.

The distinctions upon which these analytical taxonomies rest are objective and in no way subjective, since they depend upon the fixed and factual relationship between a piece of writing and a larger redactional context.

1. We know the requirements of redactors of the several documents of the rabbinic canon, because I have already shown what they are in the case of a large variety of documents. When, therefore, we judge a piece of writing to serve the program of the document in which that writing occurs, it is not because of a personal impulse or a private and incommunicable insight, but because the traits of that writing self-evidently respond to the documentary program of the book in which the writing is located.

2. When, further, we conclude that a piece of writing belongs in some other document than the one in which it is found, that, too, forms a factual judgment.

A piece of writing that serves nowhere we now know may nonetheless conform to the rules of writing that we can readily imagine and describe in theory. For instance, a propositional composition, that runs through a wide variety of texts to make a point autonomous of all of the texts that are invoked, clearly is intended for a propositional document, one that (like the Mishnah) makes points autonomous of a given prior writing, for example, a biblical book, but that makes points that for one reason or another cohere quite nicely on their own. Authors of propositional compilations self-evidently can imagine that kind of redaction. We have their writings, but not the books that they intended to be made up of those writings. In all instances, the reason that we can readily imagine a compilation that will have dictated the indicative traits of a piece of writing will prove self-evident: we have compilations of such a type, if not specific compilations called for by a given composition.

Some writings stand autonomous of any redactional program we have in an existing compilation or of any we can even imagine on the foundations of said writings. Compositions of this kind, as a matter of hypothesis, are to be assigned to a stage in the formation of classics prior to the framing of all available documents. For, as a matter of fact, all of our now extant writings adhere to a single program of conglomeration and agglutination, and all are served by composites of one sort, rather than some other. Hence we may suppose that at some point prior to the decision to make writings in the model that we now have but in some other model, people also made up completed units of thought to serve these other kinds of writings. These persist, now, in documents that they do not serve at all well. And we can fairly easily identify the kinds of documents that they can and should have served quite nicely indeed. These then are the three stages of literary formation in the making of the classics of Judaism.

This set of definitions returns us to the matter of dating documents, a problem I have now reformulated into its components: closure of the whole, definition of the protocol governing the parts, and formulation of the individual compositions that are collected into composites and ultimately included in the compilation as a whole.

Of the relative temporal or ordinal position of writings that stand autonomous of any redactional program we have in an existing compilation or of any we can even imagine on the foundations of said writings we can say nothing. These writings prove episodic; they are commonly singletons. They serve equally well everywhere, because they demand no traits of form and redaction in order to endow them with sense and meaning. Why not? Because they are essentially free-standing and episodic, not referential and allusive. They are stories that contain their own point and do not invoke, in the making of that point, a given verse of Scripture. They are sayings that are utterly ad hoc. A variety of materials fall into this – from a redactional perspective – unassigned, and unassignable, type of writing. They do not belong in books at all. By that I mean, whoever made up these pieces of writing did not imagine that what he was forming required a setting beyond the limits of his own piece of writing; the story is not only complete in itself but could stand entirely on its own; the saying spoke for itself and required no nurturing context; the proposition and its associated proofs in no way was meant to draw nourishment from roots penetrating nutriments outside of its own literary limits.

Where we have utterly hermetic writing, able to define its own limits and sustain its point without regard to anything outside itself, we know that here we are in the presence of authorships that had no larger redactional plan in mind, no intent on the making of books out of their little pieces of writing. We may note that, among the "unimaginable" compilations is not a collection of parables, since parables rarely stand free and never are inserted for their own sake. Whenever in the rabbinic canon we find a parable, it is meant to serve the purpose of an authorship engaged in making its own point; and the point of a parable is rarely, if ever, left unarticulated. Normally it is put into words, but occasionally the point is made simply by redactional setting. It must follow that, in this canon, the parable cannot have constituted the generative or agglutinative principle of a large-scale compilation. It further follows, so it seems to me, that the parable always takes shape within the framework of a work of composition for the purpose of either a large-scale exposition or, more commonly still, of compilation of a set of expositions into what we should now call the chapter of a book; that is to say, parables link to purposes that transcend the tale that they tell (or even the point that the tale makes).

Once we recognize those sizable selections of materials that circulated from one document to another, we are able to ask, can we date them to a time prior to the definition of a document's protocol and also the writings that were formulated in close adherence to, in accord with, that protocol? I think we can, and let me explain why I tend to think they were formed earlier than the writings particular to documents. The documentary hypothesis affects our reading of the itinerant compositions, for it identifies what writings are extradocumentary and nondocumentary and imposes upon the hermeneutics and history of these writings a set of distinctive considerations. The reason is that these writings serve the purposes not of compilers (or authors or authorships) of distinct compilations, but the interests of another type of authorship entirely: one that thought making up stories (whether or not for collections) itself an important activity; or making up exercises on Mishnah Scripture relationships; or other such writings as lie beyond the imagination of the compilers of the score of documents that comprise the canon. When writings work well for two or more documents therefore they must be assumed to have a literary history different from those that serve only one writing or one type of writing, and, also, demand a different hermeneutic.

My "three stages" in ordinal sequence correspond, as a matter of fact, to a taxic structure, that is, three types of writing. The first – and last in assumed temporal order – is writing carried out in the context of the making, or compilation, of a classic. That writing responds to the redactional program and plan of the authorship of a classic. The second, penultimate in order, is writing that can appear in a given document but better serves a document other than the one in which it (singularly) occurs. This kind of writing seems to me not to fall within the same period of redaction as the first. For while it is a type of writing under the identical conditions, it also is writing that presupposes redactional programs in no way in play in the ultimate, and definitive, period of the formation of the canon: when people did things this way, and not in some other. That is why I think it is a kind of writing that was done prior to the period in which people limited their redactional work and associated labor of composition to the program that yielded the books we now have.

The upshot is simple: whether the classification of writing be given a temporal or merely taxonomic valence, the issue is the same: Have these writers done their work with documentary considerations in mind? I believe I have shown that they have not. Then where did they expect their work to make its way? Anywhere it might, because, so they assumed, fitting in no where in particular, it found a suitable locus everywhere it turned up. But I think temporal, not merely taxonomic, considerations pertain.

The third kind of writing seems to me to originate in a period prior to the other two. It is carried on in a manner independent of all redactional considerations such as are known to us. Then it should derive from a time when redactional considerations played no paramount role in the making of compositions. A brief essay, rather than a sustained composition, was then the dominant mode of writing. My hypothesis is that people can have written both long and short compositions – compositions and composites, in my language – at one and the same time. But writing that does not presuppose a secondary labor of redaction, for example, in a composite, probably originated when authors or authorships did not anticipate any fate for their writing beyond their labor of composition itself.

Along these same lines of argument, this writing may or may not travel from one document to another. What that means is that the author or authorship does not imagine a future for his writing. What fits anywhere is composed to go nowhere in particular. Accordingly, what matters is not whether a writing fits one document or another, but whether, as the author or authorship has composed a piece of writing, that writing meets the requirements of any document we now have or can even imagine. If it does not, then we deal with a literary period in which the main kind of writing was ad hoc and episodic, not sustained and documentary.

Now extra and nondocumentary kinds of writing seem to me to derive from either [1] a period prior to the work of the making of Midrash compilations and the two Talmuds alike; or [2] a labor of composition not subject to the rules and considerations that operated in the work of the making of Midrash compilations and the two Talmuds. As a matter of hypothesis, I should guess that nondocumentary writing comes prior to making any kind of documents of consequence, and extradocumentary writing comes prior to the period in which the specificities of the documents we now have were defined. That is to say, writing that can fit anywhere or nowhere is prior to writing that can fit somewhere but does not fit anywhere now accessible to us, and both kinds of writing are prior to the kind that fits only in what documents in which it is now located.

And given the documentary propositions and theses that we can locate in all of our compilations, we can only assume that the nondocumentary writings enjoyed, and were assumed to enjoy, ecumenical acceptance. That means, very simply, when we wish to know the consensus of the entire textual (or canonical) community – I mean simply the people, anywhere and any time, responsible for everything we now have – we turn not to the distinctive perspective of documents, but the (apparently universally acceptable) perspective of the extradocumentary compositions. That is the point at which we should look for the propositions everywhere accepted but nowhere advanced in a distinctive way, the "Judaism beyond the texts" – or behind them.

Do I place a priority, in the framing of a hypothesis, over taxonomy or temporal order? Indeed I do. I am inclined to suppose that nondocumentary compositions took shape not only separated from, but in time before, the documentary ones did. My reason for thinking so is worth rehearsing, even though it is not yet compelling. The kinds of nondocumentary writing I have identified in general focus on matters of very general interest. These matters may be assembled into two very large rubrics: virtue, on the one side, reason, on the other. Stories about sages fall into the former category; all of them set forth in concrete form the right living that sages exemplify. Essays on right thinking, the role of reason, the taxonomic priority of Scripture, the power of analogy, the exemplary character of cases and precedents in the expression of general and encompassing rules – all of these intellectually coercive writings set forth rules of thought as universally applicable, in their way, as are the rules of conduct contained in stories about sages, in theirs. A great labor of generalization is contained in both kinds of nondocumentary and extradocumentary writing. And the results of that labor are then given concrete expression in the documentary writings in hand; for these, after all, do say in the setting of specific passages or problems precisely what, in a highly general way, emerges from the writing that moves hither and yon, never with a home, always finding a suitable resting place.

Now, admittedly, that rather general characterization of the nondocumentary writing is subject to considerable qualification and clarification. But it does provide a reason to assign temporal priority, not solely taxonomic distinction, to the nondocumentary compositions. We can have had commentaries of a sustained and systematic sort on Chronicles, on the one side, treatises on virtue, on the second, gospels, on the third – to complete the triangle. But we do not have these kinds of books. We have what we have, and those are the writings we have to date. In specifying the complexity of the problem of dating – once we abandon reliance upon attributions and allegations as to facts – I mean to suggest paths for further inquiry. The road from here to reliable conclusions on when a document reached ultimate closure, when the materials collected in the document were formulated on their own and reformulated in accord with the protocol governing their ultimate, documentary destination – that road is a very long one indeed. In the interim, we have to formulate our work of history and history of ideas with careful attention to what, out of the mass of things we do not know, we actually can say for certain. We have, in other words, to formulate our questions and our problems in response to the character of not only the evidence, but the things that the evidence as we now grasp it permits us to investigate.

3

Why Do Rabbinic Authors Cite Sayings in the Name of Particular Sages?

This lecture was given for the Theological Faculty of Helsinki University at a study day held in Åbo.

To understand the issue at hand we have to take account of two contradictory facts. First, all rabbinic documents are anonymous, and all of them include vast numbers of compositions bearing no assignments; none of the compositions of which a document is comprised is assigned to a named author; no document bears a dependable attribution to a specific person. But, by way of contradiction to these facts, every one of the documents of the Judaism of the Dual Torah produced in the formative age is characterized by numerous attributions of statements to specific figures. So individuals at the same time play no role and also dominate the representation of discourse. The literary situation is characterized by William Scott Green in the following way:

> Most rabbinic documents are unattributed works; all in fact are anonymous.... Rabbinic literature has no authors. No document claims to be the writing of an individual rabbi in his own words; and all contain the ostensible sayings of, and stories about, many rabbis, usually of several generations. Selected to suit the purposes of compilers and redactors, the documents' components are not pristine and natural. They have been revised and reformulated in the processes of transmission and redaction, with the consequence that the ipsissima verba of any rabbis are beyond recovery. Rabbinic literature is severely edited, anonymous, and collective.[1]

---

[1]William Scott Green, "Storytelling and Holy Men," in J. Neusner, ed., *Take Judaism, For Example. Studies toward the Comparison of Religions* (Atlanta, 1992: Scholars Press for South Florida Studies in the History of Judaism), p. 30.

These contradictory traits – exclusion of distinctive, personal traits of style, absolute refusal to recognize an individual in his own setting, for example, by preserving a book written by, or about, a named authority, and, at the same time, ubiquitous and persistent inclusion of names along with sayings – provoke the question at hand. If the literature were anonymous as well as collective, or if it exhibited the marks of individuality along with its constant references to named figures, we should not find puzzling the definitive trait before us. So to the work at hand.

The question is addressed to me, "Why is the Rabbinic literature so interested in coupling utterances and decisions with names?" The question finds a facile answer for those who take for granted that issues of history govern in the formulation of the Judaism of the Dual Torah. If the primary interest lies in what really happened, so that events of a specific, one-time character bear incontrovertible and compelling truth, then names are attached to sayings to indicate who really said them; then the word "really" carries the meaning, which particular authority stands behind a given statement? That premise, at the same time historical and biographical, certainly has much to recommend it, since, in our culture, with its two-century-old stress on the authority of demonstrable, historical fact, if we can show that something really happened or was truly said by the person to whom it is attributed, then much else follows. But for our sages of blessed memory, particularly in the two Talmuds, that premise will have presented considerable difficulty.

For we look in vain in the analytical documents for evidence to sustain the stated premise that people really concerned themselves with the issue of who really said what. That is to say, while sayings are attributed, the purpose of the attribution – what is at stake in it, what else we know because we know it – requires analysis in its own terms. Since, as a matter of fact, a saying assigned to one authority in document A will circulate in the name of another in document B, the one-time, determinate assignment of said saying to authority X rather than authority Y cannot be accorded enormous consequence. If the documents were broadly circulated and known, then people ought to have observed that a given saying is assigned to more than a single authority and ought also to have asked why that was the fact. But discussion on that question nowhere takes a central position in the literature. It is no more troublesome than the fact that a given authority will be assigned a given saying in two or more contexts; then, as with the Sermon on the Mount and the Sermon on the Plain, people will simply maintain (as do the true believers in the historicity of everything in the Rabbinic literature who dominate scholarly discourse in the Israeli universities and the Western yeshivot and seminaries), "he would often say...," or, "many times he said...."

Where, when, and why, then, do the names of authorities play a consequential role in the unfolding of discourse? What role is assigned to them, and what premises seem to underpin the constant citation of sayings in the names of particular masters? To answer these questions, it will hardly suffice to speculate. Our task is to turn to the documents themselves and to ask the broad question, what role do named sages play in these compilations, and on what account do specific names joined with particular statements come under discussion? That question, of course, forms a particular detail of a broader issue, which is, how come specific sages play so critical a role in the Rabbinic literature?

When we consider counterpart writings in Christian circles, by contrast, we find a very different kind of writing. There, very commonly, a named figure, whether Matthew or Paul, presents a piece of writing, and he bears responsibility for everything in that document, either as an account of what he has seen and heard, as in the case of Matthew's Gospel, or as an account of his own systematic views, as in the case of Paul's letters. True, we find anonymous writings; but such documents as Hebrews, which bears no named author, also contains no sayings assigned to specific authorities. The much later Zoroastrian law codes, which intersect in contents and at some points even in form with the Judaic ones, assign a given code to a named authority. So we should regard as emblematic and enormously consequential the constant intrusion of the names of authorities in the Rabbinic writings, beginning to end, from the Mishnah through the Bavli.

Rather than address the question in general terms, let us first ask about the role of attributions in some few specific documents: How seriously are they taken, and for what purpose? The first document, of course, is the Mishnah. There we find a principal and constitutive form, the dispute, built around the name of opposing authorities, for example, the Houses of Shammai and Hillel, or Aqiba and Tarfon, or Meir and Judah, and the like. We also find in some few passages clear evidence of the collection of statements on a given, cogent problem in the name of a specific authority, for example, Mishnah-tractate Kelim Chapter Twenty-Four is a statement of Judah's views. But, over all, the Mishnah must be described as an entirely anonymous document, which at the same time contains extensive citations of named figures. The same names occur throughout; we cannot demonstrate that a given authority was viewed as particularly knowledgeable in a specific area of law, most of the sages being treated as generalists. At the same time that names predominate everywhere, sixty-two of the sixty-three tractates are organized around not named figures but topics, and, as indicated, perhaps 98 percent of the chapters of which those tractates are made up likewise focus on subjects, not named authorities. Only tractate Eduyyot as a whole is set up around names.

If we turn to that tractate devoted to not a particular subject or problem but rather the collection of attributed sayings and stories told about authorities, what do we find? The answer is, collections of rules on diverse topics, united by the names of authorities cited therein, either disputes, for example, between Shammai and Hillel and their Houses, or sets of rulings representative of a single authority. A single representative passage shows how the document does its work:

1:2.II A.   Shammai says, "[Dough which is made] from a qab [of flour is liable] to a dough-offering [Num. 15:20]."

       B.   And Hillel says, "[Dough made] from two qabs."

       C.   And sages say, "It is not in accord with the opinion of this party nor in accord with the opinion of that party,

       D.   "but: [dough made] from a qab and a half of flour is liable to the dough-offering."

Now what is interesting here – and not characteristic of the document throughout – is the inclusion of a final ruling on the dispute, which is different from the rulings of the Houses' founders. That pattern being repeated and so shown to be definitive of the redactor's subtext, the question is raised: Why record not only the official rule, but the opinion of a named, therefore schismatic figure as well? And that of course forms the heart of the matter and tells us the document's answer to our question. First let us consider the source, then draw the conclusion it makes possible:

1:5 A.   And why do they record the opinion of an individual along with that of the majority, since the law follows the opinion of the majority?

       B.   So that, if a court should prefer the opinion of the individual, it may decide to rely upon it.

       C.   For a court has not got the power to nullify the opinion of another court unless it is greater than it in wisdom and in numbers.

       D.   [If] it was greater than the other in wisdom but not in numbers,

       E.   in numbers but not in wisdom,

       F.   it has not got the power to nullify its opinion –

       G.   unless it is greater than it in both wisdom and numbers.

1:6 A.   Said R. Judah, "If so, why do they record the opinion of an individual against that of a majority to no purpose?

       B.   "So that if a person should say, 'Thus have I received the tradition,' one may say to him, 'You have heard the tradition in accord with the opinion of Mr. So-and-so [against that of the majority].'"

The premise of this passage is simple. The law follows the position of the anonymously formulated rule. Then why attribute a rule to a named figure? It is to identify the opinion that is not authoritative, but, nonetheless, subject to consideration. Then it follows, the purpose of citing sayings in the names of authorities is to mark those positions as schismatic and not authoritative – not to validate, but to invalidate.

To test this surmise, we turn to the Tosefta's commentary on the passage of Mishnah-tractate Eduyyot that is before us. Here we find explicitly articulated the premise I identified:

1:4   A.   Under all circumstances the law follows the majority, and the opinion of the individual is recorded along with that of the majority only so as to nullify it.

        B.   R. Judah says, "The opinion of an individual is recorded along with that of the majority only so that, if the times necessitate it, they may rely upon [the opinion of the individual]" [cf. M. Ed. 1:5B].

        C.   And sages say, "The opinion of the individual is recorded along with that of the majority only so that, if later on, this one says, 'Unclean,' and that one says, 'Clean,' one may respond that the one who says it is unclean is in accord with the opinion of R. Eliezer [and the law must follow the majority, which opposed his opinion], so they say to him, 'You have heard this opinion in accord with the ruling of R. Eliezer.'"

Judah's theory of matters – that of the minority – is that the minority opinion registers, so that, under duress, it may serve as precedent; sages take the view that the very opposite consideration pertains; once an opinion is given to an individual, that opinion is to be dismissed as schismatic wherever it occurs – even when not in the name of the individual. So we find here confirmation of the surmise that at stake in assigning opinions to names is the formulation of the legal process in such a way as to permit reliable decisions to be made.

But there is a second consideration important to the Mishnah, and that emerges in another passage in the same tractate:

5:6   A.   Aqabia b. Mahalalel gave testimony in four matters.

        B.   They said to him, "Aqabia, retract the four rulings which you laid down, and we shall make you patriarch of the court of Israel."

        C.   He said to them, "It is better for me to be called a fool my whole life but not be deemed a wicked person before the Omnipresent for even one minute,

        D.   "so that people should not say, 'Because he craved after high office, he retracted.'"

The passage proceeds to specify the disputes, and then the narrative continues, reporting that because he refused to retract, sages excommunicated him:

        M.   They excommunicated him, and he died while he was subject to the excommunication, so the court stoned his bier....

5:7   A.   When he was dying, he said to his son, "My son, retract the four rulings which I had laid down."

B.   He said to him, "And why do you retract now?"

C.   He said to him, "I heard the rulings in the name of the majority, and they heard them in the name of the majority, so I stood my ground on the tradition which I had heard, and they stood their ground on the tradition they had heard.

D.   "But you have heard the matter both in the name of an individual and in the name of the majority.

E.   "It is better to abandon the opinion of the individual and to hold with the opinion of the majority."

F.   He said to him, "Father, give instructions concerning me to your colleagues."

G.   He said to him, "I will give no instructions."

H.   He said to him, "Is it possible that you have found some fault with me?"

I.   He said to him, "No. It is your deeds which will bring you near, or your deeds which will put you off [from the others]."

The crux of the matter then comes at 5:7C: Aqabia has received rulings in the name of the majority and therefore regards them as valid. So the purpose of assigning names to sayings once more is to label the unreliable ones: those in the names of individuals. And at stake, underneath, is of course the shape and structure of the tradition, which is once more stated explicitly: "I stood my ground on the tradition that I had heard...." What comes down anonymously is tradition – from Sinai, obviously – and what bears a name is other than tradition. But matters we see also prove subject to negotiation. Sages bear the obligation to remember what they heard in the name of the majority but also in the name of individuals. So the inclusion of names forms part of a larger theory of tradition and how to be guided by tradition, and the Mishnah's account of itself makes that point in so many words.

We hardly need to find that fact surprising, since the Mishnah's first apologetic, Pirqé Abot, the sayings of the fathers, points to Sinai as the origin of the Mishnah's tradition when it formulates its opening chapter. Tractate Abot in its opening chapter responds to the question: What is the Mishnah? Why should we obey its rules? How does it relate to the Torah, which, we all know, God gave to Israel through Moses at Sinai? The answer is contained in the opening sentence:

The Sayings of the Fathers Chapter One

1:1   Moses received the Torah at Sinai and handed it on to Joshua, Joshua to elders, and elders to prophets. And prophets handed it on to the men of the great assembly. They said three things: Be prudent in judgment. Raise up many disciples. Make a fence for the Torah.

What is important here is three facts. First, the verbs, receive...hand on...,
in Hebrew yield the words *qabbalah*, tradition, and *masoret*, also tradition.
There is no more lucid or powerful way of making the statement than
that: the Torah is a matter of tradition. Second, the tradition goes from
master to disciple, Moses to Joshua. So the tradition is not something
written down, it is something that lives. Third, we know that the
tradition is distinct from the Written Torah, because what is attributed to
"the men of the great assembly" (and we have no interest in who these
might be assumed to have been) are three statements that do not occur in
Scripture. In fact, among all of the sayings in the entire tractate, only
very rarely is there attributed to a sage who stands in this chain of
tradition a verse of Scripture. So the essence of "the tradition" is not
what is said, for example, citing a verse of Scripture and expanding on it,
but that a saying is said and who does the saying: a master to a disciple,
forward through all time, backward to Sinai. Torah – revelation – stands
for a process of transmitting God's will. That process is open-ended but
it also is highly disciplined.

How is the question of the origin and authority of the Mishnah
answered? The chain of tradition from Sinai ends up with names that are
prominent in the Mishnah itself, for example, Shammai and Hillel, and
their disciples, the House of Shammai and the House of Hillel. So the
message is blatant: major authorities of the Mishnah stand in a chain of
tradition to Sinai; hence, the Mishnah contains the Torah of Sinai. It is
that straightforward: through discipleship, we reach backward; through
the teaching of the sage, we reach forward; the great tradition endures in
the learning of the ages. It follows that when sayings are assigned to
sages, a quite separate issue is in play. I cite only a small sample of the
opening chapter of Abot, which suffices to make my point:

1:2   Simeon the Righteous was one of the last survivors of the great
        assembly. He would say: On three things does the world stand: On
        the Torah, and on the Temple service, and on deeds of loving
        kindness.
1:3   Antigonus of Sokho received [the Torah] from Simeon the
        Righteous. He would say: Do not be like servants who serve the
        master on condition of receiving a reward, but [be] like servants
        who serve the master not on condition of receiving a reward. And
        let the fear of heaven be upon you.
1:4   Yosé ben Yoezer of Zeredah and Yosé ben Yohanan of Jerusalem
        received [the Torah] from them. Yosé ben Yoezer says: Let your
        house be a gathering place for sages. And wallow in the dust of
        their feet, and drink in their words with gusto.
1:5   Yosé ben Yohanan of Jerusalem says: Let your house be open wide.
        And seat the poor at your table ["make the poor members of your
        household"]. And don't talk too much with women. [He referred to
        a man's wife, all the more so is the rule to be applied to the wife of

one's fellow. In this regard did sages say: So long as a man talks too much with a woman, he brings trouble on himself, wastes time better spent on studying the Torah, and ends up an heir of Gehenna.]...

1:12   Hillel and Shammai received [the Torah] from them. Hillel says: Be disciples of Aaron, loving peace and pursuing grace, loving people and drawing them near to the Torah....

1:15   Shammai says: Make your learning of the Torah a fixed obligation. Say little and do much. Greet everybody cheerfully.

1:16   Rabban Gamaliel says: Set up a master for yourself. Avoid doubt. Don't tithe by too much guesswork.

1:17   Simeon his son says: All my life I grew up among the sages, and I found nothing better for a person [the body] than silence. And not the learning is the thing, but the doing. And whoever talks too much causes sin.

1:18   Rabban Simeon ben Gamaliel says: On three things does the world stand: On justice, on truth, and on peace. As it is said, "Execute the judgment of truth and peace in your gates (Zech 8:16)."

Now the key point comes with the beginning of the Mishnah sages themselves, and that is with the pairs, five sets. What is important in this list is the pairs of names and how they are arranged:

Moses
Joshua
Elders
Prophets
Men of the Great Assembly
Simeon the Righteous
Antigonus of Sokho

1.	Yosé ben Yoezer	Yosé b. Yohanan
2.	Joshua b. Perahyah	Nittai the Arbelite
3.	Judah b. Tabbai	Simeon b. Shetah
4.	Shemaiah	Abtalyon
5.	Hillel	Shammai

Gamaliel
Simeon his son
Rabban Simeon b. Gamaliel

The numbered list carries us deep into the pages of the Mishnah itself. But there is another point not to be missed. Once the pairs end, whom do we find? Gamaliel, who is (later on) represented as the son of Hillel, and then Gamaliel and Simeon, his son, Hillel's grandson. The names Gamaliel, then Simeon, continued through this same family, of primary authorities, through Gamaliel II, ruler of the Jewish community after the destruction of the second Temple in 70 and into the second century, then his son, Simeon b. Gamaliel, ruler of the Jewish community after the defeat of Bar Kokhba in 135 – and also, as it happens, the father of Judah the Patriarch, this same Judah the Patriarch who sponsored the Mishnah. So Judah the Patriarch stands in the chain of tradition to Sinai. Not only the teachings of the sages of the Mishnah, but also the political sponsor of the document, who also was numbered among the sages, formed part of this same tradition. What the sages say in these sayings in no way contradicts anything we find in Scripture. But most of what is before us also does not intersect with much that we find in Scripture.

We see, then, two distinct but closely related considerations that operate in the persistent interest in assigning sayings to named authorities. Identifying an authority serves as a taxic indicator of the standing of a saying – classified as not authoritative; but identifying an authority bears the – both correlative and also contradictory – indication that the authority had a tradition. Enough has been said even in these simple observations to point to a broader conclusion. If we wish to ask why names are included, we have to examine the various writings that contain assigned sayings, looking for the importance accorded to attributions by the authors of the compositions and redactors of the composites of each such compilation. It suffices to note that in the later documents, a variety of positions emerges. One of the most weighty is also most surprising. In the Tosefta, we find that what is attributed in the Mishnah to a given authority will be rewritten, so that the cited sage will say something different from what he is supposed in the Mishnah to have said. Nothing in the Mishnah's statements' theory of matters prepares us for the way in which the Tosefta's authorities treat attributions. So far as they are concerned, I shall now show, while attributions set forth fixed positions on a disputed point, precisely what was subject to dispute was itself a contentious matter.

Attributions in the Tosefta bear a quite distinct task from those in the Mishnah. A set of names signifies two persistent positions, principles guiding the solution to any given problem. We find in the Tosefta two or more positions assigned to the same named authority, and these positions contradict one another. It follows that attributions bear a quite distinct sense. What they stand for, as we shall see now, is a fixed difference. Party A and Party B will differ in the same way on a variety of issues, and if we know the issues, we also know the positions to be taken by the two parties. Then all consideration of tradition is set aside; all we have in the attribution is the signification of a fixed difference, a predictable position on an unpredictable agenda of issues. A fair analogy, I think, will be the fixed difference between political conservatives and political liberals; whatever the issue, the positions are predictable. Then in place of the House of Shammai and the House of Hillel, X and Y or black and white or pigeon and turtledove would serve equally well. Neither history, nor tradition, nor designation of the accepted and the schismatic position, comes into play, when all that is at stake is the matter of invoking fixed and conventional positions. Then the attributive serves as a formal protocol, nothing more.

What we shall see in the following is that the Mishnah presents a picture of a dispute and the opinions of cited authorities, and the Tosefta provides a quite different account of what was said. The Tosefta has opinions attributed to Judah and Yosé and "others say," and at stake is three distinct positions on the law. So the framers of the Tosefta's composition exhibit access to no single tradition at all; and subject to dispute is not the outcome of a case, but the formulation of the case itself.

Besah Chapter One

A. The House of Shammai say, "They do not bring dough-offering and priestly gifts to the priest on the festival day,

B. "whether they were raised up the preceding day or on that same day."

C. And the House of Hillel permit.

D. The House of Shammai said to them, "It is an argument by way of analogy.

E. "The dough-offering and the priestly gifts [Deut. 18:3] are a gift to the priest, and heave-offering is a gift to the priest.

F. "Just as [on the festival day] they do not bring heave-offering [to a priest], so they do not bring these other gifts [to a priest]."

G. Said to them the House of Hillel, "No. If you have stated that rule in the case of heave-offering, which one [on the festival] may not designate to begin with, will you apply that same rule concerning the priestly gifts, which [on the festival] one may designate to begin with?"

M. 1:6

The Hillelites allow designating and delivering the priestly gifts owing to the priests from animals slaughtered on the festival day. The House of Shammai do not allow doing so, since the restrictions of the festival day come to bear. We shall now see a completely different picture of matters; I underline the points at which the dispute is reformulated:

A. Said R. Judah, "The House of Shammai and the House of Hillel concur that they bring [to the priest] gifts <u>which were taken up on the day before the festival along with gifts which were taken on the festival</u> [vs. M. 1:5A-C].

B. "Concerning what did they differ?

C. "Concerning [bringing to the priest on the festival] gifts <u>which were taken up on the day before the festival by themselves.</u>

D. "For the House of Shammai prohibit.

E. "And the House of Hillel permit.

F. *"The House of Shammai said, 'It is an argument by way of analogy. The dough-offering and the priestly gifts are a gift to the priest, and heave-*

offering is a gift to the priest. Just as they do not bring heave-offering [to a priest on the festival day], so they do not bring these other gifts [to a priest on the festival day]' [M. 1:6D-F].

G. *"Said to them the House of Hillel, 'No. If you have said that rule in the case of heave-offering, which one may not designate to begin with, will you say that same rule concerning the priestly gifts, which one may designate to begin with?'* [M. 1:6G]."

H. R. Yosé says, "The House of Shammai and the House of Hillel concur <u>that they do bring the priestly gifts to the priest on the festival day.</u>

I. "Concerning what do they differ?

J. <u>"Concerning heave-offering.</u>

K. "For the House of Shammai prohibit [bringing heave-offering to the priest on the festival day].

L. "And the House of Hillel permit."

> T. 1:12, ed. Lieberman, p. 283,
> lines 46-54

A. *"Said the House of Hillel, 'It is an argument by way of analogy. Dough-offering and priestly gifts are a gift to the priest, and heave-offering is a gift to the priest. Just as they do bring the priestly gifts to the priest on the festival day, so they should bring heave-offering to the priest on the festival day.'*

B. "Said the House of Shammai to them, 'No. If you have stated the rule in the case of the priestly gifts, which is permitted to be designated [on the festival], will you state that rule concerning heave-offering, which may not be designated [on the festival day]?'"

C. Others say, "The House of Shammai and the House of Hillel concur <u>that they do not bring heave-offering on a festival.</u>

D. "Concerning what did they differ?

E. <u>"Concerning priestly gifts.</u>

F. "For the House of Shammai prohibit [bringing them to the priest on the festival].

G. "And the House of Hillel permit" [= M. 1:6A-C].

> T. 1:13, ed. Lieberman, pp. 283-
> 284, lines 54-60

What we see is three distinct positions on what is at stake in the dispute of the Houses of Shammai and Hillel, and, a bit of study would show us, these positions express three distinct principles concerning what is at stake. The second century authorities are alleged to have three distinct "traditions" on what is at issue between the Houses; each then assigns to the Houses the same language in the same words, along with the same secondary arguments for its distinctive viewpoint. All that varies is the definition of that about which the Houses to begin with are conducting their dispute – no small thing!

Now that we have seen ample evidence that attributions serve, even in the Mishnah and the Tosefta, to carry out three quite distinct functions

– distinguishing regnant from schismatic opinion, identifying the traditionality of a saying, and marking off fixed points of difference concerning a variable agendum of issues – a measure of humility guides us as we revert to our original question, "Why is the Rabbinic literature so interested in coupling utterances and decisions with names?" The question has received only a preliminary answer, but the method before us is clear: we have to ask, document by document, what function is served by attributions, what importance is assigned to them, what difference the presence of an attribution makes in one context or another, and, finally, what conclusions, if any, are drawn from attributions.

Certainly a survey of the two Talmuds, with their intense interest in the consistency of positions assigned to principal authorities, alongside their quite facile practice of following the dictates of logic, not tradition at all, in switching about among various names the opinions assigned to one or another of them, will yield puzzling evidence. But the outlines of the answer are clear. We may reject as simply irrelevant to the character of the evidence any interest in preserving historical information concerning named figures, for example, for the purpose of biography. The sages of Rabbinic documents have opinions, but no biography; many individuals play critical roles in the formation of the several documentary statements, but no individual is accorded a fully articulated individuality, either as to his life, or as to his philosophy or theology.

What conclusions may we draw from this inquiry into the uses of attributions in the earliest of the Rabbinic compilations? Let us note, first, what we do not have. For the entire cadre of sages, we have not got a single biography devoted to an individual, or even the raw materials for a sustained and systematic biography. We do not possess a single document produced by a clearly identifiable individual author, a single coherent composite of any consequence at all that concerns itself with a named figure. The counterpart writings for Christianity, the Gospels, the letters of Paul, not to mention the huge collections of signed, personal, individual writings of Church Fathers, show us the documents we do not have in Rabbinic literature. The theory of authorship, of course, accounts for that fact. A document to warrant recognition – thus to be accorded authority, to be written and copied, or memorized and handed on as tradition – had to attain the approval of the sages' consensus.

That meant, every document in Rabbinic literature emerged anonymously, under public sponsorship and authorship, stripped of all marks of individual, therefore idiosyncratic, origin. Personality and individuality stood for schism, and Rabbinic literature in its very definition and character aims at the opposite, forming as it does the functional counterpart to the creeds and decisions of Church councils. Framed in mythic terms, the literature aimed to make this theological statement: sages stood in a chain of tradition from Sinai, and the price of inclusion was the acceptance of the discipline of tradition – anonymity, reasoned argument to attain for a private view the public status of a consensus statement. The very definition of tradition that comes to expression in the character of Rabbinic literature – God's revelation to Moses at Sinai received and handed on unimpaired and intact in a reliable process of instruction by masters to disciples – accounts for the public, anonymous character of Rabbinic writing.

Not a line in the entire Rabbinic literature even suggests that schismatic writing existed, even though named statements of individual authorities are preserved on every page of that literature. The point that is proven is simple. People disagreed within a permitted agendum, and the protocol of disagreement always began with the premise of concurrence on all that counted. That was, as we saw, the very goal of Rabbinic dialectics: the rationality of dispute, the cogency of theology and of law as a whole. As every named saying we have examined has already shown us, dissenting views, too, found their properly labeled position in Rabbinic literature, preserved in the name of the private person who registered dissent in accord with the rules governing the iron consensus of the collegium as a whole.

The final question raised by the ubiquity of attributions to named authorities is, what then is the standing of the named sage? We have seen that the sage is subordinate to tradition, on the one side, and the consensus of sages, on the other. That means the individual as such bore only instrumental importance; he mattered because, and only when, he served as a good example. Or his value derived from the traditions he had in hand from prior authorities. But that fact accords to the individual very high standing indeed – when the individual exemplifies the Torah, attests to tradition, or through wit in sound reasoning demonstrates the validity of a position and compels the consensus to favor his view. So attributions fulfill contradictory tasks. They both call into question the validity of what is attributed and also validate the sage as exemplar of the Torah. The sage stood at that same level of authority as did the Torah, on the one side, and the Mishnah, on the other. Therefore the failure to compose gospels alongside Midrash compilations and Mishnah exegesis is not to be explained away as an byproduct of the conception of revelation through words but not through persons that is imputed to the Judaism of the Dual Torah. Quite to the contrary, God reveals the Torah not only through words handed down from Sinai in the form of the Torah, written and oral, but also through the lives and deeds of saints, that is, sages. The same modes of exegetical inquiry pertaining to the Mishnah and Scripture apply without variation to statements made by rabbis of the contemporary period themselves.

A single example of the superficially contradictory, but deeply harmonious, meaning imputed to attributions suffices. For that purpose we turn to the way in which the rabbis of the Yerushalmi proposed to resolve differences of opinion. Precisely in the same way in which talmudic rabbis settled disputes in the Mishnah and so attained a consensus about the law of the Mishnah, they handled disputes among themselves. The importance of that fact for our argument again is simple. The rabbis, represented in the Yerushalmi, treated their own contemporaries exactly as they treated the then ancient authorities of the Mishnah. In their minds the status accorded to the Mishnah, as a derivative of the Torah, applied equally to sages' teachings. In the following instance we see how the same discourse attached to [1] a Mishnah rule is assigned as well to one in [2] the Tosefta and, at the end, to differences among [3] the Yerushalmi's authorities.

Yerushalmi Ketubot

5:1.VI A.   R. Jacob bar Aha, R. Alexa in the name of Hezekiah: "The law accords with the view of R. Eleazar b. Azariah, who stated, **If she was widowed or divorced at the stage of betrothal, the virgin collects only two hundred zuz and the widow, a maneh. If she was widowed or divorced at the stage of a consummated marriage, she collects the full amount [M. Ket. 5:1E,D].**"

B.   R. Hananiah said, "The law accords with the view of R. Eleazar b. Azariah."

C.   Said Abbayye, "They said to R. Hananiah, 'Go and shout [outside whatever opinion you like.' But] R. Jonah, R. Zeira in the name of R. Jonathan said, 'The law accords with the view of R. Eleazar b. Azariah.' [Yet] R. Yosa bar Zeira in the name of R. Jonathan said, 'The law does not accord with the view of R. Eleazar b. Azariah.' [So we do not in fact know the decision.]"

D.   Said R. Yosé, "We had a mnemonic: Hezekiah and R. Jonathan both say one thing."

E.   For it has been taught on Tannaite authority:

F.   **He whose son went abroad, and whom they told, "Your son has died,"**

G.   **and who went and wrote over all his property to someone else as a gift,**

H.   **and whom they afterward informed that his son was yet alive –**

I.   **his deed of gift remains valid.**

J.   **R. Simeon b. Menassia says, "His deed of gift is not valid, for if he had known that his son was alive, he would never have made such a gift"** [T. Ket. 4:14E-H].

K.   Now R. Jacob bar Aha [= A] said, "The law is in accord with the view of R. Eleazar b. Azariah, and the opinion of R. Eleazar b. Azariah is the same in essence as that of R. Simeon b. Menassia."

L.   Now R. Yannai said to R. Hananiah, "Go and shout [outside whatever you want].

M. "But, said R. Yosé bar Zeira in the name of R. Jonathan, 'The law is not in accord with R. Eleazar b. Azariah.'"

N. But in fact the case was to be decided in accord with the view of R. Eleazar b. Azariah.

What is important here is that the Talmud makes no distinction whatever when deciding the law of disputes [1] in the Mishnah, [2] in the Tosefta, and [3] among talmudic rabbis. The same already formed colloquy applied at the outset to the Mishnah's dispute is then held equally applicable to the Tosefta's. The process of thought is the main thing, without regard to the document to which the process applies. Scripture, the Mishnah, the sage – the three spoke with equal authority. True, one had to come into alignment with the other, the Mishnah with Scripture, the sage with the Mishnah. But it was not the case that one component of the Torah, of God's word to Israel, stood within the sacred circle, another beyond. Interpretation and what was interpreted, exegesis and text, belonged together. The sage, or rabbi, constitutes the third component in a tripartite canon of the Torah, because, while Scripture and the Mishnah govern what the sage knows, in the Yerushalmi as in the Bavli it is the sage who authoritatively speaks about them. What sages were willing to do to the Mishnah in the Yerushalmi and Bavli is precisely what they were prepared to do to Scripture – impose upon it their own judgment of its meaning.

The sage speaks with authority about the Mishnah and the Scripture. As much as those documents of the Torah, the sage, too, therefore has authority deriving from revelation. He himself may participate in the process of revelation. There is no material difference. Since that is so, the sage's book, whether the Yerushalmi or the Bavli to the Mishnah or Midrash to Scripture, belongs to the Torah, that is, is revealed by God. It also forms part of the Torah, a fully canonical document. The reason, then, is that the sage is like Moses, "our rabbi," who received torah and wrote the Torah. So while the canon of the Torah was in three parts, two verbal, one incarnate – Scripture, Mishnah, sage – the sage, in saying what the other parts meant and in embodying that meaning in his life and thought, took primacy of place. If no document organized itself around sayings and stories of sages, it was because that was superfluous. Why so? Because all documents, equally, whether Scripture, whether Mishnah, whether Yerushalmi, gave full and complete expression of deeds and deliberations of sages, beginning, after all, with Moses, our rabbi.

A few concluding observations suffice to return us to our starting point. No document in Rabbinic literature is signed by a named author or is so labeled (except in a few instances long after the fact, for example, Judah the Patriarch wrote the Mishnah) as to represent the opinion of a lone individual. In their intrinsic traits of uniform discourse all documents speak out of the single, undifferentiated voice of Sinai, and each makes a statement of the Torah of Sinai and within that Torah. That anonymity, indicative for theological reasons, comes to expression in the highly formalized rhetoric of the canonical writings, which denies the possibility of the individuation not only of the writings themselves, but also of the sayings attributed to authorities in those writings.

Books such as the Mishnah, Sifré to Deuteronomy, Genesis Rabbah, or the Bavli, that after formulation were accepted as part of the canon of Judaism, that is, of "the one whole Torah of Moses our rabbi revealed by God at Sinai," do not contain answers to questions of definition that commonly receive answers within the pages of a given book. Such authors as (the school of) Matthew or Luke, Josephus, even the writers of Ezra-Nehemiah, will have found such a policy surprising. And while Socrates did not write, Plato and Aristotle did – and they signed their own names (or did the equivalent in context). In antiquity books or other important writings, for example, letters and treatises, ordinarily, though not always, bore the name of the author or at least an attribution, for example, Aristotle's or Paul's name, or the attribution to Enoch or Baruch or Luke. For no document in the canon of Judaism produced in late antiquity, by contrast, is there a named author internal to the document. No document in that canon contains within itself a statement of a clear-cut date of composition, a defined place or circumstance in which a book is written, a sustained and ongoing argument to which we readily gain access, or any of the other usual indicators by which we define the authorship, therefore the context and the circumstance, of a book.

The purpose of the sages who in the aggregate created the canonical writings of the Judaism of the Dual Torah is served by not specifying differentiating traits such as time, place, and identity of the author or the authorship. The Judaic equivalent of the Biblical canon ("the Old Testament and the New Testament") is "the one whole Torah of Moses, our rabbi," and that "one, whole Torah" presents single books as undifferentiated episodes in a timeless, ahistorical setting: Torah revealed to Moses by God at Mount Sinai, but written down long afterward. Received in a canonical process of transmission under the auspices of a religious system, any canonical writing, by definition, enjoys authority and status within that canon and system. Hence it is deemed to speak for a community and to represent, and contribute to, the consensus of that community. Without a named author, a canonical writing may be represented, on the surface, as the statement of a consensus. That consensus derives not from an identifiable writer or even school but from the anonymous authorities behind the document as we have it. A consensus of an entire community, the community of

Judaism, reaches its full human realization in the sage. That is why the sage will be mentioned by name – but at the same time represented as exemplary, therefore subordinate; exemplary, not individual; exemplary, not schismatic. In that context writing down of that consensus will not permit individual traits of rhetoric to differentiate writer from writer or writing from writing. The individual obliterates the marks of individuality in serving the holy people by writing a work that will become part of the Torah, and stories about individuals will serve, in that context, only so far as they exemplify and realize traits characteristic of all Torah sages.

4

Form Analysis and Rabbinic Literature: The Present State of the Question

This lecture was given for the Theological Faculty of
Helsinki University at a study day held in Åbo.

I am asked to take up the theme, "The study of forms leads directly to the study of the social institutions in which the forms are used, and the groups that use and develop the forms. Which are, in your opinion, the main groups, and which are the main institutions?" The premise of form criticism or form history maintains that particular literary-rhetorical forms – patterning of words or phrases that takes place external to the particular context and meaning served thereby – conform to the requirements of particular social groups or institutions, which we may identify. Rabbinic literature, from the Mishnah through the Talmud of Babylonia, produces massive evidence to sustain the observation that compositions, and even composites, responded to fixed conventions of formulation and express.

But I cannot identify a single piece of evidence to sustain the further premise that we may link formal preferences of language to the social groups that effected those preferences. That is to say, the indicators that permit differentiation not of a documentary, but of a social, character in form history or form criticism do not come to the surface in a single Rabbinic writing, at least, not as I read those writings. That is why early on I abandoned the language "form criticism" or "form history" in favor of form analysis, that is, the material, concrete analysis of the formal traits of the writings, how they function, what subterranean conceptions they may bring to the surface, and similar analyses of a literary descriptive character. Not only so, but I shall try to demonstrate that what is to be learned from form analysis is not historical, but philosophical in character; form analysis forms a tool for the formation of

55

a history of a religion, not of the people who formulated the data of that religion. Form history trivializes, form analysis lends weight to, what is at stake.

The decisive issue for learning focuses upon differentiation, specifically, the traits we think we can identify, the way in which we interpret those points of differentiation, and, it follows, our answer to the question: What else? That is to say, once we establish that we may distinguish one composition from another by reference to patterns of language present in the one but not the other, we want to know what difference the distinction makes. My answers have told me that the differences concern not the sources of all documents, but the points of difference between one document and another. That is to say, I have found it possible to distinguish the forms of one document from those of another – the formal traits of the Mishnah from the formal traits of Sifra or of Genesis Rabbah. So form analysis has yielded documentary distinctions. Then what else I know because of these formal distinctions yields answers that concern the differences between one document and another. On the other hand, since all forms are utilized by documents of a single social venue, which is the study circle of masters and disciples, on the one side, and the "session" or metivta or rabbinic institution (however defined) on the other, I have never discovered any institutional or other points of differentiation yielded by these same formal differences. To give a single, simple example, the dispute form – statement of a problem, Rabbi X says..., Rabbi Y says... – that we find in the Mishnah compares to the formulation of disputes in, for example, the two Talmuds or Genesis Rabbah; but the formal traits of the dispute in the Mishnah prove blatant, and further, they are readily differentiated from the formal traits of the dispute in Genesis Rabbah, on the one side, and the Talmud of the Land of Israel, on the other.

If, now, we revert to the question assigned to me, "The study of forms leads directly to the study of the social institutions in which the forms are used, and the groups that use and develop the forms. Which are, in your opinion, the main groups, and which are the main institutions?" what response can I offer? First, the study of forms in the Rabbinic literature by definition as much as by result yields the trivial result that the social institutions responsible for all forms constitute a single institution, the Rabbinic estate (for lack of a better social metaphor). The main groups, by definition, come to exposure in the documents that, as a matter of hypothesis, a given group of framers and redactors wrote and compiled. The main institutions are the same: the ongoing groups that, for some four hundred years, wrote and compiled writings now found in Rabbinic documents.

Now that result, though offering little grounds for rejoicing in form critical circles in New Testament studies, allows a different, and I think, productive inquiry of its own. It concerns what we learn about groups of people – in our case, groups defined by the documents that they put forth – from the documents that they made. Specifically, are we able to move from the forms of a piece of writing to the imaginative life and the cognitive structures of the people who made a book one way, rather than another, out of materials conforming to one formal protocol, rather than some other? That is a question of not sociology or institutional history but social culture, the shared mentality of a group, otherwise unknown and in personality anonymous, who bear responsibility for a distinctive document. Form analysis yields not history but access to the social imagination of a group of rabbis, and, as a matter of fact, we are able to compare the mentality behind one document with that behind another, with results I have found stimulating and suggestive.

To show how that works, I turn to two problems, the first, description of a document in its own terms, second, comparison of two distinct documents. For the former task, I take up the Mishnah, and, for the latter, the two Talmuds. In each case what I want to know is, if I know people wrote in a certain way, what else do I know about those writers, that is, what do I know about how they saw things or constructed the world round about them? In framing the question in such a way, I have moved beyond the narrowly historical questions concerning the relationship of groups to particular forms, on the one side, and the institutional history that accounts for the persistence of forms, on the other. In my view, what I propose involves substantially less speculation concerning undemonstrable propositions, but that is for others to decide.

Let me speak first about the Mishnah. The Mishnah, a philosophical law code that reached closure at ca. A.D. 200, is divided into tractates, chapters, and paragraphs. We know when a tractate begins and ends because tractates are organized by subject matter. "Chapters" by contrast constitute conventions of printers. There is little internal evidence that the framers of the document broke up the tractates along the lines followed by the copyists and printers of medieval and early modern times. What we have within tractates are subunits on problems or themes presented by the basic topic of the tractate. These subunits or themes are characterized by the confluence of formal and substantive traits. That is to say, a given formal pattern characterizes discourse on a given substantive problem. When the topic or problem changes, the formal pattern also will be altered. What establishes the formal pattern will be three or more recurrences of a given arrangement of words, ordinarily in accord with a distinctive syntactic structure. Fewer than three such occurrences, for example, of a given mode of formulating a thought, were not found by the framers to suffice to impart that patterned formulation that they proposed to use.

The dominant stylistic trait of the Mishnah is the acute formalization of its syntactical structure, specifically, its intermediate divisions, so organized that the limits of a theme correspond to those of a formulary pattern. The balance and order of the Mishnah are particular to the Mishnah. Tosefta does not sustainedly reveal equivalent traits. Since the Mishnah is so very distinctive a document, we now investigate the intentions of the people who made it. About whom does it speak? And why, in particular, have its authorities distinctively shaped language, which in the Tosefta does not speak in rhymes and balanced, matched declarative sentences, imposing upon the conceptual, factual prose of the law a peculiar kind of poetry? Why do they create rhythmic order, grammatically balanced sentences containing discrete laws, laid out in what seem to be carefully enumerated sequences, and the like? Language not only contains culture, which could not exist without it. Language – in our case, linguistic and syntactical style and stylization – expresses a worldview and ethos. Whose worldview is contained and expressed in the Mishnah's formalized rhetoric?

There is no reason to doubt that if we asked the tradental-redactional authorities behind the Mishnah the immediate purpose of their formalization, their answer would be, to facilitate memorization. For that is the proximate effect of the acute formalization of their document. Much in its character can be seen as mnemonic. But if stylization and formalization testify to a mnemonic program, then absence of the same traits must mean that some materials were not intended to be memorized. The Mishnah, and the Mishnah alone, was the corpus to be formulated for memorization and transmitted through "living books," Tannaim, to the coming generations. The Tosefta cannot have been formulated along the same lines. Accordingly, the Mishnah is given a special place and role by those who stand behind it.

The unified and cogent formal character of the Mishnah testifies in particular to that of its ultimate tradent-redactors. We learn in the Mishnah about the intention of that last generation of Mishnaic authorities, who gave us the document as we have it. It is their way of saying things which we know for certain. From this we hope to learn something about them and their worldview. One certain fact is that they choose to hand on important materials in such a form as facilitated memorization. The second, which follows closely, is that the document is meant to be memorized. Whether or not it also was copied and transmitted in writing, and whether or not such copies were deemed authoritative, are not questions we can answer on the basis of the

Mishnah's internal evidence. The Tosefta certainly suggests that the Mishnah pericopae were copied and glossed, but its evidence does not pertain to these larger issues.

The formal rhetoric of the Mishnah is empty of content, which is proved by the fact that pretty much all themes and conceptions can be reduced to these same few formal patterns. These patterns, I have shown, are established by syntactical recurrences, as distinct from repetition of sounds. The same words do not recur, except in the case of the few forms we have specified, or key words in a few contexts. These forms have to be excised from the formulary patterns in which they occur, so that we may discern the operative and expressive patterns themselves. On the other hand, long sequences of sentences fail to repeat the same words – that is, syllabic balance, rhythm, or sound – yet they do establish a powerful claim to order and formulary sophistication and perfection. That is why we could name a pattern, he who...it is... apocopation: The arrangement of the words, as a grammatical pattern, not their substance, is indicative of pattern. Accordingly, while we have a document composed along what clearly are mnemonic lines, the document's susceptibility to memorization rests principally upon the utter abstraction of recurrent syntactical patterns, rather than on the concrete repetition of particular words, rhythms, syllabic counts, or sounds.

A sense for the deep, inner logic of word patterns, of grammar and syntax, rather than for their external similarities, governs the Mishnaic mnemonic. Even though the Mishnah is to be memorized and handed on orally, it expresses a mode of thought attuned to abstract relationships, rather than concrete and substantive forms. The formulaic, not the formal, character of Mishnaic rhetoric yields a picture of a subculture which speaks of immaterial and not material things. In this subculture the relationship, rather than the thing or person which is related, is primary and constitutes the principle of reality. The thing in itself is less than the thing in cathexis with other things; so, too, the person. The repetition of form creates form. But what here is repeated is not form, but formulary pattern, a pattern effected through persistent grammatical or syntactical relationships and affecting an infinite range of diverse objects and topics. Form and structure emerge not from concrete, formal things but from abstract and unstated but ubiquitous and powerful relationships.

This fact – the creation of pattern through grammatical relationship of syntactical elements, more than through concrete sounds – tells us that the people who memorized conceptions reduced to these particular forms were capable of extraordinarily abstract perception. Hearing peculiarities of word order in quite diverse cognitive contexts, their ears and minds perceived regularities of grammatical arrangement, repeated functional variations of utilization of diverse words, grasping from such subtleties syntactical patterns not imposed or expressed by recurrent external phenomena and autonomous of particular meanings. What they heard, it is clear, not only were abstract relationships, but also principles conveyed along with and through these relationships. For what was memorized, as I have said, was a fundamental notion, expressed in diverse examples but in recurrent rhetorical-syntactical patterns. Accordingly, what they could and did hear was what lay far beneath the surface of the rule: both the unstated principle and the unsounded pattern. This means, I stress, that their mode of thought was attuned to what lay beneath the surface, their mind and their ears perceived what was not said behind what was said, and how it was said. Social interrelationships within the community of Israel are left behind in the ritual speech of the Mishnah, just as, within the laws, natural realities are made to give form and expression to supernatural or metaphysical regularities. The Mishnah speaks of Israel, but the speakers are a group apart. The Mishnah talks of this-worldly things, but the things stand for and evoke another world entirely.

To describe that transcendent purpose, we turn to Wittgenstein's saying. "The limits of my language mean the limits of my world." The Mishnah's formulaic rhetoric on the one side imposes limits, boundaries, upon the world. What fits into that rhetoric, can be said by it, constitutes world, world given shape and boundary by the Mishnah. The Mishnah implicitly maintains, therefore, that a wide range of things fall within the territory mapped out by a limited number of linguistic conventions, grammatical sentences. What is grammatical can be said and therefore constitutes part of the reality created by Mishnaic word. What cannot be contained within the grammar of the sentence cannot be said and therefore falls outside of the realm of Mishnaic reality. Mishnaic reality consists in those things which can attain order, balance, and principle. Chaos then lies without. Yet, if we may extrapolate from the capacity of the impoverished repertoire of grammar to serve for all sorts of things, for the eleven topics of our division, for example, then we must concede that all things can be said by formal revision. Everything can be reformed, reduced to the order and balance and exquisite sense for the just match that is characteristic of the Mishnaic pericope. Anything of which we wish to speak is susceptible of the ordering and patterning of Mishnaic grammar and syntax. That is a fact which is implicit throughout our division. Accordingly, the territory mapped out by Mishnaic language encompasses the whole of the pertinent world under discussion. There are no thematic limitations of Mishnaic formalized speech.

Language in the Mishnah replaces cult, formalism of one kind takes the place of formalism of another. The claim that infinitely careful and patterned doing of a particular sort of deeds is ex opere operato an expression of the sacred has its counterpart in the implicit character of the Mishnah's language. Its rhetoric is formed with infinite care, according to a finite pattern for speech, about doing deeds of a particular sort. Language now conforms to cult then. The formal cult, once performed in perfect silence, now is given its counterpart in formal speech. Where once men said nothing, but through gesture and movement, in other circumstances quite secular, performed holy deed, now they do nothing, but through equally patterned revision of secular words about secular things perform holy speech. In the cult it is the very context which makes an intrinsically neutral, therefore secular, act into a holy one. Doing the thing right, with precision and studied care, makes the doing holy. Slaughtering an animal, collecting its blood and butchering it, burning incense and pouring wine – these by themselves are things which can be and are done in the home as much as in the cult. But in the cult they are characterized by formality and precision.

In the Mishnah, by contrast, there is no spatial context to sanctify the secular act of saying things. The context left, once cult is gone, is solely the cultic mode of formalism, the ritualization of speech, that most neutral and commonplace action. The Mishnah transforms speech into ritual and so creates the surrogate of ritual deed. That which was not present in cult, speech, is all that is present now that the silent cult is gone. And, it follows, it is by the formalization of speech, its limitation to a few patterns, and its perfection through the creation of patterns of relationships in particular, that the old nexus of heaven and earth, the cult, now is to be replicated in the new and complementary nexus, cultic speech about all things.

What the limitation of Mishnaic language to a few implicit relational realities accomplished, therefore, is the reduction of the world to the limits of language. In ritual grammar the world therein contained and expressed attains formalization among, and simplification by, the unstated but remarkably few principles contained within, and stated by, the multitudinous cases which correspond to the world. Mishnaic language makes possible the formalization of the whole of the everyday and workaday world. It accomplishes the transformation of all things in accord with that sense for perfect form and unfailing regularity which once were distinctive to the operation of the cult. Mishnaic language explores the possibility of containing and creating a new realm of reality, one which avoids abstractions and expresses all things only through the precision of grammatical patterns, that is, the reality of abstract relationships alone.

Have we come closer to a perception of the purpose for which, according to the internal testimony of our order, the Mishnah was created? In a concrete sense, of course, we have not. Mishnaic rhetoric says nothing explicit about the purpose of the rhetoric. In the simplest sense, as we noted, the proximate purpose of formalization was to facilitate the mnemonic process. Yet it is to beg the question to say that the purpose of facilitating memorization is to help people remember things. The authors of the Mishnah wants their book to be memorized for a reason. The reason transcends the process, pointing, rather, to its purpose. Nor do we stand closer to the inner intentions of the Mishnah's authorities when we raise the polemical purpose of memorization. This was to act out the claim that there are two components of "the one whole Torah which Moses, our rabbi, received from God at Sinai," one transmitted in writing, the other handed on by tradition, in oral form only. True, the claim for the Mishnah, laid down in Abot, the Mishnah's first and most compelling apologetic, is that the authority of the Mishnah rests upon its status as received tradition of God.

It follows that tradition handed on through memory is valid specifically because, while self-evidently not part of the Written Torah, which all Israel has in hand, it is essential to the whole Torah. Its mode of tradition through memory verifies and authenticates its authority as tradition begun by God, despite its absence from the written part of Torah. Both these things – the facilitation of memorization, the authentication of the document through its external form – while correct also are post facto. They testify to the result of Mishnaic rhetoric for both educational-tradental and polemical-apologetic purposes. Once we memorize, we accomplish much. But why, to begin with, commit these gnomic sayings to such language as facilitates their memorization?

In a world such as the Mishnah's, in which writing is routine, memorization is special. What happens when we know something by heart which does not happen when we must read it or look for it in a scroll or a book? It is that when we walk in the street and when we sit at home, when we sleep and when we awake, we carry with us, in our everyday perceptions, that memorized gnomic saying. The process of formulation through formalization and the coequal process of memorizing patterned cases to sustain the perception of the underlying principle, uniting the cases just as the pattern unites their language, extend the limits of language to the outer boundaries of experience, the accidents of everyday life itself. Gnomic sayings are routine in all cultures. But the reduction of all truth particularly to gnomic sayings is not.

To impose upon those sayings an underlying and single structure of grammar corresponding to the inner structure of reality is to transform the structure of language into a statement of ontology. Once our minds are trained to perceive principle among cases and pattern within grammatical relationships, we further discern in the concrete events of daily life both principle and underlying autonomous pattern. The form of the Mishnah is meant to correspond to the formalization perceived within, not merely imposed upon, the conduct of concrete affairs, principally, the meaning and character of concrete happenings among things, in the workaday life of people. The matter obviously is not solely ethical, but the ethical component is self-evident. It also has to do with the natural world and the things which break its routine, of which our division speaks so fully and in such exquisite detail. Here all things are a matter of relationship, circumstance, fixed and recurrent interplay. If X, then Y, if not X, then not Y – that is the datum by which minds are shaped.

The way to shape and educate minds is to impart into the ear, thence into the mind, perpetual awareness that what happens recurs, and what recurs is pattern and order, and, through them, wholeness. How better than to fill the mind with formalized sentences, generative both of meaning for themselves and of significance beyond themselves, in which meaning rests upon the perception of relationship? Pattern is to be discovered in alertness, in the multiplicity of events and happenings, none of which states or articulates pattern. Mind, trained to memorize through what is implicit and beneath the surface, is to be accustomed and taught in such a way as to discern pattern. Order is because order is discovered, first in language, then in life. As the cult in all its precise and obsessive attention to fixed detail effected the perception that from the orderly center flowed lines of meaning to the periphery, so the very language of the Mishnah, in the particular traits which I have specified, also in its precise and obsessive concentration on innate and fixed relationship, effects the perception of order deep within the disorderly world of language, nature, and man.

There is a perfect correspondence between what the Mishnah proposes to say and the way in which it says it. An essential part of the ethos of Mishnaic culture is its formal and formulaic sentence, the means by which it makes its cognitive statements and so expresses its worldview. Not only does ethos correspond to worldview, but worldview is expressed in style as much as in substance. In the case of Mishnaic form, the ethos and worldview come together in the very elements of grammatical formalization, which, never made articulate, express the permanence and paramount character of relationship, the revelatory relativity of context and circumstance. Life attains form in structure. It is structure which is most vivid in life. The medium for the expression of the worldview is the ethos. But for the Mishnah, ethos neither appeals to, nor, so far as I can see, expresses, emotion. Just as there is no room for nuance in general in the severe and balanced sentences of the Mishnah, so there is no place for the nuance of emotion of commitment in general.

The rhetoric of our document makes no appeal to emotion or to obedience, describing, not invoking, the compelling and ineluctable grounds for assent. This claim that things are such and so, relate in such and such a way, without regard or appeal to how we want them to be, is unyielding. Law is law, despite the accidents of workaday life, and facts are facts. The bearer of facts, the maker of law, is the relationship, the pattern by which diverse things are set into juxtaposition with one another, whether subject and predicate, or dead creeping thing and loaf of heave-offering. What is definitive is not the thing but the context and the circumstance, the time, the condition, the intention of the actor. In all, all things are relative to all things.

The bridge from ethos to worldview is the form and character of the sentence which transforms the one into the other. The declarative sentence, through patterned language, takes attitude and turns it into cognition. Mishnaic "religion" not only speaks of values. Its mode of speech is testimony to its highest and most enduring, distinctive value. This language does not speak of sacred symbols but of pots and pans, of menstruation and dead creeping things, of ordinary water which, because of the circumstance of its collection and location, possesses extraordinary power, of the commonplace corpse and the ubiquitous diseased person, of genitalia and excrement, toilet seats and the flux of penises, of stems of pomegranates and stalks of leeks, of rain and earth and clay ovens, wood, metal, glass, and hide. This language is filled with words for neutral things of humble existence. It does not speak of holy things and is not symbolic in its substance. In the Mishnah, Holy Things are merely animals a farmer has designated, in his intention, as holy. The language of the Mishnah speaks of ordinary things, of workaday things which everyone must have known. But because of the peculiar and particular way in which it is formed and formalized, this same language not only adheres to an aesthetic theory but expresses a deeply embedded ontology and methodology of the sacred, specifically of the sacred within the secular, and of the capacity for regulation, therefore for sanctification, within the ordinary.

Worldview and ethos are synthesized in language. The synthesis is expressed in grammatical and syntactical regularities. What is woven into some sort of ordered whole is not a cluster of sacred symbols. The religious system is not discerned within symbols at all. Knowledge of the conditions of life is imparted principally through the description of the commonplace facts of life, which symbolize, stand for, nothing beyond themselves and their consequences for the clean and the unclean. That description is effected through the construction of units of meaning, intermediate divisions composed of cognitive elements. The whole is balanced, explicit in detail, but reticent about the whole, balanced in detail but dumb about the character of the balance. What is not said is what is eloquent and compelling as much as what is said. Accordingly, that simple and fundamental congruence between ethos and worldview is to begin with, for the Mishnah, the very language by which the one is given cognitive expression in the other. The medium of patterned speech conveys the meaning of what is said.

So much for the form analysis of a single document. When it comes to the comparison of documents, form analysis formulates a question, which philosophical analysis must resolve. Form analysis shows how two documents are alike, but then philosophical analysis must explain how they differ. So we move from the formal study of forms to the philosophical study of the same data. The case in point derives from the Talmuds of the Land of Israel and of Babylonia, respectively. The case derives from a simple fact. The two Talmuds follow a single redactional form, being organized as commentaries to clauses or sentences of chapters of the Mishnah. They pursue a program in common, citing some of the same received formulations of rules, and using pretty much the same fixed verbal particles for the same purpose. It follows that by comparing the two documents, we may hope to compare the two distinct authorships that produced them. This, too, falls into the framework of form analysis, though the sense of analysis of forms in this case broadens from the limited sense that applies to the form analysis of the Mishnah. For what we learn here concerns not how an authorship imagines the world beyond itself – surely a considerable lesson in the study of texts – but rather how two authorships undertake in quite different ways to do the same literary work, which is the formation of a sustained commentary to a single received text.

Here I shall report as a set of generalizations the results of seven volumes of detailed comparisons between the two Talmuds' reading of the same Mishnah paragraph. These generalizations flow from the results of specific studies, presented in my *Bavli's Unique Voice* I-VII. The comparison is justified, in the framework of form analysis, by a single fact. The framers organize their ideas in the same way, around the same document, appealing to modes of formalization that, while not interchangeable, are strikingly similar.

Even though the two Talmuds use more or less the same forms to accomplish the same goal, the Bavli and the Yerushalmi in the end simply do not sustain comparison, because the Bavli is in quality and character different from the Yerushalmi, so different that the two

Talmuds are incomparable. Here is a case in which shared forms conceal deep differences, one that calls into question the assumption that a single institutional origin accounts for a given form. The two documents are diverse, for the one talks in details, the other in large truths; the Yerushalmi tells us what the Mishnah says, the Bavli, what it means, which is to say, how its laws form law, the way in which its rules attest to the ontological unity of truth, a term that will presently become clear in the context of the reading of the Bavli against the backdrop of the Mishnah. The distinction between the documents, so I have claimed, lies in the intellectual morphology that characterizes each. But the true difference between them derives from not intellection but outcome (to be sure, the product of intellection). The Bavli thinks more deeply about deep things, and, in the end, its authors think about different things from those that occupy the writers of the Yerushalmi. And yet, as is clear, the Bavli's authors find exactly the same formal protocols entirely suitable for their work.

Where the Talmuds intersect but diverge in the reading of the Mishnah paragraph, for instance in their reading of M. Gittin 1:1, we are able to identify what is at issue. Here is an occasion on which we can see the differences between the Yerushalmi's and the Bavli's representation of a conflict of principles contained within a Mishnah ruling. The Yerushalmi maintains that at issue is the inexpertness of overseas courts versus a lenient ruling to avoid the situation of the abandoned wife; the Bavli, inexpertness of overseas courts versus paucity of witnesses. How these diverse accounts differ in intellectual character and also program is hardly revealed by that brief precis. The Bavli is different from the Yerushalmi not in detail but in very character; that despite commonalities of form, which validate comparison, the two Talmuds in fact are utterly unlike pieces of writing, and that the second of the two Talmuds makes its own statement not merely because it very often says different things from the Bavli, or because it says different things in different ways (though both are the case). It stands on its own not only because its framers think differently; nor merely because their modes of thought and analysis in no way correspond to those of the Yerushalmi. The governing reason is that, for the framers of the Bavli, what is at stake in thought is different from the upshot of thought as conceived by the authors of the Yerushalmi's compositions and compilers of its composites. Specifically, for the sages who produced the Bavli, the ultimate compilers and redactors of the document, what at issue is not laws but law: how things hold together at the level of high abstraction.

What characterizes the Bavli and not the Yerushalmi is the search for the unitary foundations of the diverse laws, through an inquiry into the premises of discrete rules, the comparison and contrast of those premises, the statement of the emergent principles, and the comparison and contrast of those principles with the ones that derive from other cases and their premises – a process, an inquiry without end into the law behind the laws. What the Bavli wants, beyond its presentation of the positions at hand, is to draw attention to the premises of those positions, the reasoning behind them, the evidence that supports them, the argument that transforms evidence into demonstration, and even the authority, among those who settle questions by expressing opinions, who can hold the combination of principles or premises that underpin a given position.

Now, when we observe that one Talmud is longer than the other, or one Talmud gives a fuller account than the other, we realize that such an observation is trivial. The real difference between the Talmuds emerges from this – and I state with emphasis: *The Bavli's completely different theory of what it wishes to investigate.* And that difference derives not from intellectual morphology, but generative purpose: why the framers of the Bavli's compositions and composites did the work to begin with. The outlines of the intellectual character of the work flow from the purpose of the project, not the reverse; and thence, the modes of thought, the specifics of analytical initiative – all these are secondary to intellectual morphology. So first comes the motivation for thought, then the morphology of thought, then the media of thought, in that order.

The difference between the Yerushalmi and the Bavli is the difference between jurisprudence and philosophy; the one is a work of exegesis in search of jurisprudential system, the other, of analysis in quest of philosophical truth. To state matters simply, the Yerushalmi presents the laws, the rule for this, the rule for that – pure and simple; "law" bears its conventional meaning of jurisprudence. The Bavli presents the law, now in the philosophical sense of the abstract issues of theory, the principles at play far beneath the surface of detailed discussion, the law behind the laws. And that, we see, is not really "law," in any ordinary sense of jurisprudence; it is law in a deeply philosophical sense: the rules that govern the way things are, that define what is proportionate and orderly and properly composed.

The reason that the Bavli does commonly what the Yerushalmi does seldom and then rather clumsily – the balancing of arguments, the careful formation of a counterpoint of reasons, the excessively fair representation of contradictory positions (why doesn't X take the position of Y? why doesn't Y take the position of X? Indeed!) – is not that the Bavli's framers are uninterested in conclusions and outcome. It is that for them, the deep structure of reason is the goal, and the only way to penetrate into how things are at their foundations is to investigate how conflicting positions rest on principles to be exposed and juxtaposed, balanced, and, if possible, negotiated, if necessary, left in the balance.

The Yerushalmi is an eighteenth century fugue, the Bavli, a twentieth century symphonic metamorphosis: not merely more complicated, but rather, a different conception altogether of what music is – and can do. And while, in the end, neither kind of music is the only valid kind, taste and judgment come into play; while we value and enjoy the simplicities of the baroque, the profundities, the inventiveness, the abstraction of our own day's music speak to us and reshape our hearing. So too, while anyone can appreciate the direct and open clarity of the Yerushalmi (in those vast spaces of the text that are clear and accessible), no one can avoid the compelling, insistent, scrupulously fair but unrelenting command of the Bavli: see to the center of things, the core of mind, the workings of intellect in its own right.

Not only so, but even when the facts are the same, the issues identical, and the arguments matched, the Bavli's author manages to lay matters out in a very distinctive way. And that way yields as a sustained, somewhat intricate argument (requiring us to keep in the balance both names and positions of authorities and also the objective issues and facts) what the Yerushalmi's method of representation gives us as a rather simple sequence of arguments. If we say that the Bavli is "dialectical," presenting a moving argument, from point to point, and the Yerushalmi is static, through such a reductive understatement we should vastly misrepresent the difference. Rather, the Bavli's presentation is one of thrust and parry, challenge and response, assertion and counter-assertion; theoretical possibility and its exposure to practical facts ("If I had to rely...I might have supposed..."); and, of course, the authorities of the Bavli (not only the framers) in the person of Abbayye are even prepared to rewrite the received Tannaite formulation. That initiative can come, I should think, only from someone totally in command of the abstractions and able to say, the details have to be this way; so the rule of mind requires; and so it shall be.

The Yerushalmi's message is that the Mishnah yields clear and present rules; its medium is the patient exegesis of Mishnah passages, the provision and analysis of facts required in the understanding of the Mishnah. That medium conveys its message about not the Mishnah alone, but – through its silences, which I think are intellectual failures of millennial dimensions – about the laws. The Bavli, for its part, conveys its message in a coherent and persistent manner through its ever-recurring medium of analysis and thought. We miss the point of the message if we misconstrue the medium: it is not the dialectical argument, and a mere reportage of questions and answers, thrust and parry, proposal and counterproposal – that does not accurately convey the medium of the Bavli, not at all. Where we ask for authority behind an unstated rule and find out whether the same authority is consistent as to principle in other cases altogether, where we show that authorities are consistent with positions taken elsewhere – here above all we stand in the very heart of the Bavli's message – but only if we know what is at stake in the medium of inquiry. Happily, our sages of blessed memory leave no doubts about what is at stake.

The Bavli's voice is unique – and so is its message. But the message emerges in the medium. The Bavli attained intellectual hegemony over the mind of Israel, the holy people, because its framers so set forth their medium that the implicit message gained immediacy in the heat of argument – so that, as a matter of fact, argument about the law served as a mode of serving God through study of the Torah. But its true power derived from the message: that the truth is one. Now to set forth, in the correct context, precisely what that sentence means. And the sole valid context is, of course, the one defined for itself by the Bavli: the Mishnah, to which the Bavli's framers turned for the structure and substance of their statement.

I promised to move from form analysis to philosophical conclusion, and let me now keep that promise in a simple proposition: if the message of the first document of the Oral Torah, the Mishnah, is the hierarchical unity of all being in the One on high, then the right medium for that message is the summa of the Oral Torah, the Bavli, on account of its quest for abstraction. Matching the Mishnah's ontology of hierarchical unity of all being is the Bavli's principle that many principles express a single one, many laws embody one governing law, which is the law behind the laws. In more secular language, the intellectual medium of the Bavli accomplishes the transformation of jurisprudence into philosophy. How do the two documents work together to establish through many facts a single statement of the governing fact of being? We come at the end to our starting point; the Mishnah establishes a world in stasis: lists of like things, subject to like rules. The Bavli portrays a world in motion: lists of like things form series; but series, too, conform to rules.

Demonstrating in conclusion and in message that the truth is one, whole, comprehensive, cogent, coherent, harmonious, showing that fact of intellect – these sustained points of insistence on the character of mind and the result of thought form the goal of the Bavli's framers. In the comparison with the Yerushalmi we appreciate that the Bavli's quest for unity leads to the inquiry into the named authorities behind an unassigned rule, showing that a variety of figures can concur, meaning, names that stand for a variety of distinct principles can form a single proposition of integrity. That same quest insists on the fair and balanced representation of conflicting principles behind discrete laws, not to serve the cause of academic harmony (surely a lost cause in any age!), but to set forth how, at their foundations, the complicated and diverse laws may be explained by appeal to simple and few principles; the conflict of principles then is less consequential than the demonstration that diverse cases may be reduced to only a few principles.

Take for example the single stylistically indicative trait of the Bavli, its dialectical, or moving, argument. The dialectical argument opens the possibility of reaching out from one thing to something else, not because people have lost sight of their starting point or their goal in the end, but because they want to encompass, in the analytical argument underway, as broad and comprehensive a range of cases and rules as they possibly can. The movement from point to point in reference to a single point that accurately describes the dialectical argument reaches a goal of abstraction, leaving behind the specificities of not only cases but laws, carrying us upward to the law that governs many cases, the premises that undergird many rules, and still higher to the principles that infuse diverse premises; then the principles that generate other, unrelated premises, which, in turn, come to expression in other, still-less intersecting cases. The meandering course of argument comes to an end when we have shown how things cohere. That is what we have learned about the Bavli in this comparison of the two Talmuds.

It is therefore the incontrovertible fact that the framers of the Mishnah set forth not only cases, examples, propositions as to fact, but also, through the particulars, a set of generalizations about classification and the relationships of the classes of things that yield a metaproposition. The whole composition of thought is set forth, in the correct intellectual manner, through the patient classification of things by appeal to the traits that they share, with comparison and contrast among points of difference then yielding the governing rule for a given classification. And the goal was through proper classification of things to demonstrate the hierarchical order of being, culminating in the proposition that all things derive from, and join within, (in secular language) one thing or (in the language of philosophy of religion) the One, or (in the language of Judaism) God.

Diverse topics of the Mishnah are so represented as to make a single set of cogent points about hierarchical classification. Can the same claim be made of the Mishnah's greatest single commentary, that it, too, says one thing about many things? The answer to the "can" lies in rhetoric: do the people talk in the same way about many subjects? The answer – by this point obvious, after seven parts of a monograph on the uniqueness of discourse in the Bavli – is that they do. Both the Mishnah and the Bavli undertake to uncover and expose, in the laws of the Torah, the philosophy that the Torah reveals. That is the upshot of the two documents' powerful and reasoned, fully-instantiated polemic: many things yield one thing, and this is that one thing. Stated in the language of revelation, the Torah through many things says one thing, through many commandments, sets forth one commandment, through diversity in detail makes a single, main point. And we know what that point is. By "the integrity of truth," in secular language, we say the same thing that we express when, in mythic language, we speak, as does Sherira Gaon at the end of a long apologetic tradition, of "the one whole Torah of Moses, our rabbi." But now, by "one" and by "whole," very specific statements are made: jurisprudence reaches upward toward philosophy, on the one side, and the teachings and rules of the Torah are wholly harmonious and cogent, on the other. In the language that I have used here, the upshot is very simple: mind is one, whole, coherent; thought properly conducted yields simple truth about complex things.

Here we move beyond the limits of the analysis of the forms of rhetoric or of formal argument. The outcome of the contrast, then, is not merely the difference that the Yerushalmi is brief and laconic while the Bavli speaks in fully spelled out ways. Nor is it the difference that, in general, the Yerushalmi's presentations are not dialectical, and the Bavli's are, for even though that difference may in general prove fixed, on occasion the Yerushalmi will expand an argument through question and answer, parry and counterthrust, and the analogy of a duel will apply to the Yerushalmi, if not consistently. The difference is intellectual: the Bavli's composites' framers consistently treat as a question to be investigated the exegetical hypotheses that the Yerushalmi's compositions' authors happily accept as conclusive. All of the secondary devices of testing an allegation – a close reading of the formulation of the Mishnah, an appeal to the false conclusion such a close reading, absent a given formulation, might have yielded, to take the examples before us – serve that primary goal. The second recurrent difference is that the Bavli's framers find themselves constantly drawn toward questions of generalization and abstraction (once more: the law behind the laws), moving from case to principle to new case to new principle, then asking whether the substrate of principles forms a single, tight fabric. The Yerushalmi's authors rarely, if ever, pursue that chimera.

But what gives the Bavli its compelling, ineluctable power to persuade, the source of the Bavli's intellectual force is that thrust for abstraction, through generalization (and in that order, generalization, toward abstraction). To spell out in very simple terms what I conceive to be at issue: the way that the law behind the laws emerges is, first, generalization of a case into a principle, then, the recasting of the principle into an abstraction encompassing a variety of otherwise free-standing principles. This observation calls to mind, as I have briefly shown just now, how the Mishnah's cases time and again point toward a single abstraction, the hierarchical order of all being. Here, in the Bavli, I find the counterpart and completion of the Mishnah's deepest layer of thought, which is, the intellectual medium to match the philosophical message. The stakes of form analysis are much weightier than the historical definition suggests.

5

The Feminization of Judaism: Systemic Reversals and Their Meaning in the Formation of the Rabbinic System

This lecture was given in Swedish in Åbo and in Lund.

Rabbinic Judaism routinely finds itself represented as a wholly patriarchal, male religious system. Certainly, descriptions of Rabbinic Judaism as a male religion, subordinating women in countless ways, adduce in evidence more than ample supporting data. And yet, I shall show, at the systemic center of this patriarchal, male religious system is a deeply feminine conception of relationships.

If we may characterize masculine relationships as assertive, coercive, and aggressive, and feminine ones as suggestive, cooperative, and responsive, then the relationship between God and the human being in Rabbinic Judaism emerges as feminine. And that is not by appeal to standard, stereotyped definitions of the masculine and the feminine, since the documents themselves explicitly define the masculine as active, the feminine as passive, and the like. But then, how shall we characterize a system that maintains feminine, not masculine values? For example, God at the center does not coerce humanity, but responds freely to the gift freely given; humanity at the heart of matters does not compel God or engage in acts of force or manipulation. Human gives freely, God responds freely. Masculine relationships are conceived in terms of dominance, women's in terms of mutuality and negotiation. The right relationship with God emerges in the Dual Torah as not coerced, not assertive, not manipulative, but as one of mutuality and response, the one to the other: a transaction of responsive grace.

I. The Systemic Center: The Conception of *Zekhut*

While people suppose that the Torah forms the symbolic center of Rabbinic Judaism, and study of the Torah the critical action, so that women, excluded from academies, find no place in Rabbinic Judaism at all, in fact when we reach the systemic center, we find that "the study of Torah" does not outweigh all else, not at all. Even the stories contained in the Talmud of the Land of Israel in which the priority and sanctity of the sage's knowledge of the Torah form the focus of discourse treat study of the Torah as contingent and merely instrumental. Time and again, knowledge of the Torah forms a way-station on a path to a more distant, more central goal: attaining *zekhut,* here translated as "the heritage of virtue and its consequent entitlements." Torah study is one means of attaining access to that heritage, of gaining *zekhut.* There are other equally suitable means, and, not only so, but the merit gained by Torah study is no different from the merit gained by any and all other types of acts of supererogatory grace. And still more astonishing, a single remarkable action may produce *zekhut* of the same order as a lifetime of devotion to Torah study, and a simple ass-driver through a noteworthy act of selfless behavior may attain the same level of *zekhut* as a learned sage.

Were such stories as these located other than in the Talmud of the Land of Israel, one might find tempting the thesis that they represented an anti-rabbinic viewpoint. But rabbis told these stories, preserved them, and placed them on exhibition to expose the finest virtue they could imagine. That is why we turn for our integrating conception to that final reversal and revision of the given: just as scarce resources are made abundant, legitimate power deemed only weakness, and facts displaced by revealed truth, so the one-time moment at which *zekhut* is attained from heaven outweighs a lifetime of Torah learning. *Zekhut* formed the foundation for the Yerushalmi's conception of political economy for the social order of Israel. It and not Torah defined the whole, of which economics and politics comprised mere details. It set forth and accounts for an economics and a politics that made powerlessness into power, disinheritance into wealth. How in fact does *zekhut* function?

Zekhut is gained for a person by an act of renunciation and self-abnegation, such that heaven responds with an act of grace. Works of supererogation, which heaven cannot compel but highly prizes, *zekhut* defines the very opposite of coercion. It is an act that no one could anticipate or demand, but an act of such remarkable selflessness that heaven finds itself constrained to respond. That is why the systemic center is formed by an act, on heaven's part, of responsive grace, meaning, grace one by definition cannot demand or compel, but only provoke. When we make ourselves less, heaven makes us more; but we cannot force our will upon heaven. When we ask about the feminization of Judaism, our attention rests upon this fact: the right relationship between Israel and God is the relationship that is not coerced, not manipulated, not one defined by a dominant party upon a subordinated one. It is a relationship of mutuality, negotiation, response to what is freely given through what cannot be demanded but only volunteered. The relationship, in other words, is a feminine, not a masculine, one, when measured by the prevailing, conventional stereotypes.

It is where heaven cannot force its will upon us that *zekhut* intervenes. It is that exquisite balance between our will and heaven's will that, in the end, brings to its perfect balance and entire fulfillment the exploration of the conflict of God's will and our will that began with Adam and Eve at their last hour in Eden, and our first hour on earth. And, in context, the fact that we may inherit a treasury of *zekhut* from our ancestors logically follows: just as we inherit the human condition of the freedom to practice rebellion against God's word, so we inherit, from former generations, the results of another dimension of the human condition: our power to give willingly what none, even God, can by right or rule compel.

That is why the structure of Israel's political economy rested upon divine response to acts of will consisting of submission, on one's own, to the will of heaven; these acts endowed Israel with a lien and entitlement upon heaven. What we cannot by our own will impose, we can by the act of renunciation of our own will evoke. What we cannot accomplish through coercion, we can achieve through submission. God will do for us what we cannot do for ourselves, when we do for God what God cannot make us do. And that means, in a wholly concrete and tangible sense, love God with all the heart, the soul, the might, we have. God then stands above the rules of the created world, because God will respond not to what we do in conformity to the rules alone, but also to what we do beyond the requirement of the rules. God is above the rules, and we can gain a response from God when, on some one, unique occasion, we, too, do more than obey – but love, spontaneously and all at once, with the whole of our being. That is the conception of God that *zekhut,* as a conception of power in heaven and power in humanity, contains. In the relationship between God and humanity expressed in the conception of *zekhut,* we reach the understanding of what the Torah means when it tells us that we are in God's image and after God's likeness: we are then, "in our image," the very mirror image of God. God's will forms the mirror image of ours: when we are humble, God responds; when we demand, God withdraws.

Since, in the successor system, it is points of integration, not of differentiation, that guide us to the systemic problematic, we must therefore take seriously the contingent status, the standing of a dependent variable, accorded to Torah study in such stories as the following:

Y. Taanit

3:11.IV C. There was a house that was about to collapse over there [in Babylonia], and Rab set one of his disciples in the house, until they had cleared out everything from the house. When the disciple left the house, the house collapsed.

D. And there are those who say that it was R. Adda bar Ahbah.

E. Sages sent and said to him, "What sort of good deeds are to your credit [that you have that much merit]?"

F. He said to them, "In my whole life no man ever got to the synagogue in the morning before I did. I never left anybody there when I went out. I never walked four cubits without speaking words of Torah. Nor did I ever mention teachings of Torah in an inappropriate setting. I never laid out a bed and slept for a regular period of time. I never took great strides among the associates. I never called my fellow by a nickname. I never rejoiced in the embarrassment of my fellow. I never cursed my fellow when I was lying by myself in bed. I never walked over in the marketplace to someone who owed me money.

G. "In my entire life I never lost my temper in my household."

H. This was meant to carry out that which is stated as follows: "I will give heed to the way that is blameless. Oh when wilt thou come to me? I will walk with integrity of heart within my house" (Ps. 101:2).

Striking in this story is that mastery of the Torah is only one means of attaining the *zekhut* that had enabled the sage to keep the house from collapsing. And Torah study is not the primary means of attaining *zekhut*. The question at E provides the key, together with its answer at F. For what the sage did to gain such remarkable *zekhut* is not to master such-and-so many tractates of the Mishnah. It was rather acts of courtesy, consideration, gentility, restraint: *cortesía* in the Spanish sense, *gentilezza* in the Italian. These produced *zekhut*. Now all of these acts exhibit in common the virtue of self-abnegation or the avoidance of power over others and the submission to the will and the requirement of self-esteem of others. Torah study is simply an item on a list of actions or attitudes that generate *zekhut*.

Here, in a moral setting, we find politics replicated: the form of power that the system promises derives from the rejection of power that the world recognizes. Legitimate violence is replaced by legitimation of the absence of the power to commit violence or of the failure to commit violence. And, when we ask, whence that sort of power?, the answer lies in the gaining of *zekhut* in a variety of ways, not in the acquisition of *zekhut* through the study of the Torah solely or even primarily. But, we note, the story at hand speaks of a sage in particular. That alerts us once more to the systemic reversal that takes place at the systemic center: the sage has gained *zekhut* by not acting the way sages are commonly assumed to behave but in a humble way. In *zekhut*, a word we clearly cannot translate by an exact counterpart in American, we come to the center of a religious system in which the transformation of the individual through salvific knowledge in the end simply does not provide the compelling answer to the question of personal salvation.

Rabbinic Judaism takes shape by answering a question concerning the theory of the social order, yet we find at the heart of matters an answer addressed to individuals, one that concerns their emotions, attitudes, and sense of personal virtue. The private, the particular, the sentimental and the emotional – these are commonly portrayed as women's concerns, the public and political, those of men. Here again, the systemic center forms a paradox: a design for an Israel for eternity yields the dimensions of conduct for an Israelite in the here and now of a single, intensely private moment. None can see, none can compel, none will ever know, what he or she performs as an act of uncompelled generosity of spirit. But God knows. And God cares. That most private moment of encounter, the one to the other, with God at hand, is transformed into the most public, the most social, the most political event.

So, we see, a different question stands at center stage, and a different answer altogether defines the dramatic tension of the theatrical globe. At stake is a public and a national question, one concerning Israel's history and destiny, to which the individual and his salvation, while important, are distinctly subordinated. Not Torah study, which may generate *zekhut*, but *zekhut* itself defines what is at issue, the generative problematic of the system, and only when we grasp the answer provided by *zekhut* shall we reach a definition of the question that precipitated the systemic construction and the formation of its categories, principal and contingent alike.

II. The Character of *Zekhut*

When we come to a word that is critical to the system of those who use it and also that is beyond translation by a single, exact, counterpart in some other language, we know that we have reached the systemic center, the point at which what the system wishes to say is profoundly particular to that system. *Zekhut* in fact refers to two distinct matters, first, virtue that originates with one's ancestors and that is received from them as a legacy, that is, "original virtue," but, also, power that heaven accords to people themselves in response to uncoerced acts of grace done by those people. *Zekhut* then is scarce or common as our capacity for uncoerced action dictated, puissant or supine as our strength to refrain from deeds of worldly power decided, accomplished the systemic integration of the successor documents.

That protean conception formed into a cogent political economy for the social order of Israel the economics and the politics that made powerlessness into power, disinheritance into wealth. Acts of will consisting of submission, on one's own, to the will of heaven endowed Israel with a lien and entitlement upon heaven. What we cannot by will impose, we can by will evoke. What we cannot accomplish through coercion of heaven, trading deed for deed, we can achieve through submission, hoping for response to our freely given act of feeling, sentiment, emotion of self-renunciation. God will do for us what we cannot do for ourselves, when we do for God what God cannot make us do. In a wholly concrete and tangible sense, it is to love God with all the heart, the soul, the might, that we have. That systemic statement justifies classifying the successor system as religious in as profound and complete a way as the initial system had been wholly and restrictedly philosophical. Here, too, we move from the relationship in which one party dominates the other, to one in which each party gives what cannot be coerced, so that both parties will join freely and willingly together: one of mutuality and cooperation.

The final step in the path that began with God's profession of love for Israel, the response of the freely given, uncoerced act of love, *zekhut* stands for the empowerment, of a supernatural character, that derives from the virtue of one's ancestry or from one's own virtuous deeds of a very particular order. No single word in English bears the same meaning, nor is there a synonym for *zekhut* in the canonical writings in the original either. The difficulty of translating a word of systemic consequence with a single word in some other language (or in the language of the system's documents themselves) tells us we deal with what is unique, beyond comparison and therefore contrast and comprehension. What is most particular to, distinctive of, the systemic structure and its functioning requires definition through circumlocution: "the heritage of virtue and its consequent entitlements."

Accordingly, the systemic centrality of *zekhut* in the structure, the critical importance of the heritage of virtue together with its supernatural entitlements – these emerge in a striking claim. It is framed in extreme form – another mark of the unique place of *zekhut* within the system. Even though a man was degraded, one action sufficed to win for him that heavenly glory to which rabbis in lives of Torah study aspired. The mark of the system's integration around *zekhut* lies in its insistence that all Israelites, not only sages, could gain *zekhut* for themselves (and their descendants). A single remarkable deed, exemplary for its deep humanity, sufficed to win for an ordinary person the *zekhut* that elicits supernatural favor enjoyed by some rabbis on account of their Torah study. The centrality of *zekhut* in the systemic structure, the critical importance of the heritage of virtue together with its supernatural entitlements therefore emerge in a striking claim. Even though a man was degraded, one action sufficed to win for him that heavenly glory to which rabbis in general aspired. The rabbinical storyteller whose writing we shall consider assuredly identifies with this lesson, since it is the point of his story and its climax.

III. Systemic Remission: *Zekhut* over Torah Learning

When we come to the way in which *zekhut* is set forth, we find ourselves in a set of narratives of a rather special order. What is special about them is that women play a critical role, appear as heroines, win the attention and respect of the reader or listener. It is difficult to locate in Rabbinic literature before the Talmud of the Land of Israel – the Mishnah, the Tosefta, Sifra, for instance – stories in which women figure at all. So to take up a whole series of stories in which women are key players comes as a surprise. But there is more. The storyteller on the surface makes the man the hero; he is the center of the narrative. And yet a second glance at what is coming shows us that the woman precipitates the tale, and her action, not the man's, represents the gift that cannot be compelled but only given; she is the one who freely sacrifices, and she also is represented as the source of wisdom. So our systemic reversal – something above the Torah and the study of the Torah takes priority – is matched by a still-less-predictable shift in narrative quality, with women portrayed as principal actors.

In all three instances that follow and define what the individual must do to gain *zekhut*, the point is that the deeds of the heroes of the story make them worthy of having their prayers answered, which is a mark of the working of *zekhut*. It is supererogatory, uncoerced deeds, those well beyond the strict requirements of the Torah, and even the limits of the law altogether, that transform the hero into a holy man, whose holiness served just like that of a sage marked as such by knowledge of the Torah. The following stories should not be understood as expressions of the mere sentimentality of the clerks concerning the lower orders, for they deny in favor of a single action of surpassing power sages' lifelong devotion to what the sages held to be the highest value, knowledge of the Torah:

Y. Taanit

1:4.I F. A certain man came before one of the relatives of R. Yannai. He said to him, "Rabbi, attain *zekhut* through me [by giving me charity]."

G. He said to him, "And didn't your father leave you money?"

H. He said to him, "No."

I. He said to him, "Go and collect what your father left in deposit with others."

J. He said to him, "I have heard concerning property my father deposited with others that it was gained by violence [so I don't want it]."

K. He said to him, "You are worthy of praying and having your prayers answered."

The point of K, of course, is self-evidently a reference to the possession of entitlement to supernatural favor, and it is gained, we see, through deeds that the law of the Torah cannot require but must favor: what one does on one's own volition, beyond the measure of the law. Here is the opposite of sin. A sin is what one has done by one's own volition beyond all limits of the law. So an act that generates *zekhut* for the individual is the counterpart and opposite: what one does by one's own volition that also is beyond all requirements of the law.

In the continuation of these stories, we should not miss an odd fact. The story tells about the *zekhut* attained by a humble, poor, ignorant man. It is narrated to underline what he has done. But what provokes the event is an act of self-abnegation far greater than that willingly performed by the male hero, which is, the woman's readiness to sell herself into prostitution to save her husband. That is not a focus of the story but the given. But nothing has compelled the woman to surrender her body to save her husband; to the contrary, the marital obligations of a woman concern only conventional deeds, which indeed the Mishnah's law maintains may be coerced; failure to do these deeds may result in financial penalties inflicted on the woman in the settlement of her marriage contract. So the story of the uncoerced act of selflessness is told about a man, but occasioned by a woman, and both actors in the story exhibit one and the same virtue.

When Torah stories are told, by contrast, the point is, a man attains *zekhut* by study of the Torah, and a woman attains *zekhut* by sending her sons and her husband off to study the Torah and sitting home alone – not exactly commensurate action. Only *zekhut* stories represent the act of the woman as the counterpart and equivalent to the act of the man; and, in fact, even here, the fact that the woman's uncoerced gift is far greater than the man's – her body, merely his ass – should not go unnoticed. Once more, we find ourselves at the systemic center, where everything is reversed:

L.   A certain ass driver appeared before the rabbis [the context requires: in a dream] and prayed, and rain came. The rabbis sent and brought him and said to him, "What is your trade?"

M.   He said to them, "I am an ass driver."

N.   They said to him, "And how do you conduct your business?"

O.   He said to them, "One time I rented my ass to a certain woman, and she was weeping on the way, and I said to her, 'What's with you?' and she said to me, 'The husband of that woman [me] is in prison [for debt], and I wanted to see what I can do to free him.' So I sold my ass and I gave her the proceeds, and I said to her, 'Here is your money, free your husband, but do not sin [by becoming a prostitute to raise the necessary funds].'"

P.   They said to him, "You are worthy of praying and having your prayers answered."

The ass driver clearly has a powerful lien on heaven, so that his prayers are answered, even while those of others are not. What he did to get that entitlement? He did what no law could demand: impoverished himself to save the woman from a "fate worse than death."

Q.   In a dream of R. Abbahu, Mr. Pentakaka ["Five sins"] appeared, who prayed that rain would come, and it rained. R. Abbahu sent and summoned him. He said to him, "What is your trade?"

R.   He said to him, "Five sins does that man [I] do every day [for I am a pimp:] Hiring whores, cleaning up the theater, bringing home their garments for washing, dancing, and performing before them."

S.   He said to him, "And what sort of decent thing have you ever done?"

T.   He said to him, "One day that man [I] was cleaning the theater, and a woman came and stood behind a pillar and cried. I said to her, 'What's with you?' And she said to me, 'That woman's [my] husband is in prison, and I wanted to see what I can do to free him,' so I sold my bed and cover, and I gave the proceeds to her. I said to her, 'Here is your money, free your husband, but do not sin.'"

U.   He said to him, "You are worthy of praying and having your prayers answered."

Q moves us still further, since the named man has done everything sinful that one can do, and, more to the point, he does it every day. So the singularity of the act of *zekhut*, which suffices if done only one time, encompasses its power to outweigh a life of sin – again, an act of *zekhut* as the mirror image and opposite of sin. Here again, the single act of saving a woman from a "fate worse than death" has sufficed.

V.   A pious man from Kefar Imi appeared [in a dream] to the rabbis. He prayed for rain and it rained. The rabbis went up to him. His householders told them that he was sitting on a hill. They went out to him, saying to him, "Greetings," but he did not answer them.

W.   He was sitting and eating, and he did not say to them, "You break bread, too."

X. When he went back home, he made a bundle of faggots and put his cloak on top of the bundle [instead of on his shoulder].

Y. When he came home, he said to his household [wife], "These rabbis are here [because] they want me to pray for rain. If I pray and it rains, it is a disgrace for them, and if not, it is a profanation of the name of heaven. But come, you and I will go up [to the roof] and pray. If it rains, we shall tell them, 'We are not worthy to pray and have our prayers answered.'"

Z. They went up and prayed and it rained.

AA. They came down to them [and asked], "Why have the rabbis troubled themselves to come here today?"

BB. They said to him, "We wanted you to pray so that it would rain."

CC. He said to them, "Now do you really need my prayers? Heaven already has done its miracle."

DD. They said to him, "Why, when you were on the hill, did we say hello to you, and you did not reply?"

EE. He said to them, "I was then doing my job. Should I then interrupt my concentration [on my work]?"

FF. They said to him, "And why, when you sat down to eat, did you not say to us 'You break bread too'?"

GG. He said to them, "Because I had only my small ration of bread. Why would I have invited you to eat by way of mere flattery [when I knew I could not give you anything at all]?"

HH. They said to him, "And why when you came to go down, did you put your cloak on top of the bundle?"

II. He said to them, "Because the cloak was not mine. It was borrowed for use at prayer. I did not want to tear it."

JJ. They said to him, "And why, when you were on the hill, did your wife wear dirty clothes, but when you came down from the mountain, did she put on clean clothes?"

KK. He said to them, "When I was on the hill, she put on dirty clothes, so that no one would gaze at her. But when I came home from the hill, she put on clean clothes, so that I would not gaze on any other woman."

LL. They said to him, "It is well that you pray and have your prayers answered."

Here the woman is at least an equal player; her actions, as much as her husband's, prove exemplary and illustrate the ultimate wisdom. The pious man of V, finally, enjoys the recognition of the sages by reason of his lien upon heaven, able as he is to pray and bring rain. What has so endowed him with *zekhut*? Acts of punctiliousness of a moral order: concentrating on his work, avoiding an act of dissimulation, integrity in the disposition of a borrowed object, his wife's concern not to attract other men and her equal concern to make herself attractive to her husband.

We note that, at the systemic center, women find entire equality with men; with no role whatever in the study of the Torah and no possibility of attaining political sagacity, women find a critical place in the sequence of actions that elicit from heaven the admiring response that *zekhut* embodies. Indeed, a second reading of the stories shows that the hero is second to the heroine; it is the woman who, in each case, precipitates the occasion for the man's attainment of *zekhut*, and she, not he, exemplifies the highest pinnacle of selfless virtue. It follows, once more, that those reversals that signal the systemic center culminate in the (for so male a system as this one) ultimate reversal: woman at the height. Just as Torah learning is subordinated, so man is subordinated; *zekhut*, the gift that can be given but not compelled, like love, in an unerring sense must be called the female virtue that sets atop a male system and structure.

IV. The Yerushalmi's Household of Israel and the Heritage of *Zekhut*

In the Talmud of the Land of Israel, Israel the people emerges above all as a family, the social metaphors of people, nation, kingdom, giving way to the one social metaphor that a feminine Judaism must select for itself. Coming to the Talmud of the Land of Israel and associated Midrash compilations, we turn first to the conception of the *zekhut* that has been accumulated by the patriarchs and been passed on to Israel, their children. The reason is that the single distinctive trait of *zekhut*, as we have seen it to this point, is its transitive quality: one need not earn or merit the supernatural power and resource represented by the things you can do if you have *zekhut* but cannot do if you do not have it. One can inherit that entitlement from others, dead or living. Moses not only attains *zekhut* but he also imparts *zekhut* to the community of which he is leader, and the same is so for any Israelite.

Zekhut speaks of not legitimate but illegitimate violence, not power but weakness. In context, time and again, we observe that *zekhut* is the power of the weak. People who through their own merit and capacity can accomplish nothing, can accomplish miracles through what others do for them in leaving a heritage of *zekhut*. And, not to miss the stunning message of the triplet of stories cited above, *zekhut* also is what the weak and excluded and despised can do that outweighs in power what the great masters of the Torah have accomplished. In the context of a system that represents Torah as supernatural, that claim of priority for *zekhut* represents a considerable transvaluation of power, as much as of value. And, by the way, *zekhut* also forms the inheritance of the disinherited: what you receive as a heritage when you have nothing in the present and have gotten nothing in the past, that scarce resource that is free and unearned but much valued. So let us dwell upon the definitive character of the transferability of *zekhut* in its formulation, *zekhut abot*, the *zekhut* handed on by the ancestors, the transitive character of the concept and its standing as a heritage of entitlements.

It is in the successor documents that the concept of *zekhut* is joined with *abot*, that is, the *zekhut* that has been left as Israel's family inheritance by the patriarchs or ancestors, yielding the very specific notion, defining the systemic politics, its theory of the social entity, of Israel not as a (mere) community (for example, as in tractate Abot's reference to Moses's bestowing *zekhut* upon the community) but as a family, with a history that takes the form of a genealogy, precisely as Genesis has represented that history. Now *zekhut* was joined to the metaphor of the genealogy of patriarchs and matriarchs and served to form the missing link, explaining how the inheritance and heritage were transmitted from them to their heirs. Consequently, the family, called "Israel," could draw upon the family estate, consisting of the inherited *zekhut* of matriarchs and patriarchs in such a way as to benefit today from the heritage of yesterday. This notion involved very concrete problems. If "Israel, the family" sinned, it could call upon the "*zekhut*" accumulated by Abraham and Isaac at the binding of Isaac (Genesis 22) to win forgiveness for that sin. True, "fathers will not die on account of the sin of the sons," but the children may benefit from the *zekhut* of the forebears. That concrete expression of the larger metaphor imparted to the metaphor a practical consequence, moral and theological, that was not at all neglected.

The *zekhut* deriving from the patriarchs or *zekhut abot,* emerges in a statement of the legitimate power – sufficient to achieve salvation, which, in this context, always bears a political dimension – imparted by the *zekhut* of the ancestors. That *zekhut* will enable them to accomplish the political goals of Israel: its attaining self-rule and avoiding government by gentiles. This statement appeals to the binding of Isaac as the source of the *zekhut*, deriving from the patriarchs and matriarchs, which will in the end lead to the salvation of Israel. What is important here is that the *zekhut* that is inherited joins together with the *zekhut* of one's own deeds; one inherits the *zekhut* of the past, and, moreover, if one does what the progenitors did, one not only receives an entitlement out of the past, one secures an entitlement on one's own account. So the difference between *zekhut* and sin lies in the sole issue of transmissibility:

Genesis Rabbah

LVI:II.5 A. Said R. Isaac, "And all was on account of the *zekhut* attained by the act of prostration.

   B. "Abraham returned in peace from Mount Moriah only on account of the *zekhut* owing to the act of prostration: '...And we will worship [through an act of prostration] and come [then, on that account] again to you' (Gen. 22:5).

C. "The Israelites were redeemed only on account of the *zekhut* owing to the act of prostration: And the people believed...then they bowed their heads and prostrated themselves' (Ex. 4:31).

D. "The Torah was given only on account of the *zekhut* owing to the act of prostration: 'And worship [prostrate themselves] you afar off' (Ex. 24:1).

E. "Hannah was remembered only on account of the *zekhut* owing to the act of prostration: 'And they worshipped before the Lord' (1 Sam. 1:19).

F. "The exiles will be brought back only on account of the *zekhut* owing to the act of prostration: 'And it shall come to pass in that day that a great horn shall be blown and they shall come that were lost...and that were dispersed...and they shall worship the Lord in the holy mountain at Jerusalem' (Isa. 27:13).

G. "The Temple was built only on account of the *zekhut* owing to the act of prostration: 'Exalt you the Lord our God and worship at his holy hill' (Ps. 99:9).

H. "The dead will live only on account of the *zekhut* owing to the act of prostration: 'Come let us worship and bend the knee, let us kneel before the Lord our maker' (Ps. 95:6)."

The entire history of Israel flows from its acts of worship ("prostration") beginning with that performed by Abraham at the binding of Isaac. Every sort of advantage Israel has ever gained came about through that act of worship done by Abraham and imitated thereafter. Israel constitutes a family and inherits the *zekhut* laid up as a treasure for the descendants by the ancestors. It draws upon that *zekhut* but, by doing the deeds they did, it also enhances its heritage of *zekhut* and leaves to the descendants greater entitlement than they would enjoy by reason of their own actions. But their own actions – here, prostration in worship – generate *zekhut* as well.

VI. Responsive Grace

Zekhut comes about through deeds of a supererogatory character – to which heaven responds by deeds of a supererogatory character: supernatural favor to this one, who through deeds of ingratiation of the other or self-abnegation or restraint exhibits the attitude that in heaven precipitates a counterpart attitude, hence generating *zekhut*, rather than to that one, who does not. The simple fact that rabbis cannot pray and bring rain, but a simple ass driver can, tells the whole story. The relationship measured by *zekhut* – heaven's response by an act of uncoerced favor to a person's uncoerced gift, for example, act of gentility, restraint, or self-abnegation – contains an element of unpredictability for which appeal to the *zekhut* inherited from ancestors accounts. So while one cannot coerce heaven, he or she – for women as much as men enjoy full access to *zekhut*, though they do not to the study of the Torah – can through *zekhut* gain acts of favor from heaven, and that is by doing what heaven cannot require of me. Heaven then responds to one's attitude in carrying out his or her duties – and more than those duties. That act of pure disinterest – giving the woman one's means of livelihood – is the one that gains for me heaven's deepest interest.

So *zekhut* forms the political economy of the religious system of the social order put forward by the Talmud of the Land of Israel, Genesis Rabbah, Leviticus Rabbah, and related writings. Here we find the power that brought about the transvaluation of value, the reversal of the meaning of power and its legitimacy. *Zekhut* expresses and accounts for the economic valuation of the scarce resource of what we should call moral authority. *Zekhut* stands for the political valorization of weakness, that which endows the weak with a power that is not only their own but their ancestors'. It enables the weak to accomplish goals through not their own power, but their very incapacity to accomplish acts of violence – a transvaluation as radical as that effected in economics. And *zekhut* holds together both the economics and the politics of this Judaism: it makes the same statement twice.

VII. The World Upside Down and Right Side Up: The Power of the Weak

Here we find the ultimate reversal, which the moves from scarcity of real estate to abundance of Torah learning, the legitimacy of power to the legitimacy of weakness, in perspective are shown merely to adumbrate. "Make God's wishes yours, so that God will make your wishes his... Anyone from whom people take pleasure, God takes pleasure" (Abot 2:4). These two statements hold together the two principal elements of the conception of the relationship to God that in a single word *zekhut* conveys. Give up, please others, do not impose your will but give way to the will of the other, and heaven will respond by giving a lien that is not coerced but evoked. By the rationality of discipline within, we have the power to form rational relationships beyond ourselves, with heaven; and that is how the system expands the boundaries of the social order to encompass not only the natural but also the supernatural world.

Treating every deed, every gesture as capable of bringing about enchantment, the successor system imparted to the givens of everyday life – at least in their potential – remarkable power. The conviction that, by dint of special effort, one may so conduct himself or herself as to acquire an entitlement of supernatural power turns one's commonplace circumstance into an arena encompassing heaven and earth. God responds to an individual's – and holy Israel's – virtue, filling the gap – so to speak – about oneself and about one's entire family that we leave when we forebear, withdraw, and give up what is one's own: our space, one's self. When one does so, then God responds; one's sacrifice then evokes memories of Abraham's readiness to sacrifice Isaac; devotion to the other calls up from heaven what by demanding one cannot coerce. What imparts critical mass to the conception of *zekhut*, that gaining of supernatural entitlements through the surrender of what is mine, is the recasting, in the mold and model of that virtue of surrender, of the political economy of Israel in the Land of Israel. That accounts for the definition of legitimate power in politics as only weakness, economics as the rational increase of resources that are, but need not be, scarce, valued things that are capable of infinite increase.

God here gains what the philosophical God of the Mishnah lacks, which is personality, active presence, pathos and empathy. The God of the religious system breaks the rules, accords an entitlement to this one, who has done some one remarkable deed, but not to that one, who has done nothing wrong and everything right. So a life in accord with the rules – even a life spent in the study of the Torah – in heaven's view is outweighed by a single moment, a gesture that violates the norm, extending the outer limits of the rule, for instance, of virtue. And who but a God who, like us, feels, not only thinks, responds to impulse and sentiment, can be portrayed in such a way as this?

> "So I sold my ass and I gave her the proceeds, and I said to her, 'Here is your money, free your husband, but do not sin [by becoming a prostitute to raise the necessary funds].'"
> They said to him, "You are worthy of praying and having your prayers answered."

No rule exhaustively describes a world such as this. Here the law of love is transcended, for love itself is now surpassed. Beyond love is the willing, uncoerced sacrifice of self: love of the other more than the love of self, love of the Other most of all. Feminine Judaism relates to God as lovers relate to one another: giving not in order to receive, receiving only in order to give.

What is asked of Israel and of the Israelite individual now is truly Godly restraint, supernatural generosity of soul that is "in our image, after our likeness": that is what sets aside all rules. And, since as a matter of simple fact, that appeal to transcend the norm defined not personal virtue but the sainthood of all Israel, living all together in the here and in the now, we must conclude that, within Israel's society, within what the Greco-Roman world will have called its *polis*, its political and social order, the bounds of earth have now extended to heaven. In terms of another great system composed in the same time and in response to a world-historical catastrophe of the same sort, Israel on earth dwells in the city of God. And, it must follow, God dwells with Israel, in Israel: "today, if you will it."

Life in conformity with the rule, obligatory but merely conventional, did not evoke the special interest of heaven. Why should it? The rules describe the ordinary. But (in language used only in a later document) "the All-Merciful really wants the heart," and that is not an ordinary thing. Nor was the power to bring rain or hold up a tottering house gained through a life of merely ordinary sanctity. Special favor responded to extraordinary actions, in the analogy of special disfavor, misfortune deemed to punish sin. And just as culpable sin, as distinct from mere error, requires an act of will, specifically, arrogance, so an act of extraordinary character requires an act of will. But, as mirror image of sin, the act would reveal in a concrete way an attitude of restraint, forbearance, gentility, and self-abnegation. A sinful act, provoking heaven, was on that one did deliberately to defy heaven. Then an act that would evoke heaven's favor, so imposing upon heaven a lien that heaven freely gave, was one that, equally deliberately and concretely, displayed humility.

Zekhut as the power of the powerless, the riches of the disinherited, the valuation and valorization of the will of those who have no right to will. *Zekhut* arms Israel with the weapons of woman: the strength of weakness, the power of patience and endurance, the coercion that comes about through surviving, come what may. This feminine Judaism's Israel a family, its God a lover and beloved, its virtue uncoerced, its wisdom uncompelled – this Judaism served for those long centuries in which Judaism addressed a people that could not dominate, but only reason; that could not manipulate, but only hope; that could not guarantee results, but only trust in what would be. In the context of Christian Palestine, Jews found themselves on the defensive. Their ancestry called into question, their supernatural standing thrown into doubt, their future denied, they called themselves "Israel," and the land, "the Land of Israel." But what power did they possess, legitimately, if need be through violence, to assert their claim to form "Israel"? And, with the holy land passing into the hands of others, what scarce resource did they own and manage to take the place of that measure of value that now no longer was subjected to their rationality? Asserting a politics in which all violence was illegitimate, an economics in which nothing tangible, even real property in the Holy Land, had value, the system through its counterpart categories made a single, simple, and sufficient statement.

We now appreciate the entire systemic reversal that we find at the very heart of Rabbinic Judaism. Study of the Torah, which only men could do, emerges as contingent; the life of obedience to the commandments proves necessary but not sufficient; Israel's relationship to God finds its definition not in what it must do, but in what it alone can decide to do, not commanded, not coerced, but also not so positioned as to dominate or manipulate. This Judaism values relations that are mutual and negotiated, cooperative, suggestive, not assertive, coercive, or aggressive. The conception of *zekhut* came to the fore to integrate of the system's theory of the way of life of the social order, its economics, together with its account of the social entity of the social order, its politics. The remarkable actions – perhaps those of omission more than those of commission – that produced *zekhut* yielded an increase in the scarcest of all resources, supernatural favor, and at the same time endowed a person rich in entitlements to heavenly intervention with that power to evoke that vastly outweighed the this-worldly power to coerce in the accomplishment of one's purpose. It is no wonder that, at the systemic apex, woman and the virtue that is natural to her situation now sits enthroned. The right relationship to God is one of responsive grace and love freely given, one that is not subject to conditions, but that embodies perfect commitment.

6

The Foundations of Jewish Existence

A Public Lecture for the Community of Åbo/Turku.

By the phrase, "foundations of existence," I mean, the basis, in shared ideas, attitudes, sentiments, and emotions, for the life of a group. When people explain to one another who and what they are, the answer defines the foundations of their life together. When Jews explain who and what is "Israel," or the particular "Israel" they claim to embody, they define the foundations of their Jewish existence. And every group of Jews tacitly or articulately makes it statement concerning its character as "Israel."

But what sort of "group" is an "Israel"? By "group," I mean, persons who identify themselves as part of a common social entity, different from other social entities round about. "Social entity" forms the loosest and most general language I can find; I mean two or more people who see one another as forming a distinct subset of undifferentiated humanity – different from the rest of the people round about. The premise at hand then maintains that people form a distinct group by reason of intellectual definitions they find compelling. And the still-deeper presupposition in play insists that ideas matter, emotions count, sentiments and attitudes dictate behavior in the world of conduct, not only conviction. Persuade people to view matters in one way, rather than in some other, and they will adopt policies and carry out actions that express in concrete terms the view people hold of themselves as an identifiable group.

I regard that proposition as a fixed star, beyond the need for argument; people whose convictions exclude the principle that attitudes and ideas govern social behavior and come to expression in the concrete modes of public conduct, acceptable or not, that define a group will find simply irrelevant everything I have to say; those who, like me, regard as definitive socially shared attitudes, emotions, and ideas will recognize the urgency of the issue at hand. For the task before us requires an analysis of the various intellectually governing sets of ideas, attitudes, sentiments, and emotions that tell Jews in particular that they differ from others (for our purpose, simply "non-Jews") and that explain to Jews why they should persist in their distinct group existence.

When people recognize as a simple fact of life, beyond all analysis or need of argument, that they do form a social entity, however they classify that entity, then they affirm as self-evident a set of propositions – ideas and attitudes. They further will share feelings – emotions, sentiments, definitions of virtuous or improper response – that endow ideas with the authority of sensibility. But that is not to propose that the simple fact of life – forming a social entity – forms the consequence of decisions made every day. A social entity comes about not by decision but by increment, over time. To the contrary, over long centuries, in conditions of stability and order, attitudes and ideas explain the status quo, sustaining by their formulation of self-evidently true propositions a social order that no one in any event can imagine otherwise than what it is. And when new ideas find a hearing, that is because the received vision has lost its power self-evidently to explain how things should be; how they are is no longer how people perceive they ought to be. So I should not mean to suggest that ideas come first, the social order only later on; but I also do not mean that ideas serve merely to defend, explain, and ratify a social given. In the interplay between how things are and how people imagine they ought to be, attitudes, emotions, and sentiments, together with the propositions they generate, shift in character. Ideas no longer describe, they also prescribe; they no longer state the obvious, they insist upon what is not yet in being at all.

To make this point concrete, I point out that the three governing policies in contemporary Jewish affairs – Zionism, Reform Judaism, and Orthodox Judaism – all carry on their discourse in the language of ideas: for Zionism, debates concerning public policy; for Reform Judaism, arguments having to do with ethnic preference; and for Orthodox Judaism, sustained theological affirmation, respectively. And the great forces that shape Jewry today, that move people to give huge sums of money and devote their lives to the achievement of certain common purposes, all give expression to specific ideas. Techniques of fund-raising only manipulate sentiments that are already compelling; all ferocious debate flows from deeply-shared common viewpoints. No one argues with an outsider.

Zionism begins as a conception, that the Jews form a people, one people, who should constitute a political entity, a state, and not merely a supernatural community of faith. Reform Judaism as we know it in America – and it is the dominant formulation of the condition of Jewish continuity in America – begins as a conception that people should do what is personally meaningful to them, but that one thing that should and does matter to them is that they are Jewish, whatever they make of that fact. Orthodox Judaism without compelling conviction concerning God and the Torah is inconceivable. Not only so, but without these generative ideas – the Jews as a political entity, the Jews as an ethnic group, the Jews as a holy people – the activities, programs, and public policies of the State of Israel, the organized American Jewish community, and world-wide Orthodox Judaism, respectively cease to make any sense at all.

Now, as a matter of fact, these three competing formulations of the ideas and attitudes that form the foundations of social existence for Jewish social entities find hearings among quite distinct groups, and what is self-evident here is incomprehensible nonsense elsewhere. Zionism sees the Jews as a politically empowered entity, located in the ancestral homeland; its theory of Jewish existence defines the future in a clear way. The State of Israel forms the center of the Jewish People, one people; takes priority over what happens anywhere else; defines the purpose of "being Jewish" wherever Jews are. Orthodox Judaism, or the Judaism of the Dual Torah, oral and written (as I prefer to call it) defines the Jews as Israel, meaning the holy people of whom the Torah speaks and to whom the Torah (oral and written) is given by God. Israel is Israel by virtue of the Torah of Sinai. In neutral categories, the Jews form a religious group, defined by the law and theology of the Torah. Any Jew may take a place in this "holy Israel" by reason of birth of a Jewish mother, but this "holy Israel" of the Torah has its own view of the meaning of the history and destiny of Israel, the holy people of God. Reform Judaism, or American Judaism outside of its small Orthodox sector, defines the Jews as a distinct ethnic group, different from other ethnic groups in the ethnic complex of American society. This ethnic group is bound by a common history, which yields lessons bearing ineluctable meaning about why Jews must continue to be Jewish but not imposing patterns of life – where should I live, what should I do with my life – or of thought as do Zionism and the Judaism of the Dual Torah.

Now Reform Judaism in particular, and American Judaism in general, have placed heavy reliance upon allegedly shared emotions and sentiment, common responses and concerns in forming a social identity for their particular "Israel." Unlike Zionism, with its appeal to facts of power and politics, and the Judaism of the Dual Torah, with its insistence on God as the source for the social order of holy Israel, the Judaism represented by Reform, on the one side, and the generalized American Judaism of Holocaust and Redemption, on the other, finds its source of energy in a supposedly shared set of attitudes and concerns, for example, Jews care for one another. On that same account, they devote valued resources to the welfare of one another. Not only so, but their perception of sharing existence with others by reason of their being Jewish generates a sense of connection between Jews in one place and Jews in every other place. But that appeal to what we may call an ethnic definition of Jewish existence – not commandments but customs, not political imperatives but a community of fate (by contrast to the Judaism of the Torah, on the one side, and the Zionism of the state of Israel, on the other), proves amorphous.

For the perception that Jews share existence together derives not only, or mainly, from the presence of other Jews, whom one sees and knows everyday. It flows from the conception, not founded on everyday experience, that Jews form a group even when they do not see one another, bear responsibilities even for persons whom they have never seen and probably will never see. And, finally, that same shared existence, so Jews maintain, links individuals or groups in a given place and time to other groups in former times, not only in other places in the here and now. Consequently, Jews impute to themselves, that is, perceive about themselves what they call history, claiming a past that they hold in common with persons who otherwise are strangers, and who derive from that past messages and meanings to which they appeal in framing the present.

Now, as a matter of fact, this appeal to allegedly shared ethnic traits of sentimentality and emotion persuades only when the facts of life conform: Do people really share common concerns, attitudes, or emotions? Unlike Zionism, which appeals to the palpable facts of the State of Israel, and unlike the Judaism of the Dual Torah, which hears the commanding voice of Sinai, this ethnic Jewishness ("Judaism" being the wrong word) relies heavily upon the intangibilities of this one's caprice and that one's memory. Lacking an imperative deriving from this worldly politics or other worldly perception and conviction, the ethnic definition of Jewish existence proves subjective and acutely personal. That accounts for Reform's stress on a theology of utter personalism – doing what I find personally meaningful this minute – and American Judaism's insistent appeal to emotion stirring events – the Holocaust, on the one side, the state of Israel's wars, on the other.

These somewhat abstract remarks become concrete once more when we contemplate the foundations of the shared life of Jews viewed as an ethnic group. Within this view, which is both "spiritual" by contrast to Zionism and also insubstantial by contrast to the Judaism of the Dual Torah, Jews imagine a common existence, and in their minds are not perceived as isolated individuals having in common a socially irrelevant trait, for example, a matter of common belief in this or in that. Jews' existence together rests not on maintaining some arcane and esoteric "tradition," but on a powerful and concrete claim to constitute a social entity, in fact, a social group with shared traits of fact, not only imputed ones of imagination. Now if we ask ourselves how and where we locate the structures of mind and imagination that impart to the Jews a common existence, where do we find them? Our search leads us first to the here and the now, and only then to the intangible worlds of imagination, intellect, and sentiment. For we do well to start with what we know and can acknowledge as fact. So we consider the exterior, and the interior, structures of Jewish existence in the ethnic model.

The exterior structures of Jewish existence comprise granite foundations, walls composed of hard rock, a roof of steel. For the shared public experience of Jews, both in Sweden or Finland and in the United States, rests upon the correct public perception of Jews forming a group with identifiable traits, traits that people can know in the real world of action. These traits we may call political, since they do not rest on the assent of individuals but are imputed by common consent. Jews are understood, and understand themselves, to form a political entity in countries in which social difference is permitted to take political form. In the United States, for example, Jews tend to vote the same way and therefore are perceived as a voting group, which is very much a political entity. They are understood to share a set of concerns and to favor a set of public policies, therefore again to share a political existence. That political character of the Jews' entity identifies Jews as a political group, not a party, self-evidently, but, rather, one of the components of which, in the political realities of the United States, a political party is composed. That political character of the Jews' group defines the granite foundation of the exterior existence of the Jews. But politics and public policy are not only national. They frame dimensions of the Jews' life as a community. In the public life of organizations and institutions, centers and societies, the Jews form a public entity, sustain a politics. Here too, especially here in the life of shared association in organizations and institutions, I identify the firm foundations of Jewish existence in its exterior lines. It follows that the exterior foundations of Jewish existence in the ethnic model appear solid and secure.

The solid walls that form the outer bounds of the house of Jewish existence bear both interior and exterior surfaces, but, being boundaries, they correspond in setting limits. The gentile world defines those limits. Jews' exterior existence meets the unmarked, but clearly perceived, frontier of difference, whether real or merely imagined, that is given a negative and even a hostile interpretation. I refer on the outside of the exterior wall to anti-Semitism, which is a fact of the life of Jews wherever they live in minority status. Dislike of the unlike in the case of Jews bears many particularities, but it is the simple fact that the exterior existence of the Jews finds demarcation of an impenetrable order in the frontier of hatred. The inner walls of that same house of Jewish existence are surfaced by the appropriate counterpart to anti-Semitism, which is the Jews' own perception of themselves as different by reason of being Jewish, and which is Jews' own negative interpretation of that difference. That wall on the inner surface of the exteriority of Jewish existence comprises Jewish self-hatred, the Jewish counterpart to anti-Semitism. The walls, alas, stand firm and sustain, holding within, the shared existence of Jews who otherwise scarcely live within the house at all.

And the roof, that covers the whole, in our day and age, of course, is the State of Israel. The outer structure of Jewish existence, its exterior dimensions, wherever Jews live, takes shelter under that single overriding and paramount concern. Since nearly all Jews everywhere concur that the State of Israel is not a state of Jews, but the Jewish state. As to states of Jews, these we can have simply by declaring certain neighborhoods into states within the United States of America or the Finland, or into tiny nations, Jewish Luxembourgs, for instance. But *the* Jewish state – that is different. All affirm that the State of Israel is the Jewish state, and, because of its location, identification, and character, is the only nation-state that is, or can ever be, the Jewish state. And it is, further, the only overseas nation-state, whether for Jewish Americans or Jewish Finlandians, for which any of us cares. It encompasses almost all Jews, and it holds together and defines the existence of all Jews, everywhere in the world. Accordingly, it forms the roof, the shelter, within which, in its exterior architecture, Jewish existence takes place.

But we are not Zionists, because we do not make our lives in the State of Israel. That leaves, as the furniture for the interior existence of our particular Israel, our sector of the Jewish people, either ethnic Jewishness or theological Judaism. In the American context I identify ethnic Jewishness with Reform and Conservative Judaisms, on the one side, and the American Judaism of Holocaust and Redemption, on the other, and theological Judaism with Orthodox Judaism in its intellectual modes, yeshiva-Orthodoxy, on the one side, integrationist Orthodoxy such as is practiced in France and Britain and in middle class synagogues in the United States, on the other.

It is in that context that I ask, what of the interiorities of Jewish existence in the ethnic mode? Where can we locate the interior structures of Jewish existence? Here the answers are more difficult to discern, and, indeed, even defining what we should identify as an answer is not an easy exercise. For when we ask not about political structures, public attitudes, international realities, such as the shared exterior existence of the Jews reveals, we move into a world of intangibles. That is not to say we cannot touch these intangibles. We can. We have access to shared attitudes that are not political, not public, not affairs of nation states. And these attitudes, we may posit, also form the frame and take the measure of Jewish existence. But attitudes that yield to action do not fall within the interior of that existence. They restate, in terms of values or feelings, things we are prepared to do. What about attitudes that do not touch actions in such a way as to lead to public policy? And what about those interior matters of intellect and emotion, sentiment and inner, never public feeling, above all, imagination? These form the critical mass of interiority: the center of the atom when it is not a molecule (to appeal to outdated physics for a metaphor).

Here we find ourselves facing a crisis. The ethnic definition of Jewish existence clearly has lost its power to persuade. That is shown in two decisive ways. First, people vote not only with their feet but with their hearts. Jews marry gentiles in unprecedented proportions. The ethnic foundations of Jewish existence show large cracks; the ethnic explanation of who is Israel and why someone should be Jewish does not persuade Jews to keep things going; the children of intermarriages ordinarily opt for no religion or for a religion other than Judaism; and the ethnic tie is quickly severed. The ethnic theory of Jewishness turns out to serve a circumstance and an occasion, that is, the circumstance of atheist Jews living outside the state of Israel, who have warm memories of a Judaic past and who also do not choose to settle in the state of Israel. That explanation – appealing to Holocaust and Redemption – speaks of the past, on the one side, or to experiences outside of perceived reality, on the other; no wonder it no longer persuades.

But the ethnic definition fails in yet another way. Jews no longer form an ethnic group bearing its own compelling definition in the way in which they once did. They do not speak a language that is both common to themselves and different from the languages of others round about, the way in which in various parts of eastern European, ethnic groups, such as Swedish-speaking Finns, or Hungarian-speaking Rumanians, do. If they are ethnic groups, then the Jews are something else. The much flaunted conception that the Jews form a community of fate rests upon a shared experience of Jew-hatred or Jew-baiting or political anti-Semitism. In the Western democracies where most ethnic Jews now live, these experiences of a hostile world do not define everyday experience for most Jews most of the time, and I daresay, Jew-hatred rarely impinges on the consciousness of Jews in general. So the common experience, the common fate, the common heritage apart from a national or a religious one – these evaporate when we come to examine them.

Now in insisting that Israel, the state, or Israel, the holy people, or Israel, the ethnic group, form distinct conceptions, each with its distinctive theory of Jewish existence, I run counter to the convention that treats "the Jews" and "Israel" and "the state of Israel" and "holy Israel" of the Torah as pretty much one and the same thing. Christian theology and secular nationalist ideologies in general fail to find self-evident the categorical structure that I have set forth up to this point. And yet, it is clear to me, if we do not distinguish the national from the ethnic from the religious, then we confuse things, by treating different things as though they were the same thing. And then our capacity for lucid argument suffers. For the worst thing we can do is to treat separate things as though they were the same thing.

Now when it comes to "Israel," that one word, meant to refer to a this-worldly social group, turns out to cover more than one thing. It was the genius of the founders of the state of Israel to call the nation "Israel." But "Israel" covers more than that one nation. "Israel" speaks also of the entire Jewish people, wherever they live; it speaks of the land where the State of Israel is located, since people may say, "I am going to Israel," and mean, "to Tel Aviv." Israel in the liturgy of Judaism, moreover, clearly stands for a holy people, not a place, on the one side, or a particular nation, on the other. "The rock of Israel" for example is not a particular boulder in Holon or Beer Sheva; nor does it refer to the God of the State of Israel nor the State of Israel. The phrase refers to the God who is made manifest to Israel, the holy people, through the Torah – and that language has no this-worldly dimensions or implications whatsoever.

Treating "Israel" as the ethnic group, the nation, and the holy people, all at once, forms not only an error in the use of language, but a theological judgment made by Christianity, and that is one of the reasons that "Israel" is so broadly understood to refer to everything all together and all at once, rather than several things that, as I argue, are to be kept distinct from one another. For Christian theology takes as its starting point in the conflict with Judaism the position that "Israel" is ethnic, but the Gospel, universal. Hence treating Christianity in wholly this-worldly terms, that theology commonly explains how Christianity improved upon Judaism by bringing to all the peoples of the world what had originally been kept for only one people alone. So "Israel" refers to the ethnic group, a particular people, defined in quite this-worldly terms. And the contrast between the ethnic Judaism and the universalist Christianity follows, imposing on language in general that confusion among the several distinct meanings of "Israel" that strikes me so forcefully as the source of botched thinking about critical questions.

My illustrative case – to show how high are the stakes in the debate on the ethnic as against the theological definition of "Israel" – derives from a friendly account of Judaism in the initial conflict with Christianity, James D.G. Dunn's *The Partings of the Ways between Christianity and Judaism and their Significance for the Character of*

Christianity.[1] Dunn takes as his question the explanation of "how within the diversity of first-century Judaism, the major strand which was to become Christianity pulled apart on a sequence of key issues from the major strand which was to become rabbinic Judaism." The parting of the ways "began with Jesus, but without Easter and the broadening out of the gospel to the Gentiles," the break may not have taken place at all. How, then, does Dunn explain the parting of the ways? He appeals to the particularity and ethnicity of Judaism, as against the metaethnic, universalizing power of Christianity to reach out beyond the ghetto walls of an ethnic Israel. Here is his language:

> For the Judaism which focused its identity most fully in the Torah, and which found itself unable to separate ethnic identity from religious identity, Paul and the Gentile mission involved an irreparable breach.[2]
>
> *Christianity began as a movement of renewal breaking through the boundaries first within and then round the Judaism of the first century.* At its historic heart Christianity is a protest against any and every attempt to claim that God is our God and not yours, God of our way of life and not yours, God of our "civilization" and not yours...against any and every attempt to mark off some of God's people as more holy than others, as exclusive channels of divine grace.[3]

Dunn's premise is that "Israel" found definition in both an "ethnic" and a religious identity. But as a matter of fact, distinguishing the "ethnic" from the religious aspect of "Israel" for the documents of the Dual Torah simply defies reason. There is no ethnic Israel that is distinct from a religious Israel at all, not in the sources that attest to the Judaism of which Dunn speaks. So what I find in Dunn's formulation of matters is the explicit claim that Judaism (or: Rabbinic Judaism) takes second place in the hierarchy of religions because it is ethnic, while Christianity overspreads the bounds of ethnic identification. That is profoundly anachronistic, on the one side, and wrong-headed in its view of Judaism, on the other. But Dunn cannot be blamed for seeing what Jews today themselves perceive about their group. If he sees Judaism as an ethnic religion, it is, to begin with, because Jews regard themselves as an ethnic group. If he makes the distinction between the ethnic and the religious "Israel," well, so do we.

But what if "Israel" in the language of Judaism refers to an entity of precisely the same type as "church" or "mystical body of Christ" in the language of Christianity? Then the judgments of Dunn prove simply

---

[1]Philadelphia, 1991: Trinity Press International.

[2]James D.G. Dunn's *The Partings of the Ways between Christianity and Judaism and their Significance for the Character of Christianity* (Philadelphia, 1991: Trinity Press International), p. 230.

[3] *Ibid.*, pp. 258-9.

unintelligible. What is wrong with his formulation is that, as a matter of fact, Dunn does not grasp the meaning of "Israel" as a category. He sees the social metaphor, "Israel," as ethnic in the narrow, this-worldly sense of the word: a particular people, different from other people by reason of its genealogy, customs, social traits, and the like. And so would be the case, were it not for a simple fact. Ethnic identity is transmitted genealogically, but a place in "Israel" so far as the Torah is concerned is reserved for every gentile who accepts the unity of God and the yoke of the Torah, God's revealed will for humanity.

Our sages of blessed memory understand "Israel" to refer to all those who share the inheritance of Abraham and Sarah, who are called to the Torah, who dwell under the wings of the Shekhinah of God's presence. "Israel" is a supernatural entity for the Judaism of the Dual Torah, and, so far as I know, every other Judaism before modern times – a supernatural entity, not an ethnic one. The distinction is critical when we consider the appropriate category for this "Israel." Is Israel a this-worldly people, with customs and ceremonies, or is it a supernatural social entity, people called to form a holy community by God at Sinai, that is, comparable to a Church?

This "Israel" forms the counterpart to Church or Nation of Islam, not to the Albanians or the Italians or the Algerians or the Swedes; to become part of "Israel" one affirms a faith, one need not undertake a long process of territorial, cultural, or ethnic assimilation; and such a process, by itself, will not serve. The entire corpus of the law of the Mishnah attests to the supernatural character of "Israel" – the very "Israel after the flesh" – of which the New Testament speaks as well. Not only so, but, as a matter of fact, the supernatural character of the social entity, "Israel," counterpart to the supernatural character of that this-worldly, mystical body of Christ we know as the Church, is attested on every page of the Prayerbook of Judaism and in every pertinent line of the Mishnah, Midrash compilations, and Talmuds. Dunn's formulation of matters is possible only in entire ignorance of the religious character of the religion, Judaism, and the supernatural meaning that that religion's language imputes to the word "Israel."

For the Judaism of the Dual Torah "Israel" is no more a merely ethnic category than "Christ" is a political one ("king of the Jews" indeed!) or than "the Church" is a sociological (for example, an institutional) one. When, therefore, we read Dunn's language with that fact in mind, then, as I just said, what he says simply becomes unintelligible:

> For the Judaism which focused its identity most fully in the Torah, and which found itself unable to separate ethnic identity from religious identity, Paul and the Gentile mission involved an irreparable breach....

The premise of "separate ethnic identity from religious identity" is that religious identity ever was ethnic at all. Dunn's premise is that in antiquity, the people of whom Dunn writes ("the Jews") could have grasped that "Israel" formed a social category that was counterpart and comparable to any other social category, whether nation or cult. But for Rabbinic Judaism "Israel" formed a category that was sui generis, supernatural, and entering "Israel" by coming under the wings of the Shekhinah bears nothing in common with joining an ethnic group.[4]

Holy Israel really does maintain that "God is our God"; that we know God through the Torah; that what we practice is not a secular "way of life," made up of customs and ceremonies. Christianity is represented as a religion, Judaism as something else, and that representation forms a misrepresentation made possible only by a complete misunderstanding of the sense and meaning of the word "Israel" in the writings of Judaism; but it is made necessary by the secular task of explaining Christianity in a wholly this-worldly setting. Alas, what is necessary is not always possible; what is necessary is not always sufficient; and what is necessary may impose its own logic on what is so.

When we dance with the Torah on the Day of the Rejoicing over the Torah, we are not doing a funny, exotic, ethnic dance. And when we sing out the words of the Torah, we are not singing our beloved folk songs. When Christians sing hymns, these are not folk songs, though they sing in idioms of various nations. And when Israel sings the Torah, the song is not one of sentiment. Holy Israel meets God in the Torah, which is God's self-manifestation to Israel and humanity. And the encounter takes place in song, a medium of not culture but divine revelation. The conduct – the singing – of holy Israel in the synagogue and academy or yeshiva in the hour of the giving and the receiving of the Torah marks the moment and the locus at which Israel meets God. In the words and music, gesture and movement, dance and drama and sentiment of that moment, God is made manifest in the congregation of Israel. What has this to do with the characterization of Judaism as an ethnic religion?

The Lord God, creator of heaven and earth, is Lord of the dance; all persons are welcome to join in God's dance. And there has never been a time in the history of Judaism in which some persons, here and there, did not join in the song. However strange their voices, they blended in and found a place in the harmony of the singing, in the chorus formed of

---

[4] I have spelled out these matters, comparing the theories of Israel of a number of Judaic systems, in my *Judaism and its Social Metaphors. Israel in the History of Jewish Thought* (New York, 1988: Cambridge University Press).

Israel. The Lord God, who gives the Torah when it is sung in the synagogues and in the academies of holy Israel, has sung to us the song we sing. And when, in the fullness of time, we hope and believe, the Lord God will send the savior and redeemer, it will be to do all the things the prophets said, wholly in accord with the revelation of the Torah. To that Judaism, the distinction between "Israel" the holy people and the gentiles will fall away, when the Lord is one and the Name one. And with that Judaism, invidious comparisons of the kind that Dunn makes prove out of place.

This brief excursus serves to underline the point at which I began. "Israel" emerges in three distinct formulations within the three living accounts of Jewish existence today, the national, the ethnic, and the holy. Certainly the national definition of "Israel" excludes Jews outside of the state of Israel, but also aspires to encompass them. The religious definition of "Israel" does the same; it is both exclusive and inclusive, on its own terms. The ethnic is only inclusive, defining everyone in, and no one out – but with this proviso. The ethnic imputes to everyone the same innate traits of emotions and attitude, experience and response to experience; being innate, they do not have to be explained; but, being innate, they also cannot be conveyed through rational, public argument, on the one side, or imparted through equally rational, public, action on the other.

That is to say, theological Judaism explains its views and seeks to persuade all Jews to adopt them; it also will make a place for gentiles to adopt them, as I have already stressed. Nationalist Judaism explains its views and defines what someone must do to conform to them: take up residence in, and citizenship of, the State of Israel. But what must I do if I am to enter into "ethnic Judaism," which involves neither territorial transfer nor religious conversion? Ethnic assimilation proves exceedingly difficult to accomplish, when it involves inchoate responses to unstated stimuli, not to mention a taste (in some circles) for a certain kind of cooking. The phrase "kosher style" captures the anomaly of the ethnic basis for Jewish existence. Theological Judaism knows kosher and traif, and most foods can be one or the other. Nationalist Judaism for its own reasons finds the same language anomalous. But ethnic Jewishness can tell us precisely what it means by "kosher style" – so long as the definition ignores the situation of those Jews who did not know that one kind of pickle was Jewish, and another, goyish. The subtleties and implicit, self-evident but inarticulable refinements of ethnic Jewishness in the end appeal to a mystic bond, not to a tangible connection. Either one feels it or one does not; what one feels one cannot convey to others; what one is supposed to feel, others cannot communicate either.

For reasons of theory, therefore, and not only for considerations of social policy, it follows that, among the three foundations for Jewish existence that presently confront Israel worldwide, political, religious, and ethnic, the two that flourish in the state of Israel, the nationalist and the religious, prove solid and enduring – though for contradictory reasons. And the ethnic presently appears to defy the laws of sociology, on the one side, and the affirmations of Zionism and of Judaism, on the other. Since for the vast majority of Jews in the golah, whether in Europe or in Latin America, the South Pacific or the United States, ethnic Jewishness prevails – the ethnic, not the nationalist or the religion, thus not Zionism in its Israeli formulation or Judaism in its enduring (I believe, eternal) one, the issue is clearly drawn. How are people to sustain their collective life on the flawed foundations of mere personal preference for what is familiar? I do not know the answer to that question, but I also do not think that anyone else does. In my judgment Jewish existence may take shape on the foundation of the State of Israel or may find its realization in the holy Israel of the Torah. For reasons of theology, not sociology, I dismiss as trivial and therefore also demeaning that Israel of ethnic preference, the future of which, even now, sociology calls into doubt.

Part Two

TWO BELLARMINE LECTURES

7

The Spirituality of the Talmud: How Does Holy Israel Know God?

Explaining to outsiders how, within the religious life of a given sacred community, the faithful know God requires use of the imagination on the part of the other or outsider. The outsider has to ask, how would I feel, if I were there – when the outsider is somewhere else. But the question demands response, for we are used to the mode of thought of "let's pretend" and "imagine that"; it is how we liberate our sensibility. The shared, human imagination forms the bridge from heart to heart, what is most private turning out to be what is most human and therefore common. What would I see if I saw my vision with the other's eyes – performing that mental experiment forms the task of exposition. What would I see if I saw with my eyes the other's vision, the world of the other through the clarification or distortion of my spectacles, then defines the labor of comprehension.

This is especially important in the world of religious sensibility. In religion we speak the language of uniqueness, but we address the human condition. We have by definition to find analogies to convey what is a particular vision to a world that is, from our angle of sight, undifferentiated. And doing so is demanded by the nature of the religious calling: to share, to love with open arms. Not only so, but communicating our very particular spirituality acquires importance when we see the other as analogous to ourself. The dark side of religions' reciprocal encounter we know full well; but the bright side – the will to compare, contrast, illuminate and gain illumination – continues to beguile. And well it should, when, as in the case of Judaism and Christianity, two religions look back on two millennia of intimacy, and, now for the first time, look forward to an age of amity as well.

Let us speak in particular of classical things, of the age when the faith got going, the time of Christian beginnings, on the one side, the representation by the Talmud of Babylonia of the entirety of the Torah of Sinai, on the other. Seeking to see things as the other does becomes possible, for Catholic Christianity and Talmudic Judaism as for all monotheisms, because we profess in common to love and worship one and the same God, whom we know through the Torah, Christianity through Christ, and Islam through the record of the Quran. We can share because, on our own, each of us affirms the other in a way in which we can affirm no religion besides these three. For while every way to God by definition takes a unique path, all our three roads lead to the same Heavenly City, and pilgrims along each one of them recognize one another's badges and emblems. A shared imagination links us all: we see ourselves in God's image, after God's likeness. That entails a shared arrogance: we compliment ourselves, we diminish God, when we say so. But we hold in common a sublime vision of what we, humanity, can and ought to be. Now that same act of supererogatory, commanding imagination also draws us apart, since, after all, we really do believe different things about one and the same unique God, and we also see the other as different from ourselves, and in all honest, we are constrained to judge the other as in error to the extent of the difference.

The issue of spirituality, which I take to mean, how we know God, where we find God, in the here and now, defines the critical arena for thought. For that is where religion makes its difference, setting forth its judgments about the living God in the concrete terms of attitude, sentiment, emotion, and imagination: the honest encounter. In other ways religion shapes this world in worldly ways; but in this way, religion stands back, and God takes over. So when we speak of spirituality, it is my premise that the "we" are people who not only believe that there is a God, but who welcome the encounter with God in their lives of prayer and study. That is to say, here is an occasion of not sociology or anthropology or religion or even theology, but a logos of another kind altogether.

Here I stand as a Jew by theology, not only by sociology, that is, as a practicing Jew or Judaist. I speak as a Jew who practices a Judaism, in contrast to a Jew who practices no religion or an ethnic culture. And what that means is, I know God through the Torah. The "I" bears no consequence. Holy Israel meets God in the Torah, which is God's self-manifestation to Israel and humanity. Speaking in Israel, the holy people (not to be confused with the State, the ethnic group, or all the other "Israels" the world has to sort out), I know God not because I find God in the Torah. The decision is not mine; faith does not begin with me. Rather, among all of Holy Israel, I know (not find) God in the Torah, because that is the premise and established fact in the context of the faith of Holy Israel (the supernatural entity, not to be confused with the secular categories, Jewish People, State of Israel, and the like). Holy Israel finds its definition in the encounter with God at Sinai: all who stand there and declare, "We shall do and we shall obey." In Holy Israel God is made manifest in the Torah. Where and how the Torah takes place in my life, of what that encounter with God consists, and how, through the Torah, I know God (not find God, but know God) – these tasks of explanation define my task in laying out what I conceive to be the soul of the spirituality of Judaism for the illumination of faithful Christians, Catholic Christians in particular.

Now for Christians, and in particular, for Catholic Christians formed in the classical age of the faith, that statement both registers but also puzzles. Knowledge of God in the here and now forms a claim, a concept, Catholic Christians find comfortable, since, after all, among most Christians, they know God here on earth through the second person of the Trinity, Jesus Christ, God Incarnate. But familiarity distorts. I speak of Torah, not person, and what it means to know God the way you know God through Jesus Christ certainly proves difficult to convey, when I seem to be talking about a book. After all, who ever opened a book and met God, the way, in the body of the faithful who form the mystical body of Christ, in the sacrifice of the Eucharist, in the imitation of Christ in the everyday, Christians mean to know God? Can all this rich encounter find its counterpart in a book?

Torah stands for us for what Christ conveys to you, in the simple, perfectly functional sense that we know God through the Torah, you know God through Christ, God Incarnate. If you then were to conclude, then for holy Israel, the Torah is God Incarnate, you would of course draw a wrong and misleading conclusion. And yet, the record is clear, we of Holy Israel are possessed of a spirituality, not only a sociology, and the God-centered lives that some among us lead focus upon the Torah; there, we do not read about God – a third-person, anonymous transaction. There we see the face of God, a second-person, personal transaction. And seeing the face of God is not the same thing as coming to a correct conclusion as to a matter of fact or tradition. Seeing the face of God means, to stand in the presence of God. I do not invent; this claim concerning the Torah is explicit, as in the following:

A.   R. Halafta of Kefar Hananiah says, "Among ten who sit and work hard on Torah the Presence comes to rest,

B.   "as it is said, 'God stands in the congregation of God' (Ps. 82:1).

C.   "And how do we know that the same is so even of five? For it is said, 'And he has founded his group upon the earth' (Am. 9:6).

D.   "And how do we know that this is so even of three? Since it is said,
       'And he judges among the judges' (Ps. 82:1).

E.   "And how do we know that this is so even of two? Because it is
       said, 'Then they that feared the Lord spoke with one another, and
       the Lord hearkened and heard' (Mal. 3:16).

F.   "And how do we know that this is so even of one? Since it is said,
       'In every place where I record my name I will come to you and I
       will bless you' (Ex. 20:24)."

Abot 3:6

The passage does not speak about finding the word of God, let alone
facts or rules or laws. It says, in laboring in the Torah, I meet God's
presence.

Clearly we speak of comparable encounters, and if I were to say that
the second person of the Trinity and the Shekhinah form counterparts for
us, respectively, that claim, while imprecise, would also prove within
comprehension. But comparing what is like also underlines difference;
the Shekhinah and Jesus Christ God Incarnate stand for entirely distinct
statements. How, then, am I to convey in an accessible manner the
spirituality of this grand and ancient faith? This is where imagination is
required, on the one side, and the sense for comparison and contrast, on
the other. I have to ask you to imagine what you would know about
God, and how you would know it, if in place of ways in which you know
God, you took other paths, carrying you in the same direction.

To explain to you, therefore, how we of Holy Israel, God's first love,
formed at Sinai in an eternal covenant set forth by the Torah, know God
calls upon an act of imagination on your part – the sort of imagination
that permits us to share what is most private, distinctive, and, when we
speak about God, unique. We differ because we disagree about God.
But then, without negotiating difference, we also may comprehend the
other because we hope to learn, from the other, something about
knowing God that, before the encounter with the other, we did not know.
What, then, out of the resources of the Torah, can I teach Christians about
God?

To grasp the answer to that question, you have to imagine how you
would know God if God came to you not incarnate, in the person of Jesus
Christ God Incarnate, the second person of the Trinity, but in another
way altogether. For where we are marks the starting point of an act of
imagination. To make matters concrete, let me specify what I take to be
three critical kinds of knowledge of God that Christianity gains in Jesus
Christ, God Incarnate. With him whose name is legion, specifying three
points of encounter obviously cannot imply exclusion; the three I choose
come to me from the first record of Christ on earth, the Bible, because
that is public and accessible to outsiders. Rather than imputing the result

of impressions and haphazard observations, being of a scholarly mind, I like to look into books to find out what's going on out there. So, not being a Christian, I require authoritative statements of that knowledge, for which I turn, quite naturally, to Scripture's record, not exhaustive (tradition, the magisterium providing knowledge of God as well) but necessary and authoritative. When I look at the biblical account of Christ Incarnate, I find the knowledge of God in three distinct forms, and consequently to explain how holy Israel knows God in the Talmud's representation of the Torah, I shall have to set forth the same three categories as definitive.

God Incarnate among the legion of names, that is, categories or classifications, in Scripture comes to us as master of the Torah, in Matthew; as embodiment of Israel, its this-worldly adumbration of an other-worldly, supernatural "history," inclusive of the history of its worship of God in the holy Temple and its liturgy, in the Letter to the Hebrews, and as the embodiment of intellect, logos, in John. Then, speaking for Christians, what should I know about God, and how should I know it, if I did not know God incarnate as the fountain of enduring wisdom, as the embodiment of Israel's supernatural history and divine service, and as the word made flesh, in the here and now, the physicalization of that inner fittingness and order of all being that the word "logos" conveys? How would the world lose its sense, its perspective, its inner structure, without Jesus Christ as recorded in Matthew, John, and Hebrews?

Matthew's Jesus sets forth, in the Sermon on the Mount, supernatural wisdom, Torah, in the way in which Moses does on Sinai. But Matthew's Jesus exceeds the Moses of the Written Torah, asking for more than Moses required. Spirituality then consists in loving one's neighbor as one's self, and God with all one's heart and soul and mind. But God incarnate here surpasses the Torah: you have heard it said..., but I say to you. Matthew's Jesus invites not intellectual assent but existential imitation. Sell all you have and follow me, take up your cross and follow me – what should Christians know about the utter, selfless devotion we owe to God, about God's profound yearning for our love, God's wild love for us, without Jesus Christ upon the mount, whether Galilee, whether Golgotha? What should they know about right and wrong, without Matthew's Jesus Christ, God Incarnate, there to show, not alone to say, there is a difference. We, Israel, respond to God's wild passion, and in the Torah we expose ourselves to that yearning: Where and how?

What should we know about God in time and history, and how should we know it, without the account of God incarnate in the Letter to the Hebrews, with its account of the tale of heaven and earth and of Christ in between, the story of creation and of Israel mediated through the Son? Here is the high priest, here is the perfect offering, here is the Temple: "We have such a high priest, one who is seated at the right hand of the throne of the Majesty in heaven, a minister in the sanctuary and the true tent which is set up not by man but by the Lord," "a single sacrifice for sins...for all time." And as to Israel, "through Christ humanity becomes Israel: by faith Abel offered to God a more acceptable sacrifice than Cain, by faith Noah...took heed; by faith Abraham obeyed; by faith Abraham when he was tested offered up Isaac; by faith Moses...by faith the people...by faith Jericho...by faith Rahab...and all these, though well attested by their faith, did not receive what was promised, since God had foreseen something better for us." Here is God's Israel, and what should we know without this reshaping of the entire past in the light of God incarnate? We Israel confront events and perceive truth, and in the Torah, we find God in time.

We come, finally, to the spirituality of intellect formed in that mysterious and awesome statement, "In the beginning was the Word, and the Word was with God, and the Word was God. He was in the beginning with God; all things were made through him, and without him was not anything made that was made. In him was life, and the life was the light of men." Now among the many senses of this "logos" that was made flesh in Jesus Christ, one surely will secure general approval among the learned (and in John's Gospel, as on the others, I do not number myself as learned), and that is, "logos" as the sense and order and logic of all things, how things make sense, from creation forward. I offer as my sense of "the Word" in the context of this discussion here the word Torah in the meaning imputed at this explicit statement about the Torah and God:

I.1   A.   "In the beginning God created" (Gen. 1:1):

      B.   The word [translated beginning, reshit] means "workman."

      C.   [In the cited verse] the Torah speaks, "I was the work plan of the Holy One, blessed be He."

      D.   In the accepted practice of the world, when a mortal king builds a palace, he does not build it out of his own head, but he follows a work plan.

      E.   And [the one who supplies] the work plan does not build out of his own head, but he has designs and diagrams, so as to know how to situate the rooms and the doorways.

      F.   Thus the Holy One, blessed be He, consulted the Torah when He created the world.

      G.   So the Torah stated, "By means of 'the beginning' [that is to say, the Torah] did God create..." (Gen. 1:1).

      H.   And the word for "beginning" refers only to the Torah, as Scripture says, "The Lord made me as the beginning of his way" (Prov. 8:22).

Genesis Rabbah I:I.1

I understand the point to be that the Torah forms the design of the world; God looked into the Torah and created the world. I understand "logos" here to bear the sense that the Word was made flesh, the Torah embodied or incarnate. The relevance of this passage to my larger argument is then simple: What should we know about God, and how should we know it, without the knowledge of Jesus Christ as the embodiment of the Torah, the explanation of the world as God made it?

These three rough characterizations of three principal manifestations of God in the Bible afford access to God through God Incarnate. Matthew's account of God Incarnate introduces us to God in the here and now of a man who teaches things: wisdom, rules for right conduct and love for the other, the laws of the Kingdom of Heaven. Matthew's God Incarnate has both taught and exemplified that wisdom, the laws of life ("It has been told to you, humanity, what is God, and what the Lord requires of you"). We, too, know God in the course of human events ("history"). Hebrews' account of God Incarnate speaks of history and faith, the deep meaning of events. We, too, know the pattern of truth adumbrated by consequential moments in time, such as have happened in and to Israel, events precipitated by faith ("You alone have I known among all the families of humanity, therefore I will visit upon you all your iniquities"). John's God incarnate introduces us to God through the perfection of things, the deepest logic, the inner structure of existence. So too, we know God in the profound logic of the universe, its mathematics of order and structure ("The heaven declares the glory of God").

And these various chapters in the knowledge of God through God Incarnate evoke response in us – Holy Israel – in the worldly ethics, the other-worldly sacrifice; in the perspective of time in the standpoint of eternity; and in the deep sense for the manifestation of God in the order of nature and the logic of human events that invoke awe and reverence. Spirituality forms an act of intellect and sentiment only when these join, an act of adoration and reverence in response to the presence of knowledge. Christianity responds to the knowledge of God afforded through Christ Incarnate (whether in Scripture, whether in the Eucharist, whether in the magisterium, but never solely factual or narrowly intellectual, it goes without saying). We respond to the knowledge of God afford through the Torah. What we know reveals parallels of scale.

How in the Torah (that is, the native category for which the academic and public category is Judaism) do we know God? To understand the answer to that question, we have first to ask, what, exactly, do we mean by "the Torah"? The answer, for Catholic Christians, proves easy to grasp. To the Judaism that is normative, the Judaism that finds its authoritative re-presentation in the Talmud of Babylonia, the Torah comes to Israel in two media, written and oral, for which the concepts of

Scripture and tradition form a serviceable counterpart. Specifically, when Moses received the Torah from God at Sinai, God conveyed, and Moses received, the Torah in two forms, the written, which we now have to begin with in the Five Books of Moses, the first meaning of the word Torah; but also, the oral. The oral part of the Torah is set forth in the following statement, also in tractate Abot:

A. Moses received Torah at Sinai and handed it on to Joshua, Joshua to elders, and elders to prophets.
B. And prophets handed it on to the men of the great assembly.
C. They said three things: (1) "Be prudent in judgment. (2) "Raise up many disciples. (3) "Make a fence for the Torah."

Mishnah-tractate Abot 1:1

Now what is striking in this statement is two facts. First, Torah is described as not only written but also oral tradition. Second, the Torah comes down to us not only through figures known in Scripture, such as Joshua or elders or prophets, but also "men of the great assembly," and, whoever these may have been, they clearly are not known to us in Scripture. Third, what the men of the great assembly leave as their increment of Torah is not a verse of Scripture but a free-standing word of advice. And, more consequential still, the same chain of tradition begun in the sentence before us proceeds onward through time, ending up with the names of important authorities who figure in the Mishnah, the first document in this Judaism accorded the status of Torah, that is, the first writing down of what is presented as an originally oral part of the Torah.

Now, clearly, when we speak of "Torah," we mean something other, more than Scripture alone. The Torah reaches us through a chain of tradition made up of masters and disciples, and in the Rabbinic writings, the relationship of disciple to master is portrayed as identical to the relationship between Moses and God, or between Aaron and Moses:

A. *Our rabbis have taught on Tannaite authority:*
B. What is the order of Mishnah teaching? Moses learned it from the mouth of the All-powerful. Aaron came in, and Moses repeated his chapter to him and Aaron went forth and sat at the left hand of Moses. His sons came in and Moses repeated their chapter to them, and his sons went forth. Eleazar sat at the right of Moses, and Itamar at the left of Aaron....
D. Then the elders entered, and Moses repeated for them their Mishnah chapter. The elders went out. Then the whole people came in, and Moses repeated for them their Mishnah chapter. So it came about that Aaron repeated the lesson four times, his sons three times, the elders two times, and all the people once.

> E. Then Moses went out, and Aaron repeated his chapter for them. Aaron went out. His sons repeated their chapter. His sons went out. The elders repeated their chapter. So it turned out that everybody repeated the same chapter four times.
>
> Bavli Erubin 54B

Here is a different kind of portrait of imitation of God: what we imitate about God is the wording of teachings (which of course we are to carry out), and how we encounter God is in the labor of using our minds.

Now how far do we stand from the mountain in Galilee, when we meet the sage who repeats the Torah of Sinai? We know God through study of the Torah, we meet God in the Torah. And what distance separates us from that place of the perfect offering, the Temple in heaven, the perfect priest, when we know that, when we study Torah, it is as if we made an offering on the altar of the Temple? And what can lead us more deeply into the structure and the order of being than the Torah, serving as it does to record what God had in mind in making the world? The mathematics of existence, the events of time viewed by faith, the lessons of eternity set forth in the here and now of ordinary time – these messages of God Incarnate in the second person of the Trinity find their counterparts in the physicalization of the Torah in the person of the sage, the realization of the Torah in two media, the recasting of events into the rules of the social order, and the recognition of the Torah as the here and now record of what was in God's mind in the order of creation.

To make that point I need not refer to what I have already said about the presence of God where the Torah is studied or about the Torah as counterpart to John's logos. But it pays to dwell for a moment on the matter of finding, in the writings of the Oral Torah, a counterpart to the conceptions of Hebrews, since that is not a matter quite so familiar or accessible as the others. To understand what is at stake, we have to notice what lies on the surface of Hebrews, which is a rather odd juxtaposition, the combination of two distinct topics, the history of Israel, the meaning of the Temple and its rite: priesthood, sacrifice, holy place itself. The union of the two – history, in the form of Israel's history, nature, in the form of Israel's holy celebration of the gifts of nature in the rite of the Temple – draws our attention to the one book of the Written Torah in which the specification of the rite – what is offered, by whom the offerings are made, where the offerings are to take place, when the rites are carried on – is joined together with the meaning of Israel's history. Any reading of the book of Leviticus, with its climactic chapter, the historical-prophetic ones of Chapter 26, will provoke the question, how do our sages of blessed memory (as the masters of the Torah are known), read Leviticus, with its union of cult and prophecy, nature and history?

The counterpart to Hebrews I find in Leviticus Rabbah, which joins nature to history, the cult to events in the life of Israel, and, which, like Hebrews, means to set forth fundamental knowledge of God in the form of the rules of Israel's existence. The message of Leviticus Rabbah is that the laws of history may be known – the counterpart to Hebrews' "by faith," and that these laws, so far as Israel is concerned, focus upon the holy life of the community. A startling trait of the Letter to the Hebrews is its composition of facts into lists, and Leviticus Rabbah makes its points through list making, too. These lists then through the power of repetition make a single enormous point or prove a social law of history. The catalogues of exemplary heroes and historical events – in both Hebrews and Leviticus Rabbah – serve a further purpose. They provide a model of how contemporary events are to be absorbed into the biblical paradigm. Since biblical events exemplify recurrent happenings, sin and redemption, forgiveness and atonement, they lose their one-time character. At the same time and in the same way, current events find a place within the ancient, but eternally present, paradigmatic scheme.

What we have in Leviticus Rabbah is the result of the mode of thought not of prophets or historians, but of philosophers and scientists and theologians – the generalizing sciences. The framers propose not to lay down, but to discover, rules governing Israel's life. As we find the rules of nature by identifying and classifying facts of natural life, so we find rules of society by identifying and classifying the facts of Israel's social life. In both modes of inquiry we make sense of things by bringing together like specimens and finding out whether they form a species, then bringing together like species and finding out whether they form a genus – in all, classifying data and identifying the rules that make possible the classification. That sort of thinking lies at the deepest level of list making, which is work of offering a proposition and facts (for social rules) as much as a genus and its species (for rules of nature). Once discovered, the social rules of Israel's national life of course yield explicit statements, such as that God hates the arrogant and loves the humble. The logical status of these statements, in context, is as secure and unassailable as the logical status of statements about physics, ethics, or politics, as these emerge in philosophical thought. What differentiates the statements is not their logical status – as sound, scientific philosophy – but only their subject matter, on the one side, and distinctive rhetoric, on the other.

Our sages of blessed memory in Leviticus Rabbah transformed Scriptural history from a sequence of one-time events, leading from one place to some other, into an ever-present mythic world. No longer does Scripture speak of only one Moses, one David, one set of happenings of a distinctive and never-to-be-repeated character. Now whatever happens of which the thinkers propose to take account must enter and be absorbed into that established and ubiquitous pattern and structure founded in Scripture. It is not that biblical history repeats itself. Rather, biblical history no longer constitutes history at all, that is, history as a linear, purposeful, continuous story of things that happened once, long ago, and pointed to some one moment in the future. Rather it becomes an account of things that happen every day – hence, an ever-present mythic world. In this way the basic trait of history in the salvific framework, its one-timeness and linearity, is reworked into the generative quality of sanctification, its routine and everyday, ongoing reality. When history enters a paradigm, it forms an exercise within philosophy, the search for the rules and regularities of the world.

This excursus considerably advances my argument, for what I have shown through strong exemplification is how in our encounter with the Torah, we know God: the wisdom of the ages, the meaning of time in eternity, and the word made into the world, that Catholic Christians know through God Incarnate in the aspects set forth in Matthew, Hebrews and John. And yet, thus far, I have left unanswered the principal question, the one of authentic spirituality, the encounter with God in the Torah, counterpart to Christians' encounter with God in Jesus Christ. Answering that question requires us to step outward from books to the lived life of the religious faithful, just as knowing how Christians fully encounter God requires us, in the Catholic setting, to attend to the Eucharist and the other celebrations of Jesus Christ, Lord of the Dance, that the Catholic Church offers its faithful in the sacraments.

Clearly, I have to point to the times and places in which the Torah rises out of books and takes on that sacramental, liturgical reality that for us stands for the sacramental meeting. Where and when does the Torah meet Israel in God's presence? Phrasing the question in that way produces an obvious answer: where the Torah is proclaimed to Holy Israel, assembled to meet God, in the synagogue; and where the Torah speaks to Holy Israel, assembled to learn, to study the record of God's revelation of the Torah, wherever holy Israel assembles to study the Torah, in Talmud study circles anywhere, or in the study hall of the yeshiva or Talmudical academy or rabbinical school. A brief account of what takes place defines the spirituality of the Talmud in terms that now, I hope, Christians can fully appreciate. And, since spirituality forms the here and now of theology, let me also spell out what I conceive to be the theology of the Talmud: its medium, its message.

Holy Israel meets God in the Torah, which is God's self-manifestation to Israel and humanity. The spirituality of holy Israel takes the form of music: when we sing, we sing to God; when we sing, we sing God's song. I do not mean those statements in any poetic sense, but in a material way. If you come to the synagogue, you will find that the Torah – here, the five books of Moses – is not read like prose, but declaimed, chanted in song. If you come to a Torah study session in a synagogue or a yeshiva, you will find that the Torah – there, the Oral Torah, the Talmud – is not read but sung, and the debates that follow form a choreography of intoned words, received patterns of gesture, ritual arguments, an opera. So our encounter with God in the Torah, written and oral alike, takes place in song. In ancient times, none would have had to be told that fact: it was ordinary to sing books, not to say them or to read them silently. From antiquity onward, music carried the words, and, sometimes (as in the spirituality of Hasidism), melody without words bore meaning, too.

Performed music always is an event, ephemeral but perfect for its moment, not to be replicated, magical, enchanted and transforming – acutely present in tense and effect. And so is the moment of encounter in the Torah. And that is natural, too, for the meeting with God in song. For the language of revelation – the native category is "the giving of the Torah" – uses the present tense. When in the synagogue the reading of the written part of the Torah is prefaced with a blessing, the obligatory blessing speaks of the eternal action that is continuous and present: "...who gives the Torah." The academy or yeshiva receives its part – the oral part – of the Torah as a set of claims about the truth that pertains for all time, but especially, at this moment of reasoned encounter. The immediacy of the giving of the Torah accounts for the vitality of contention in that setting. So in both loci God gives the Torah to Israel – not gave, but gives. The principal setting for the self-manifestation of God therefore is in today's synagogue liturgy and in the contemporary labor of learning in the academy or yeshiva.

The spirituality of the Talmud – now understood as the re-presentation of the entire Torah, Oral and Written – may therefore be set forth in a few words. The governing facts about the Torah come to us from the vivid activities of synagogue and yeshiva: what happens in those places when the Torah is received in prayer, proclamation and learning. That Israel meets God in the Torah in particular when in a setting of piety and reverence the Torah is sung tells us that Israel encounters God in song. Israel therefore sings its way across the ages to heaven. That is what it means to allege (in descriptive language) that the theological voice of Judaism sings, or, in the language of faith, God sings to Israel.

I say, "God sings," because when received with reverence by holy Israel the Torah always is sung; I call the Torah God's song, because the Torah is given ("revealed") by God in an act of self-manifestation. So the Torah itself proclaims: "I am the Lord your God...," "The Lord spoke to

Moses, saying, 'Speak to the children of Israel and say to them...,'" "I will make all my goodness pass before you and will proclaim before you my name, 'The Lord,' and I will be gracious to whom I will be gracious and will show mercy on whom I will show mercy. But you cannot see my face." These and companion proclamations leave no doubt for holy Israel that in the Torah is God. Israel receives the Torah to meet God. And when Israel sings the Torah, God is present. This yields four propositions, with which I close:

1. THE IMMEDIACY OF REVELATION, THE HERE AND NOW OF SONG: How do Sinai at one time in the past and the giving of the Torah in the here and now? What chemistry of the present moment unites them so as to surpass the paradox of past and present in one and the same moment? Music comes into being at the moment of performance; written out notes are not music, any more than map is territory, as I said. Music is intensely present; that is its only used tense. That is why music forms the right medium for that message, because God's self-manifestation in the Torah takes place in the immediate and acutely present tense. It is not merely an event remembered out of the long-ago past, a paradigm to be reenacted; nor is the Torah imitated or acted out, as though recapitulated. To the contrary, these ways of recovering the past are hardly appropriate, since the Torah in the synagogue and academy comes not out of the past but out of the very present, as God is present (in the language of Halafta cited before). None of this forms an inert fact of history, but a truth concerning how things are and Who is here.

2. THE SONG IS A VERY SPECIFIC ONE: Why do I insist that revelation is specific and propositional, not general and merely the revelation that there is the Presence? Specific words are sung and made to sing in a particular way; here is not singing in general – mere exuberance, an invention of the moment, la la la – but a tradition of music matching the circumstance and the sentiment. The way the words are sung is closely prescribed by ancient tradition; the melodies are very old, the conventions of punctilious sound and precise matching of word to music bearing the authority of the ages. Nothing so captures the union of tradition and the present than the fact that the musical modes come from ancient tradition, but are recreated in age succeeding age as

though made up that morning. I can think of no more accurate a metaphor then for the realization of the Torah in the here and now than music; absent the performer, the notes lie dead on the page, black marks on white paper. Performed properly, the notes carry us into the mind of the composer, but they also recreate the mind of the composer in our very presence.

3.   SUNG THEOLOGY: So it is with the sung theology of Judaism, the theological voice of the Torah at that very place, in that very moment, at which the Torah is pronounced. When the words are rightly sung, pronounced with precision, in proper rhythm and vocal pattern, then the Torah's message comes in the words and in the music, both. Without song, with the Torah merely read, revelation does not take place; there is no reason then to recite a blessing, as we do to revere the act. For the Torah read, not sung, is a mere book, with inert information. When the Torah is proclaimed, declaimed, sung out, then it is Torah – revelation. And that cannot serve merely as an act of remembrance; the moment of revelation can never be merely reenacted nor recapitulated, but only renewed in the freshness of the song – not new but always renewed, just as music when played realizes its eternal present. It is not played so that we may remember how Mozart made up and played this music, but so that we may encounter this music, this very music, in the here and now of the living moment.

4.   GOD SINGS: Come to a synagogue on a Sabbath, Monday, or Thursday, or on a holy day or festival, and you will hear the Torah not read but sung, loud and clear, in an ancient chant, the melody matching the natural sounds of the words. The song is of the Torah ordinarily is sung with great punctiliousness, and where that is not the case, it is a disgrace to the community that receives God in a slovenly way. The Torah, removed from its holy ark, carried in choreographed parade around the synagogue, is proclaimed, declaimed, in formal song. Then it is held up, and the congregation sings back, "This is the Torah that Moses set before the children of Israel at the command of the Lord." In between the dance before and the display at the end, the Torah is sung out to the people, week by week, through the year: "In the beginning God created the heaven and the earth..." through "And there arose not a prophet since in

Israel like unto Moses, whom the Lord knew face to face...."
So goes the song of the Torah from Genesis through
Deuteronomy, song out of the scroll of the Torah. So much
for the written part of the Torah, sung as God's song in the
synagogue. It is easy to witness or at least to imagine how
the Written Torah is sung in the synagogue. What about
singing the oral part of the Torah in the academy?

5.   ISRAEL RESPONDS IN SONG: In the academy the music is less
readily imagined, and, in the ordinary circumstance, people
not part of the yeshiva world are not likely to find their way
to hear the music. In Torah study in a yeshiva, argument
takes the form of song, reasoning is reinforced in the upward
and the downward movement of the melodic line, and
conclusions are drawn in crescendo. True, what you would
hear in a yeshiva would be music of an other-than-
conventional sort. It is a hot music, not a cool music. But
you need listen only briefly to grasp that the sound is
organized, with rhythms, with measures and beats, with
upward and downward passages, with hesitations and
movement, words spoken largo, allegro, adagio, sostenuto,
then agitato – yes, always agitato.

Israel the people is holy Israel in singing God's song. Israel's God is
a God who sings, neither in the storm nor in the thunder, but in the voice
that pierces the silence, the thin voice, the urgent voice. The thin, halting,
nervous, quavering chirping of the bar or bat mitzvah, called for the first
time to read the Torah to the community assembled for prayer in the
synagogue, is the voice that Moses heard from the cleft in the rock.
Moses, denied the vision he sought, heard instead the voice to proclaim
the name: "I will proclaim before you my name, 'The Lord.'" It is the
still, small voice that Elijah heard – that same Elijah present at the
circumcision of the covenant, that same Elijah who at the end of time will
announce the coming of the Messiah.

8

What Should We Want to Know from the Gospels?

An Outsider's View of New Testament Studies

The Bellarmine Lecture I Did Not Give.

The real issue in New Testament studies must be, how can we define the character of Christianity and explain its advent? That question concerns anyone, Christian and otherwise, who proposes to account for how things are in the world we know, since Christianity in its various forms constitutes a paramount religion in the here and now and, furthermore, has defined the character of Western civilization. Why the cathedrals, the art and music, the political structures and the theory of the worth of life, and, in other-worldly terms, why the views we take to be commonplace concerning the character of God and the definition of humanity in God's image? These come to the West through Christianity, without which none can even begin to imagine what the West might have become. So quite naturally we expect those who study its first documents to tell us how Christianity came into being; it is not a question urgent for Christians alone.

The question finds its answer these days in personalized accounts of a supposedly historical Jesus, distinguished from the Christ of faith, on the one side, and, among the enemies of Christianity, the story of how the simple truths of Jesus were corrupted by the diabolical Paul into a Christianity Jesus himself never contemplated. Leaving aside consideration of the bases and premises of these accounts, we focus upon the premise. For many today, the generative question is, who, really, in this-worldly, historical terms, was (not *is*) Jesus (not Jesus *Christ*). So the advent of Christianity as a historical problem finds its definition in entirely personal terms. In one way, that definition accords with the theological datum of Christianity – the religion founded by Christ. But in another, it defies the conceptual datum of all historical study, which finds itself unable to concede heroes do all that much in history, or to write history principally in personalist categories. Christianity therefore finds itself studied in a manner unfamiliar for other global historical movements; its theological given is treated as secular fact, but then its history is formulated in a way different from histories of all counterpart, massive and influential, formations of human civilization. The confusion does not end there.

The premise yields a further, rather odd conception. It is that if we know who the historical Jesus was, then we can explain Christianity. But that is not the outcome of contemporary work on the life and teaching of Jesus.   For accounts of the historical Jesus – a Reform Jew, a Mediterranean peasant, a marginal Jew, and the like – rarely carry with them answers to the question, whence and why Christianity? The Jesus of history, commonly presented as separate from the Church that the Gospels' accounts maintain he founded, turns out incommensurate to the Christ of faith (to use current language), and New Testament studies answer every question but the urgent one.   It follows that New Testament studies invest their best energies in answering the wrong question: Who was the man who made the Church is replaced by, who was the man who never even contemplated the church, and, given accounts of who he was in this life and time, could never have imagined what became of his teachings? In simple language, New Testament studies are so formulated as to subvert to begin with the very integrity of the phenomenon they propose to investigate.

Some may argue that Gospels' research, focused as it is on the life and teachings of a particular man, does not even ask the question about Christian origins that I identify as paramount. That allegation strikes me as implausible, since, if the issue of Jesus is not Christ, then why should it matter to anyone, as it self-evidently matters to nearly everyone? But for the moment, let us postulate that it means to tell us, whence and why Christianity. Then, reducing a religion to a chapter in the history of a particular time and person (biography) rests on these premises:

    1.   Religions, including Christianity, originate in what identifiable persons really did at some specific "starting point." We therefore explain the beginnings of a religion by appeal to the activity of a founder. That premise adopts a

radically personalist view of history, rare in other contemporary writing.

2. Religions then project to a large screen the traits of personality and conviction of the founder. Since they are something that some one person founded, in historical time, we can recover the facts concerning that unique moment. Here again, religion is private and individual, gaining adherents through intensely subjective decisions in response to a personality or character or immediate encounter.

3. Religions form the appropriate object of wholly this-worldly explanation, so that the same causes or factors that we invoke when we wish to account for psychological, economic, political, or institutional events suffice to explain, also, religious ones. Religions in their collectivity then are not really religious; that middle range of the social world is excluded. Religions are private and personal, or they are wholly comparable to this-worldly institutions, political movements, for instance, or data of sociology or economics or mass psychology.

It follows that these three premises turn out to personalize religion, emphasizing not its vast, social expression but its beginnings in a private person's life and activities, and they furthermore insist upon its profound secularity, its this-world-ness, rejecting at the outset a religion's own account of its supernatural origin. That is a further basis for explaining why, in my view, Gospels' scholarship produces results that prove monumentally beside the point, answering everything but the main thing.

Then, some may claim in behalf of Gospels' research, the results speak for themselves. For we have learned to do other than merely paraphrase our sources, repeating in historical language the supernatural account that they set forth for us. So while lives of Jesus turn out because of their intense interest in the person of Jesus himself not to answer the main question – whence Christianity – they have at least brought us closer to the man, Jesus, if not to Jesus Christ, the second person of the Trinity. But that allegation hardly compels assent. But whether or not we know Jesus better than we did before because we now supposedly know who he really was and what he really did – as distinct from what the faithful have known all along – remains open to doubt. For, as a matter of historical fact, the results of the quest have produced nothing short of chaos. As many as are the scholars who have written lives of

Jesus, so many are the Jesuses whom we know now but did not know before the quest began.

In general, a review of the upshot of the question for the historical Jesus yields the simple observation, which every history of the quest for the historical Jesus has yielded, that each generation gets the Jesus that it wants; pretty much every scholar comes up with the historical Jesus that suits his taste and judgment. That was the conclusion a century ago reached by Albert Schweitzer, at the end of nearly a hundred years of lives of Jesus. And today, the distinguished Gospels' scholar Luke Timothy Johnson concludes his reading of the splendid current books of Dominic Crossan and John Maier with the observation that, once more, we have a Jesus for our times: "Does not Crossan's picture of a peasant cynic preaching inclusiveness and equality fit perfectly the idealized ethos of the late twentieth-century academic? Is not both authors' hope for a historical foil to theology or faith still fundamentally a theological, rather than a historical project?"[1] Discouraged, some ask, "What is left to believe in Jesus after the scholars have done with him?"[2] And, invariably, the answer proves less incisive than the question – and revealing of not precisely what the questioner had in mind at all.

What happens, however, if we reconsider the premises that shape New Testament, and particularly Gospels, research? I begin with the premise that our work conforms to the paradigm of secular history, which explains events in entirely this-worldly terms and insists that, in those terms, what has happened can indeed be accounted for? What happens when we view religions as not personal but shared response – to God, for example, or to a prophet – and abandon the acute personalism that characterizes the focus on the man Jesus in favor of a different generative question altogether? What happens, finally, when we recognize that the history of a religion and the history of a city or a social or political institution or a battle for that matter really form quite distinct kinds of knowledge? The way in which we explain the history of a city – this happened first, then that happened, which shaped the third thing – and the very thing that we explain proves incongruous not only to how we explain the history of a religion, but what we propose to account for. What happens, in other words, if the history of a religion yields neither biography (writ large) or narrative history?

---

[1]Luke Timothy Johnson, "A Marginal Mediterranean Jewish Peasant," *Commonweal* April 24, 1992, p. 26.

[2]Philip L. Culbertson, *Journal of Ecumenical Studies* 1991, 28:1ff. His question is better than his answer. He has "a Pharisaic context for the historical Jesus," but exactly what he means by "Pharisaic" he does not tell us, and he is alarmingly ignorant of nearly all of the scholarship on that subject done in the past twenty years.

When, in the framework of studying a religion within the framework of the history of religion, by contrast, other premises come into play, a different mode of explanation is invoked to take up a quite different, equally secular question. First, we have to explain without explaining away; explain without reductionism. We have, second, to explain something other than the sequence of events that led to the event at hand or to the formation of the institution we claim to explain. When I come to the matter of Christianity, I want to know not where it came from – for that would explain nothing about the shape and structure of the faith – but how it came to be what it is, whether in the first or any subsequent Christian century. The history of the religion, Christianity, is the story of how theology made a world – a multitude of worlds – and formulated the issues and the purposes of life for not private persons hither and yon but massive social structures and entire social orders. Opening the Gospels, we find ourselves deep in the heart of a living faith, sorting out for itself the issues of its nascent life in appeal to the teachings of the founder.

The rich repertoire of teachings, whether harmonized or subjected to a process of selection, attest to the enormous impact of a remarkable personality; but they by their nature and even their secular character impose upon us that same sense of awe and wonder, of humility at the limits of knowledge, that the word mystery entails, as we feel before the great works of nature and the great events of human history. We are prepared, I think, to live with not ignorance but respect for what we do not know or cannot fully account for in ordinary ways. If that is so before the personal moments of life and death, surely we can bring to the study of a great religion that same reverence for mystery that defines the condition of our knowledge of other fundamental things. When a religion speaks of its founder as God incarnate, it strikes me as monumentally irrelevant to be told what he ate for breakfast, or what, among the many things that religion treasures from God incarnate, he is supposed (by humanity very carnate indeed) really to have said, as against the many things we are alleged to be able to discern to be human, therefore fraud. All great scholars bear in common the deep-seated trait of humility before the unknown; the mark of the great scholar is the capacity to say, this I think I know, that I'm sure I do not know; and the more a scholar says, "I don't know – yet," the more formidable that scholar's intellectual dimensions.

Then what do I maintain Gospels' scholarship should take for its problem? My question to the Gospels is formulated in response to what the Gospels mean to tell us. It therefore commences with an account of the principal traits of Christianity, viewed in its full, historical formulation, and I look back to the points of origin to find out how in the view of the first recorded generation of Christians, Christianity reached its entirety, its integrity, its enormous dimensions in civilization.[3] And to that question, Jesus the man, alleged by Gospels' scholarship to be accessible through ordinary historical research, hardly provides a commensurate answer. Jesus Christ, who founded the Church – "Thou art Peter, and upon this rock..." – or Jesus Christ, who was crucified, died, rose from the dead – these form the Christianity that commands attention. If, then, I had to identify the three traits of Christianity that any historical-religious account of not origins but original traits and condition will present and explain, they are [1] the Church with its vision of the whole of humanity within a single polity; [2] the Churches, with their remarkable diversity (the fissiparous quality of the faith); and [3] the figure of Christ himself, his variety, his capacity to speak in many languages messages that prove commensurate here and there. The allegation that Christianity broke the Judaic ethnic mode (a false indictment and an uncomprehending one, as I shall show presently) forms a negative way of addressing this positive trait: the many voices bearing a single message (though defining that single message proves parlous) that Christianity put forth even from its first recorded writings.

So to revert to my starting point, if we regard religion as a given, a principal factor in the formation of the social order, then we formulate the question of origins not as a problem of historical fact involving a private person, however holy – did he really do this, did he really say that? – but as an issue of description of facts of the social order: What did people do together, in the here and now, in the formative phases of the religious community that, in its writing as in other artifacts, we come to know in due course? The question of origins is social, concerning the formation of the Church and the churches, and not reductively biographical.[4] It registers when we take up documents a community values and analyze those documents as public artifacts. The documents themselves constitute facts of history, things people made at some determinate moment, for some specific, socially relevant purpose, and that is by definition. But our concern shifts from astringent interest in removing the detritus of time and change in quest of the original object. We examine the artifacts as facts in themselves: this is what people

---

[3]That accounts for my theory of the Judaeo-Christian dialogue, spelled out in my *A Rabbi Talks with Jesus. An Intermillennial, Interfaith Exchange* (New York, 1993: Doubleday). Jewish Book Club Main Selection, February, 1993.

[4]In the context of the study of Christianity as the formation of a single man, God-incarnate, arguing about what Jesus really said or did (e.g., to Peter in founding the Church of Rome) represents a theological debate, not a historical inquiry. But that strikes me as so self-evident as not to require further attention.

believed, and here is their account of the world that they were in process, in the very beginning, of forming for themselves.

So let me state in a few words the positive program I advocate for New Testament studies. They really should focus on the earliest period of Christianity and tell us about that. Looking backward, we know now what few outside the believers could ever have conceived then. It is that Christianity is important in this world because it has defined the course of much of the history of the West and of the world. Questions of history and origins then must focus upon the starting point of traits that would prove decisive and definitive: the sense of oneness, the equally strong capacity to divide and osmose. If we see religion as public, social, something people do together, something that defines the social world people share, then our concern is for the faith of the faithful, not the history of the formation of its components. For the critical issue emerges in the here and now of the life of the believing community. The pre-history of the bits and pieces – the detritus of time – that have taken shape in one way, rather than in some other, proves of mild and contingent interest; it makes no contribution to the hermeneutics that will guide our reading of the texts. In this context, three other premises, in place of those of history, come to the fore:

1. Religions may originate with their founders, but by the time we know them, they have become communities, often diverse and conflicting, and all we really know for certain concerns not the specific starting point in some one, individual and unique person's action, but the diverse ways in which social entities have taken shape around, and given expression to, that religion.[5]

2. Religion by definition is social and not personal, this-worldly in the phenomena we can examine. Therefore that about religions that we can in fact study concerns not the traits of a single, unique founder, but the effects, in the here and now of religious communities, of whatever people heard and remembered, valued and put into effect.

3. The kind of information we should require to determine what a specific individual really said or did commonly takes second place to the kind of information communities provide about their perceptions and commitments, on the one side,

---

[5]Even religions born in the full light of day (or, in their own language, recovered) produce schism and debate, disputation on the intention and desire of the founders; the history of the Latter Day Saints Church (the Mormons) is a fine example; but Islam serves equally well.

or their hermeneutics in the reading of the received writings
of actual persons, on the other.   It must follow that
hermeneutics of texts takes priority, in the study of religions'
beginnings, over the kinds of historical inquiry into
economics, politics, institutions and their past, that historians
pursue and historians of religion tend to treat as marginal.
But, as Joseph Cardinal Ratzinger has reminded us in his
Ingersoll Lecture, hermeneutics is the child of theology.

Christianity as we know it, in every period of its history, takes on the
character it has had specifically because of what people believed Jesus
Christ really said and did.   The true explanation for the origin of
Christianity and its character comes to us in the entire record of
Christianity, every detail of which is factually, historically true, telling us,
as it does, what real Christian communities really maintained was the
fact and really preserved and handed on as the record of what Jesus
Christ as (their) Christianity frames matters really made.   For reasons I
have now spelled out, as an outsider, I want New Testament research to
tell me about Christianity, but much that I hear misses the point of the
Christian Bible in general, and the Gospels in particular.

I wonder, indeed, whether New Testament research, as distinct from
Church history, has given us even now a rich picture of the origins of
Christianity, which it claims in the end to deliver.   For the contrast
between the reading of history and the writing of the history of the
religion, when it comes to Christianity, proves stunning.   For what we
have in place of history of religion – that is, an explanation of the origin
of Christianity – in Gospels' research is the answer to a different question
altogether: what the man, Jesus, said and did, in contrast to what the
churches have believed he said and did.   Only when we turn to Church
historians, among whom I should point to Harnack as a principal figure
in my own education, do we begin to learn something about Christianity,
as distinct from the life and times of an itinerant Galilean sage and
wonder worker such as Gospels' research repeatedly yields for us.

And that (admittedly invidious) contrast underscores my point about
the failure of learning.   It is not because of raising unbelief to the level of
a scholarly norm – believing Christians need not apply for more than a
few professorships in New Testament studies.   It is rather than in
drawing a distinction between the Christ of faith and the Jesus of history,
Gospels' research at the very outset of its work announces that it wants
to focus on anything but Christianity in all its worldly presence; that
research declares itself disinterested in Christianity ("the Christ of faith")
but concerned only for the man, Jesus, in this world, in this life, in that
time, in that place: before the resurrection, before even the founding of

the Church, and long before the formation of those numerous churches, here, there, everywhere, that came in consequence of whoever and whatever the man Jesus was.

Since my proposition here runs against the current of learning today, let me elaborate on my objections to the trivialization of the Gospels that takes place in much contemporary New Testament scholarship. While the quest for the historical Jesus forms a brief chapter in Christian theology of our own times, it matters because it has defined how the Gospels will be read in the secular academy and many Christian seminaries. Annual meetings where scholars debate and vote (using black, gray, pink, and red balls for what he certainly didn't say, probably didn't say, may have said, and certainly said) are routine; the Holy Spirit is pretty busy nowadays. Where have we learned to make this distinction, and why, and to whom, does it matter? The gospels themselves present points of disharmony, but Christians for centuries satisfied themselves with harmonies of the Gospels. The stories of the miracles have challenged faith, but Christians took it as a mark of grace that they believed. The same data that have impressed scholars in the past two centuries made no profound impression on believers for eighteen prior ones. At the beginning of the kind of historical study that promised to distinguish fact from fiction, myth or legend from authentic event, got underway that Protestant theologians, mainly in Germany, undertook to write lives of Jesus that did not simply paraphrase the gospels but stood in judgment of them. An attitude of systematic skepticism brought to the gospels considerations that prior generations scarcely conceived. These considerations engaged theological professors in universities in Europe and in some U.S. divinity schools and university Religious Studies departments in particular, with the result that a different reading of the gospels replaced the paramount one.

The Christ of the Church's faith – that is, in my language, the study of Christianity and its paramount qualities – gives way to "a Mediterranean Jewish peasant," on the one side, or "a marginal Jew," on the other. And these are only two of the many pictures of Jesus (not longer Jesus Christ) that two hundred years of critical historical scholarship have painted. As many as are the scholars who have written lives of Jesus, so many are the Jesuses whom we know now but did not know before the quest began, all of them smaller than the Gospels' figure, every one of them an entirely this-worldly figure; and, in our country at least, not one of them a figure a conservative can admire for his politics, only for his sentimentality, as a matter of fact. The one fact that this famous "quest for the historical Jesus" has established beyond doubt about Jesus is that each generation gets the Jesus that it wants; pretty much every scholar comes up with the historical Jesus that suits his taste and judgment. The Gospels' four portraits, intersecting and concentric in many ways, have become legion.

My objections to Gospels' research with its insistence that information of only one kind matters are two, one concerning the nature of the study of religion and its history, the other concerning the impact, upon Judaism and the study of Judaism, of Gospels' studies.

The first objection is that the historians and biographers in fact undertake a theological task, but they do so without the rigorous modes of thought of well-crafted theology. This unbelieving historical quest actually takes up the critical theological question, for surely no question bears more profound theological implications for Christians than what the person they believe is the incarnate God really, actually, truly said and did here on earth! But then historical method, which knows nothing of the supernatural and looks upon miracles with unreserved incredulity, is then required to answer them. The premises of this historical question (did it really happen, did he really say it?) rule out nearly the whole of Christian faith. For these are the perfectly routine, historical premises that govern the work as they would any other:

1. Any statement we may wish to make about Jesus is just another fact of history, like the fact that George Washington crossed the Delaware on Christmas eve, 1775;

2. Facts of that kind form the entire historical truth about Jesus;

3. Facts about Jesus bear the same weight and consequence as facts about George Washington (which is why points one and two are true); he is the same as any other man we investigate through ordinary, secular sources.

But statements (historical or otherwise) about the founders of religions present a truth of a different kind. Such statements are not only more important, bearing weightier implications. They also appeal to sources of a character distinct from the sources that record what George Washington did on a certain day in 1775. The sources are classified as revelation, not mere information; they claim, and those who value them believe, that they originate in God's revelation or inspiration. Asking the Gospels to give historical, not gospel truth confuses theological truth with historical fact, diminishing it to the modest measurements of this world, treating Jesus as precisely the opposite of what Christianity has always known him to be, which is, unique. Where else do supposedly critical historians take up phenomena they know to begin with are unique? Uniqueness claims, after all, signal entry into the heart and soul of faith. The philosophical, generalizing, rule-seeking program of social science, including history, hardly proves a comfortable venue for such claims, or for the consideration of them.

When we speak of "the historical Jesus," therefore, we turn out to dissect a sacred subject with a scalpel of secular research, and in the profound confusion of categories of truth the patient dies on the operating table; the surgeons have forgotten why they made their cut and in their confusion have removed the heart and forgotten to put it back. The statement, one and one are two, or, the Constitutional convention met in 1787, is simply not of the same order as the statement "Moses received the Torah at Sinai" or "Jesus Christ is son of God." What historical evidence can tell us where or not someone really rose from the dead, or what God said to the prophet on Sinai? I cannot define a historical method congruent to the work of telling us how to sort out claims that God's son was born to a virgin girl. And how can historians, used to telling us the causes of the Civil War (whether 1642-1651 or 1861-1865) really speak of miracles, men rising from the dead, and other matters of broad belief among some, utter incredulity among others? Historians working with miracle stories turn out what is either paraphrastic of the faith, or indifferent to it, or merely silly. Theological truth about what is unique and matters of fact about what conforms to the rules of nature speak in different ways about altogether different issues; derive from different sources of information and verification; yield each its implications for its own realm of reality, the one eternity, the other the here and now of commonplace fact.

For, if faithful Christians today find surprising the distinction between the Jesus of history and the Christ of faith, they continue an ancient tradition of faith, for no one before modern times knew that the one was and is not the same as the other. No Christianity before modern times, and only some in modern times, produced this kind of writing, though all of them have studied the life and teachings of Jesus. But the theological context defined by "the Church," meaning, whichever Christianity pursued the study, formed the framework of learning. Christology was never confused with quite secular biography until the nineteenth century. Distinguishing between the Jesus of history and the Christ of faith will have earlier produced utter incomprehension.

And yet, in Protestant Christianity from the early nineteenth century and Roman Catholic Christianity from World War II, professors of the faith, as distinct from the (mere) faithful, have taken for granted the Gospels' Jesus and the actual man, who really lived and taught and died, are not one and the same person. They came to the faithful armed with the authority of scientific learning, bearing as their weapon the prestige accruing to the objective, rational, dispassionate sorting out of facts. So from their laboratory they turned to tell the faithful who Jesus really was.

Their work – surprising and scandalizing simple believers – bore the marks of secular learning, but at no point did a merely this-worldly and secular agenda dictate their program.

Instead of interpreting one saying in light of another and the whole in light of tradition or creed or theological premise, Gospels scholarship proposed to distinguish, by various criteria, between things Jesus really said and things that the Church, responding to its own concerns, attributed to him later on. This intense historical study is grounded in these premises, all of them inimical to historic Christianity – a hermeneutic that is the misbegotten child of an anti-Christian theology:

1. Not only is it the fact that Church tradition is null, only Scripture matters;

2. And, more to the point, the faith of the Church is null, and only the declarations of historians concerning historical fact carry weight in formulating the faith;

3. So historical facts by themselves bear theological consequence;

4. Historical facts must undergo a rigorous test of skepticism, the donation of the Enlightenment (how could a whale swallow Jonah, and what else did he have for lunch that day); and

5. Historical facts cannot comprise supernatural events, a secularizing principle that is the gift of nineteenth century German historical learning ("exactly how things were" by definition cannot include rising from the dead) taken over by theological science.[6]

---

[6]Joseph Cardinal Ratzinger, in a variety of important and authoritative papers, such as his Ingersoll Lecture, has made these points – quite properly, in the setting of Catholic faith, but, in context, in the context of the claim to not theological truth but merely critical historical knowledge advanced in the quest of the historical Jesus (see his "L'interpretazione biblical in conflitto. Problemi del fondamento ed orientamento dell' esegesi contemporanea," in Ignace de la Potterie, Romano Guardini, Joseph Ratzinger, Giuseppe Colombo, and Enzo Bianchi, *L'Esegesi christiana oggi* (Rome, 1992), pp. 93-125). The method itself dictates scandalous results: "La fede non è un elemento costitutivo del metodo e Dio non è un fattore di cui occorre tener conto nell'avvenimento storico." At the same time, exegesis forms an important requirement of theology: "The more prudent among systematic theologians seek to produce a theology independent, so far as is possible, from exegesis: "Ma quale valore può avere una teologia che si separa dale proprie fondamenta?" So, Ratzinger argues, it is necessary to raise the question of hermeneutics: "La spiegazione del processo storico non sarebbe che una parte del compito dell'interprete; l'altra sarebbe la comprensione del

At the outset of the scholar's venture these rules dictate the result, since by definition they exclude most of what Christians by faith know to be truth: the miracles, the resurrection, the givenness of the Gospels' truth, the (admittedly Catholic) conception that the Bible is the gift of the Church, alongside that other gift, tradition. Before work gets underway, nothing is left of what makes Jesus into Christ, unique, wholly man, wholly God, God incarnate, and all the other things that define Christ for Christianity, and Christianity for the world beyond. Within such premises, the character as fundamentally secular and incredulous life of "the historical Jesus" is dictated by such a criterion. But then the quest begs the question: On that basis should Christians concern themselves with this particular Jesus at all (who, for both Meier and Crossan would have voted for left-wing Democrats)? And to whom does the life of a marginal Jew or a Mediterranean Jewish peasant matter very much anyhow (or a Galilean rabbi, or a homosexual magician, or any and all of the other historical Jesuses that people have produced)?

Not only so, but these premises set a standard of secular historicity that religious writings setting forth a religious faith, speaking in terms of uniqueness and the supernatural, such as the Gospels cannot, and should not, attempt to meet. For, after all, all the givens dismiss what to the evangelists is critical: here is a unique man, who said and did what no one else ever said or did; these things happened in the way the Church has preserved them (also) in the Gospels, tradition being a valid source; these things really did happen as the narrative says (would the Gospels lie?); and Jesus Christ assuredly performed miracles in his lifetime and rose from the dead (ours is the story of God among us). No corroborating evidence, you object? But by definition there can be none; by faith we are saved.

So to conclude this part of my argument: much New Testament scholarship seeks a secular, this-worldly explanation for a perfectly secular this-worldly fact. But that explanation effects the reduction of early Christianity to issues other than those of religion, and, further, it imposes an anti-Christian theological hermeneutic that, outside the framework of Christianity, bears no meaning whatsoever. For my part,

---

testo nell'oggi. Di consequenza, occurrerebbe indagare sulle condizioni del comprendere stesso così da giungere ad una attualizzazione del testo che vada oltre una 'anatomia del defunto' puramente storica." How, he asks, is it possible to come to a comprehension which will not be founded on the arbitrary decisions of my own presuppositions, "una comprensione che me permetta veramente d'intendere il messaggio del testo, restituendomi qualcosa che non viene da me stesso?" The answer is a correct hermeneutics: "'so l'ermeneutica' deve diventare convincente, occorre innanzitutto che scopra un'armonia tra l'analisi storica e la sintesi ermeneutica."

as I have stressed, I am inclined in the end to see the matter of the historical Jesus as a chapter in the problem, how do we account for Christianity? And all the answers to that question begin in either a religious or an unbelieving attitude, depending upon whether supernatural or this-worldly facts are going to serve as suitable sources of explanation.

Why does this outsider take an interest in such matters? The reason is that Gospels' research has a very serious affect upon the study of Judaism. For I come to the field as an outsider with a specific interest of my own. It is that New Testament scholarship persistently defines not only the historical Jesus, but also the historical Judaism in the context of which Jesus did his work; with a historical Jesus, that Judaism bears the burden of explanation of what Jesus meant when he said such and so, or that to which, or more commonly, against which, he reacted in making such a statement. No longer God incarnate, Jesus is turned into a prophetic critic of a Judaism that scholars invent, along with their historical Jesus, to make this-worldly sense of things. New Testament scholarship therefore forms a source of anti-Judaism as free-flowing as the Gospel of John or the sermons of John Chrysostom – but with the prestige of footnotes.

Why does the denigration of Judaism, or (as I shall show), the condescending defense of a Judaism defined in Protestant terms, take the place of a Christian theological hermeneutics, such as Cardinal Ratzinger proposes? The reason is simple. Since Christianity does not define the issue, but only the this-worldly figure of Jesus does, the Judaism of the time comes under sustained examination in all biographies of Jesus. If he is a Reform rabbi, then he is given what to reform – corruption, hypocrisy, pharisaism with a small p; and if he is a marginal Jew, he is assigned his valid reasons for rejecting the norms and moving to the fringe. In New Testament studies until the present day, with important exceptions, Judaism serves as Brand X to the new, improved product, Christianity.

I do not think that, in the history of scholarship on religion in general, we can point to a comparable case in which one religion's historians so systematically defame and denigrate another religion as do Christianity's for Judaism. And, for the purpose, a single Judaism, fabricated as point of origin and counterpart for that single, uniform Christianity represented by Jesus himself, is essential. Because of the premise of a single founder of a single religion, a single contrary religion has to be defined, hence "Judaism," a word with no counterpart in Hebrew, a word that stands for an invented and not a native category. And, as I have indicated, what a despicable Judaism! Part of Christianity's difficulty in understanding why "the Jews rejected Jesus" (not to say, crucified him!), lies in the character of the Judaism invented for the occasion; no normal human being could espouse such a fraudulent faith, and it is no wonder that medieval Christianity speculated on whether or not the Jews could be deemed human at all, bearing as they did so inhuman a religion.

Now it may be taken to be perfectly natural to treat Jesus in the context of his own setting, hence "Judaism." But what is natural is hardly congruent to the supernatural character of the claim that God has taken human form, and that Jesus Christ was, and is, God incarnate. A different theology from the secular one shows what is at stake. If in the formation of Christianity, God's work is at hand, then there is no need to denigrate the Judaism of that time; but only if not has Christianity to be portrayed as a reform movement of a degraded faith, a renewed Judaism, that is all. But the Church fathers took the view that there never had been "Judaism," but only the unfolding of Christianity, that is, of Jesus Christ, in and through Israel, its prophets, its Torah, its holy people.[7] Any New Testament scholar will have to account for "Israel after the flesh," but the unbeliever will have to impute very negative qualities to Judaism, while the faithful need not do so, even though, as a matter of fact, they, too, commonly do.

Then the issue must resolve itself in these terms: Why Christianity? And that is secondary to, what is Christianity? The generality of New Testament scholarship draws invidious comparisons between Judaism and Christianity, and it goes without saying, Jesus and Judaism. But surely, if you believe in the faith as God's grace, you do not have to find this-worldly validation for it, while if not, you do. It may be that studies of the history of New Testament scholarship will yield a rough rule that Protestant scholarship tends to treat Judaism (whatever they mean by "Judaism") as reformed or improved by a this-worldly Jesus; Catholic scholarship in the classical tradition understands that, theologically, the whole of the received Israelite tradition was brought to fulfillment, therefore understood in a new way; it has no need to denigrate the Judaism of that period, taking a supernatural, rather than a supersessionist, view of matters. That would then account for the simple fact that it was the Catholic, not the Protestant, Church that produced the world-shaking statement, *Nostra Aetate.*

---

[7]That is not to suggest supersession is a new doctrine! But supersessionism represents a theological doctrine, not a historical judgment based on the supposed, worldly corruption of Judaism. Supersessionism that dismisses Israel after the flesh in favor of the spiritual Israel formed of the mystical body of Christ bears within itself no logical necessity to dismiss on grounds of worldly venality what to begin with it cannot take seriously. A distinction between theological dispute and factual characterization has at some point to be drawn.

These tentative suggestions set the stage for a forthright response to the obvious question, what is at stake to you as an outsider to Christianity in the character of study about the origins of Christianity? I come to the subject as a historian of religion in antiquity, but the subject bears deep meaning to me as a practicing Judaist and a loyal Jew. For it would be disingenuous to allege that, as a scholar of religion, all studies of religion interest me. To the contrary, Christianity occupies far more attention of mine – and of nearly all scholarship on religion in general – than any other religion. I cannot imagine my formulating a presentation on "what we should know from the Gathas," and, in general, essays on scholarship on the Quran fall far short in volume and intensity of concern of the counterparts on the Gospels. What is at stake for me as a practicing Judaist – a Jew who practices Judaism – is already obvious: study of the origins of Christianity, including the so-called "historical Jesus," invariably address the character of Judaism in that time, and what people say about Judaism in the first century always spills over into judgments made about Judaism, and the Jews, in our own day. I need not elaborate on that point. Anyone familiar with the Gospel of John knows the horror of the fact that some of the New Testament books incite to Jew-hatred, and at every period in the history of New Testament scholarship, from the beginning to the present, the New Testament has served to provoke teachings of contempt for Judaism, with consequences I hardly need rehearse here. So the stakes are very high.

To define those stakes, I turn back to the acutely present moment and point to two concrete case that illustrates my point: the study of Judaism in times past finds itself profoundly affected by the premises of New Testament scholarship; the characterization of Judaism at all times by Christianity finds its definition in questions of origin. Two cases suffice to define the stake contemporary Judaism, and the study of ancient Judaism as well, have in the character of New Testament studies.

First, let me show through one representative case what difference it makes that New Testament scholarship takes as its task the characterization of the Judaism that Jesus the man supposedly rejected or reformed, or did not really reject or reform at all (depending on the attitude of the scholar). Since the anti-Semitism and anti-Judaism of New Testament scholarship in times past hardly require rehearsal, let me take a case of the opposite: the effort to present the Judaism of the day in a light that Christians will deem favorable. Protestant Christianity from Luther forward claimed to reform a Christianity altogether taken over by ritualism, the letter killing the spirit. So Protestant scholarship described the Judaism of the first (and all subsequent) centuries as ritualistic, lifeless, dead, a religion for shopkeepers, keeping tabs on righteous deeds in the balance against sins, and on and on and on. Not only so, but the entire history of Judaism, inclusive of ancient Israel, was formulated as the story of the thesis, prophecy, the antithesis, law, and the synthesis, which hardly requires identification.

Since the Judaism we practice, that defined in the Dual Torah, Oral and Written, does believe God cares what we do, not only what we believe, Judaism provided a perfect cover for a sustained Protestant attack on Catholic Christianity. Everything they wrote about Judaism pertained equally to any other religion of works as much as faith, and much that passed for scholarship served a violent polemic anti-Semitic only in its garb, but heart and soul, anti-Catholic. Now to counter that attack on Catholicism through the flank of Judaism, in our own day, some scholars have taken the opposite turn. Rather than conceding that Judaism was (and is) a religion of works as much as faith, Judaism would be represented as covenantal; it would no longer serve as a surrogate for Catholic Christianity.[8] Judaism really is not legalistic at all, because the laws express loyalty to the covenant, and Judaism is a religion of covenantal nomism; it is that supposedly acceptable covenantal nomism accounts for the stress on correct observance, which should not be represented therefore as magical, coercive, a defiance of grace, or pharisaical (with a small p). We therefore ought not to denigrate Judaism as a legalistic religion, since the law really did not matter all that much. That polemic in behalf of Judaism, emerging from New Testament scholarship, has yielded two results: [1] an attitude of condescending judgment of a religion that (like Roman Catholic Christianity) really does maintain that God cares about what we do, not only what we believe, and that how we do what we do matters very much; and [2] out and out misrepresentation of the facts. For the first of my two illustrative cases I take a presently prominent Protestant New Testament scholar and apologist for a Judaism of his own invention, E.P. Sanders.[9]

His condescension toward the law and those who kept (and now keep) the Torah is expressed in the following language, which surpasses, in condescension and self-absorption, any lines I have ever read, whether philo- or anti-Semitic in origin, about Judaism and the Pharisees:

> I rather like the Pharisees. They loved detail and precision. They wanted to get everything just right. I like that. They loved God, they

---

[8]I do not know how "covenantal nomism" would differentiate Judaism from Catholicism, with its affirmation of works and faith as well, but that is not our problem here.

[9]My systematic critique of his views is in *Judaic Law from Jesus to the Mishnah. A Systematic Reply to Professor E.P. Sanders* (Atlanta, 1993: Scholars Press for South Florida Studies in the History of Judaism).

thought he had blessed them, and they thought that he *wanted* them to get everything just right. I do not doubt that some of them were priggish. This is a common fault of the pious, one that is amply displayed in modern criticism of the Pharisees. The Pharisees, we know, intended to be humble before God, and they thought that intention mattered more than outward show. Those are worthy ideals. The other pietists strike me as being less attractive than the Pharisees. The surviving literature depicts them as not having much of a program for all Israel, and as being too ready to cultivate hatred of others: learn *our* secrets or God will destroy you. But probably they weren't all that bad, and we can give them credit for loving God and being honest.

Mostly, I like the ordinary people. They worked at their jobs, they believed the Bible [sic! he means, the Old Testament, of course], they carried out the small routines and celebrations of the religion; they prayed every day, thanked God for his blessings, and on the sabbath went to the synagogue, asked teachers questions, and listened respectfully. What could be better? Every now and again they took their hard-earned second tithe money to Jerusalem, devoutly performed their sacrifices, carried the meat out of the temple to share with their family and friends, brought some wine and maybe even some spirits, and feasted the night away. Then it was back to the regular grind. This may not sound like much, but in their view, they were living as God wished. The history of the time shows how firmly they believed in God, who gave them the law [he means, the Torah] and promised them deliverance.

In the world series of condescension toward the Jewish People and Judaism, Sanders here wins the gold medal. "I rather like the Pharisees" – indeed. Sanders comes from small-town Texas, and some think he talks like a hick. If coming to his defense, someone were to say, "But he's had speech lessons," he would understand why most Jews would rather not have supercilious friends of his kind.

Sanders provides a striking instance of how in order to re-form Judaism of the first century into a religion that Protestant Christians can respect, that same Judaism is simply misrepresented as to its essential character. For that purpose I shall address a much controverted subject, the importance of purity in ancient Judaism. Since Protestants claim to find difficult the appreciation of a religion that concerns itself with rite, not only right, the notion of cultic purity (the Judaic counterpart to priestly celibacy) is particularly disagreeable. In defending the Judaism of the day from the anti-Judaic polemic of Liberal Protestantism, Sanders wishes to minimize purity and maintain that considerations of cultic purity proved trivial; hence Protestants should not be put off by the descriptions of the role of purity in the earlier Rabbinic literature that I have set forth in various works of mine.

In portraying the laws of uncleanness, Sanders stresses that uncleanness in some instances in and of itself is a sin. Accordingly, he reads uncleanness as a moral category. Quite correctly, in describing the Old Testament account of uncleanness Sanders carefully stresses that "most impurities do not result from the transgression of a prohibition, although a few do."[10] He accurately emphasizes that an impure person is not a sinner; contact between an impure and a pure person is not ordinarily considered a sin. Once he has so represented biblical law, however, Sanders proceeds to allege the following:

> One should ask what was the situation of a person who disregarded the purity laws and did not use the immersion pool, but remained perpetually impure. Here it would be reasonable to equate being impure with being a "sinner" in the sense of "wicked," for such a person would have taken the position that the biblical laws need not be observed.[11]

That statement contradicts the judgments Sanders makes in his précis of the biblical representation of uncleanness, except for a single matter, which is sexual relations between husband and wife when the wife is menstruating. That is penalized by extirpation (Lev. 20:18), as Sanders says, and represents an exception, again explicitly specified by Sanders:

> But as a general rule, those who became impure...did not, as long as they lived their ordinary lives, sin. Normal human relations were not substantially affected.[12]

Here is a minimization and a trivialization of the topic that occupies a fourth of the entire volume of the Mishnah, purities. Now in order to harmonize the judgment made here with the position taken immediately following, Sanders gives an example, but, as we shall see, the example exemplifies only its own case:

> All the laws of purity and impurity are to be voluntarily observed. If, for example, a husband and wife agreed not to observe the prohibition of intercourse during menstruation, no one would ever know unless they announced the fact. If the woman never used the immersion pool, however, her neighbors would note that she was not observant.... Not intending to be observant is precisely what makes one "wicked"; but the wickedness comes not from impurity as such, but from the attitude that the commandments of the Bible need not be heeded.
>
> Thus these biblical purity laws, which most people seem not to have observed, did not lead to a fixed view that the common people were sinners.[13]

---

[10]E.P. Sanders, *Jesus and Judaism* (Philadelphia, 1985: Fortress), p. 183.
[11]Sanders, p. 184.
[12]Sanders, p. 183.
[13]Sanders, p. 184-5. The Fathers According to Rabbi Nathan Chapter Two contains an explicit statement in accord with Sanders's example here, drawn from the privacy of marital relations.

In fact, the case exhausts the category; the only Old Testament purity law that by definition and unavoidably must affect conduct outside of the cult is the one that serves Sanders's claim that being impure may be equated with being a sinner in the sense of wicked.

Sanders's categorization of impurity as (sometimes) an issue of morality leaves open the question of how (at other times) we should classify the matter. The answer to that question will prove diverse, as we move from one Judaism to another. No one need doubt, for example, that Sanders's reading of uncleanness as sin will have found, in the Essene Judaism of Qumran, a broader scope than merely menstrual uncleanness, and eschatological immersion from sin, so prominent a motif in the description of John the Baptist, assuredly conforms to Sanders's view. But were we to interrogate the Judaism represented, as to its initial statement, by the Mishnah, we should come up with a quite different view of matters.

Sanders's effort to trivialize and marginalize purity requires him to ignore ample evidence that purity and impurity for the Mishnah's account of the Torah occupy a critical position. It is a position I have characterized as ontological, not eschatological, expressive of a profound conviction about the true character of the life of holy Israel (a subject to which we shall return). Sanders's trivialization, in the language just now cited, makes me wonder what we are to make of the explicit rule that if we are cultically unclean, we cannot recite our prayers, specifically, the Shema – "Hear, Israel, the Lord our God, the Lord is one" – and the obligatory Prayer said three times a day. Perhaps "normal human relations were not affected" – a judgment that defies entire tractates of the Mishnah. But surely God will have missed the prayers of the unclean person, for the Mishnah is explicit on that point, in the following language, which distinguishes among levels of uncleanness, lesser, then greater, in determining how prayers were to be recited:

3:4 A. One who has had a seminal discharge recites [the Shema] silently.
     B. And he may not recite either blessings before [the Shema] nor [the blessings] after it.
     C. And [as for] the meal, he may recite the grace after it, but may not recite the blessings before it.
     D. R. Judah says, "He may recite the blessings before them [before the Shema and the meal] and after them."

3:5 A. If he was standing in [recitation of] the prayer
     B. and remembered that he had had a seminal emission,
     C. he should not interrupt [his recitation].
     D. Rather he should shorten [it].
     E. If one went down to immerse himself –
     F. if he can come up [from the pool] and cover himself and recite [the Shema] before the sun rises –

G.   he should come up and cover himself and recite.

H.   But if not, he should cover himself in the water and recite.

I.   But he should not cover himself in foul water or in water used for soaking [flax],

J.   unless he has poured into it [some fresh] water.

K.   And how far should one distance himself from them [from foul water] and from excrement [before he may recite]?

L.   Four cubits.

3:6   A.   A Zab who had an emission,

B.   a menstruating woman who discharged semen,

C.   and a woman who had intercourse and had a menstrual discharge

D.   require immersion [before they may recite the Shema].

E.   But R. Judah exempts [them from the requirement of immersion].

The passage recognizes two forms of uncleanness. If one suffers the lesser, which is, uncleanness by reason of seminal emission, then one set of restrictions pertain; if the greater, a different and more stringent set come into play. In the latter case, one cannot recite the Shema at all until attaining cleanness. How these facts square with Sanders's evaluation of matters is hardly obvious. His trivialization of the role of the purity laws hardly prepares us to anticipate so weighty an impact of purity taboos upon the everyday life of ordinary people (at least, those ordinary people who kept these laws at all, and clearly, many did not).

So much for New Testament scholarship on Judaism: condescending and misrepresentative. But there is a deeper problem still: all New Testament scholarship under Protestant auspices, and much under Catholic as well (particularly in the USA), has chosen to explain the origin of Christianity and its character by finding this-worldly contrasts with an inferior Judaism. Christianity then is viewed not on its own terms and in its own perspective – the authentic religion of Israel, adumbrated at Sinai, prophesied in Israelite prophesy – but as a more legitimate offspring of "biblical Judaism" than the Judaism of the day. Here, in particular, as I said before, "Judaism" comes to center stage as brand X, to be contrasted to the new, improved, religion of Christianity. In that way, a this-worldly, historical explanation is fabricated to answer the question that, in times past, Christianity answered in supernatural terms (if, to be sure, supersessionist ones). Specifically, nearly the whole of New Testament scholarship concurs that "Judaism" was ethnic, so failed; Christianity was universal, so succeeded.

If Sanders provides a fine example of condescension toward Judaism, on the one side, and out and out misrepresentation of the facts, on the other, then we turn to a more sophisticated scholar for a fine example of theological apologetics in historical guise. The invidious comparison of Judaism to superior Christianity emerges even in the most sympathetic and "pro-Jewish" scholarship. My case rests on James D.G. Dunn's *The*

Partings of the Ways between Christianity and Judaism and their Significance for the Character of Christianity.[14]   Dunn takes as his question the explanation of "how within the diversity of first-century Judaism, the major strand which was to become Christianity pulled apart on a sequence of key issues from the major strand which was to become rabbinic Judaism."   The parting of the ways "began with Jesus, but without Easter and the broadening out of the gospel to the Gentiles," the break may not have taken place at all. How, then, does Dunn explain the parting of the ways? He appeals to the ethnicism of Judaism, as against the power of Christianity to reach out beyond Israel.   Here is his language:

> For the Judaism which focused its identity most fully in the Torah, and which found itself unable to separate ethnic identity from religious identity, Paul and the Gentile mission involved an irreparable breach.[15]
>
> *Christianity began as a movement of renewal breaking through the boundaries first within and then round the Judaism of the first century.* At its historic heart Christianity is a protest against any and every attempt to claim that God is our God and not yours, God of our way of life and not yours, God of our "civilization" and not yours...against any and every attempt to mark off some of God's people as more holy than others, as exclusive channels of divine grace.[16]

What I find in Dunn's formulation of matters is the explicit claim that Judaism (or: Rabbinic Judaism) takes second place in the hierarchy of religions because it is ethnic, while Christianity overspreads the bounds of ethnic identification.

What is wrong with this formulation is that, as a matter of fact, Dunn does not grasp the meaning of "Israel" as a category. He sees the social metaphor, "Israel," as ethnic in the narrow, this-worldly sense of the word: a particular people, different from other people by reason of its genealogy, customs, social traits, and the like. And so would be the case, were it not for a simple fact.   Ethnic identity is transmitted genealogically, but a place in "Israel" so far as the Torah is concerned is reserved for every gentile who accepts the unity of God and the yoke of the Torah, God's revealed will for humanity.

What we should want to know from the Gospels is not how superior Christianity was, or is, to Judaism, but how Christianity came about – an account framed in its own terms. And if this outsider may offer a final

---

[14]Philadelphia, 1991: Trinity Press International.

[15]James D.G. Dunn's *The Partings of the Ways between Christianity and Judaism and their Significance for the Character of Christianity* (Philadelphia, 1991: Trinity Press International), p. 230.

[16] *Ibid.*, pp. 258-9.

word of counsel to New Testament studies, it is simple: stop beating up on "Judaism" in order to explain a religion that you may not in fact affirm at all. We cannot help your unbelief; our flaws are our own. Your God (if you believe in God) did not correct them. Two thousand years of scholarly bully boys have not won any arguments that count. For at issue in the theological study of religion – and when Christians study Christianity, or Jews Judaism, theology forms the provocation and the goal – are questions of eternity: how we know God, how we are in God's image, how God wants us to be. The Torah has answered those questions for holy Israel, Jesus Christ has answered those questions for those who, upon the rock, have built his Church. God will in the fullness of time settle our ongoing argument. There is no this-worldly, historical explanation that can truly serve any one of us, not Christianity, not Judaism, not Islam, not Bible, Torah, or Quran. To the Church, Israel after the flesh lies beyond all comprehension, and to Israel, Christianity and Islam find no reasonable explanation by the canons of reasoned faith made known to us in the Torah. But these three facts – three religions that in common claim to worship the one, unique, and same God and to proclaim that one, unique God's will to humanity – form a mystery. None of us adopts relativism and remains true to our respective vocations. All cannot be right, and the intellect of frail humanity can scarcely make sense of the disagreeable, intractable facts that confront each one. So we must live with incomprehension, or, in supernatural language I prefer, with mystery. We all must thank God, who knows the mysteries of the world (in the language of our liturgy) and who judges us all with love and mercy and accords grace to each, beyond anyone's most imagined merits.

Part Three

ÅBO RESEARCH

9

Judaism beyond the Texts, or Judaism behind the Texts? Formulating a Debate

Some scholars just now claim that there is a "Judaism out there," beyond any one document, to which in some way or other all documents in various ways and proportions are supposed to attest. And that Judaism out there, prior to, encompassing all documents, each with its "Judaism in here" imposes its judgment upon our reading of every sentence, every paragraph, every book. A reading of a single document therefore is improper. All documents have to be read in light of all other documents; none sustains a distinctive reading; a hermeneutics serving one explains all the others. This view may be framed in the phrase, "Judaism beyond the texts," which is to say, we have to read the various documents to find evidence of the nurturing, sheltering Judaic system that transcends them all and encompasses each one equally well. To discover that Judaism, we have to identify the premises and presuppositions of documents and their contents, for when we find out what the documents take for granted, we are led into the documentary matrix, which is to say, that Judaism that comes prior to any particular Judaic system, that Judaism to which all Judaisms subscribe.

The contrary view begins with the same question, which is to say, what do we know from a text about its framers' premises and presuppositions? That is precisely the question that precipitates research into the Judaism beyond the texts. But it is answered in a different way, by reason of a different premise. The premise of those who ask presuppositions to tell us about a Judaism beyond a given document is that a text tells us something beyond itself. But those who ask the premises to attest to the inner structure of thought on which a document's details rest insist that a text, inclusive of its premises and presuppositions, attests only to itself: its framers' views, its authors' conceptions. What lies beyond the text we cannot know from any one text, or from all of them put together. Accordingly, research on the character and consequences of the premises of a document will have to turn inward, asking about the Judaism behind the text, the system presupposed by a given document. Since my research in Åbo carried forward the issue just now outlined, an account of events in my study of Judaism in Finland will cover the question at hand. So let me explain how it came to the fore and what is at stake.

A considerable debate concerning the Judaism supposedly implicit in, and beyond, any given document of that Judaism, presently enlivens all scholarship on the literature of formative Judaism. Specifically, people wonder whether and how we may describe, beyond the evidence of what an authorship has given us in its particular piece of writing, what that authorship knew, had in mind, took for granted, and otherwise affirmed as its larger "Judaism." Nearly fifteen years ago I precipitated matters in my *Judaism: The Evidence of the Mishnah.* Specifically, I proposed to describe the system and structure of a given document and ask what "Judaism" – way of life, worldview, address to a defined "Israel" – emerged from that document. The notion that documents are to be read one by one and not as part of a larger canonical statement – the one whole Torah of Moses, our rabbi, for example – troubled colleagues, and not without reason. For reading the literature, one book at a time, and describing, analyzing, and interpreting the system presented by a document that to begin with invited systemic analysis set aside received notions in three ways.

First, as is clear, the conception of the document as part of a prior and encompassing tradition now met competition. Second, I dismissed the prevailing notion that we may describe on the basis of whatever we find in any given document a composite, "Judaism" (or some qualification thereof, for example, classical, rabbinic, Talmudic, normative, what-have-you-Judaism). Third, I treated as merely interesting the received and hitherto commanding tradition of exegesis, imputing to the ancient texts meanings not to be tampered with.

For example, I translated fully half a dozen tractates of the Bavli without referring in any systematic way (or at all) to Rashi's interpretation of a single passage, let alone accepting at face value his reading and sense of the whole. I dismissed as pertinent only to their own times the contributions of later authorships to the description of the Judaism attested by earlier documents. These things I did for good and substantial reason, which Western academic learning has recognized since the Renaissance: the obvious fallacy of anachronism being the compelling and first one, utter gullibility as to assertions of received writings, an obvious second. But, further, I maintain, along with nearly the whole of academic secular learning, that each document derives from a context, and to begin with is to be read in that context and interpreted, at the outset, as a statement of and to a particular setting. Constructs such as -*isms* and -*ities* come afterward (if they are admitted into discourse at all). Not only so, but in the case of ancient Judaism, a mass of confused and contradictory evidence, deriving from Jews of a broad variety of opinion, requires not harmonization but sorting out. The solution to the disharmonies – a process of theological selection, for example, of what is normative, classical, Talmudic, rabbinic, or, perhaps, Jewish-Christian, Hellenistic-Jewish, and the like – no longer solved many problems.

From this quest for "the Judaism beyond" the documents, so familiar and so much cherished by the received scholarly and theological tradition, with no regret I took my leave. My absence was soon noticed – and vigorously protested, as is only right and proper in academic discourse. One statement of the matter derives from the British medievalist, Hyam Maccoby:

> Neusner argues that since the Mishnah has its own style and program, nothing outside it is relevant to explaining it. This is an obvious fallacy. The Mishnah, as a digest, in the main, of the legal...aspect of rabbinic Judaism, necessarily has its own style and program. But to treat it as something intended to be a comprehensive compendium of the Oral Torah is simply to beg the question. Neusner does not answer the point, put to him by E.P. Sanders and myself, that the liturgy being presupposed by the Mishnah, is surely relevant to the Mishnah's exegesis. Nor does he answer the charge that he ignores the aggadic material within the Mishnah itself, for example, Avot; or explain why the copious aggadic material found in roughly contemporaneous works should be regarded as irrelevant. Instead he insists that he is right to carry out the highly artificial project of deliberately closing his eyes to all aggadic material, and trying to explain the Mishnah without it.[1]

Maccoby exhibits a somewhat infirm grasp upon the nature of the inquiry before us. If one starts with the question, "What does the authorship of this book mean to say, when read by itself and not in light of other, *later* writings?" then it would be improper to import into the description of the system of the Mishnah in particular (its "Judaism" – hence "Judaism: the evidence of the Mishnah") conceptions not contained within its pages.[2] Tractate Abot, for one instance, cites a range

---

[1]Writing in the symposium, "The Mishnah: Methods of Interpretation," *Midstream* October, 1986, p. 41. Maccoby's deplorable personal animadversions may be ignored.

[2]I stated explicitly at no fewer than six points in the book my recognition that diverse ideas floated about, and insisted that the authorship of the Mishnah can

of authorities who lived a generation beyond the closure of the (rest of the) Mishnah and so is ordinarily dated[3] to about 250, with the Mishnah dated to about 200. On that basis how one can impute to the Mishnah's system conceptions first attaining closure half a century later I do not know. To describe the Mishnah, for example, as a part of "Rabbinic Judaism" is to invoke the premise that we know, more or less on its own, just what this "Rabbinic Judaism" is and says.

But what we cannot show we do not know. And, as a matter of established fact, many conceptions dominant in the final statements of Rabbinic Judaism to emerge from late antiquity play no material role whatsoever in the system of the Mishnah, or, for that matter, of Tosefta and Abot. No one who has looked for the conception of "the Oral Torah" in the Mishnah or in the documents that succeeded it, for the next two hundred years, will understand why Maccoby is so certain that the category of Oral Torah, or the myth of the Dual Torah, applies at all. For the mythic category of "Oral Torah" makes its appearance, so far as I can discern, only with the Yerushalmi and not in any document closed prior to that time, although a notion of a revelation over and above Scripture – not called "Oral Torah" to be sure – comes to expression in Abot. Implicitly, moreover, certain sayings of the Mishnah itself, for example, concerning rulings of the Torah and rulings of sages, may contain the notion of a secondary tradition, beyond revelation. But that tradition is not called "the Oral Torah," and I was disappointed to find that even in the Yerushalmi the mythic statement of the matter, so far as I can see, is lacking. It is only in the Bavli, for example, in the famous story of Hillel and Shammai and the convert at b. Shab. 30b-31a, that the matter is fully explicit. Now, if Maccoby maintains that the conception circulated in the form in which we know it, for example, in the Yerushalmi in truncated form or in the Bavli in complete form, he should supply us with the

---

have entertained such ideas. But the statement that they made in the Mishnah did not contain them, and therefore was to be read without them. Alas, the few reviews that the book did receive contained no evidence that the reviewers understood that simple, and repeated caveat. Jakob J. Petuchowski in *Religious Studies Review* for July, 1983, subjected the book to a savage attack of trivializing and with vast condescension imputed to the book precisely the opposite of its message, as, we see, does Maccoby.

[3]I take responsibility for not a single date in any writing of mine, culling them all from available encyclopedia articles, in the notion that those articles, e.g., the splendid one by M.D. Heer in *Encyclopaedia Judaica* s.v. *Midrash*, represent the consensus of learning at this time. I do not know why Maccoby and Sanders reject the consensus on Abot, since, to my knowledge, neither of them has published a scholarly article on the dating of the document. But I believe my position accords with what is presently "common knowledge." If it does not, I should rapidly correct it.

evidence for his position.[4] As I said, what we cannot show we do not know. And most secular and academic scholarship concurs that we have no historical knowledge a priori, though in writing Maccoby has indeed in so many words maintained that we do. In fact the documents of formative Judaism do yield histories of ideas, and not every idea can be shown to have taken part in the statement of each, let alone all, of the documents. But those who appeal to a Judaism out there, before and beyond all of the documents, ignore that fact.

Sanders and Maccoby seem more certain of the content of the liturgy than the rest of scholarship, which tends to a certain reserve on the matter of the wording and language of prayer. Maccoby's "roughly contemporaneous" aggadic works cite the Mishnah as a completed document, for example, Sifra and the two Sifrés, and so therefore are to be dated in the period beyond the closure of the Mishnah.[5] Unless we accept at face value the attribution of a saying to the person to whom a document's editorship assigns it, we know only that date of closure for the contents of a document. True, we may attempt to show that a saying derives from a period prior to the closure of a document; but we cannot take for granted that sayings belong to the age and the person in whose name they are given. These are simple truisms of all critical learning, and, once we understand and take them to heart, we find it necessary to do precisely what I have done, which is to read each document first of all on its own and in its framework and terms.[6]

---

[4]Maccoby may not have read my *Torah: From Scroll to Symbol in Formative Judaism* (Philadelphia, 1985: Fortress Press). There I survey the materials that stand behind the statements made here.

[5]I utterly ignore Mekhilta deR. Ishmael, because of the important article by Ben Zion Wacholder on the date of the document, published in 1969 in *Hebrew Union College Annual*. I have not worked on that Mekhilta and have yet to see any scholarly discussion of Wacholder's most interesting arguments in behalf of the view that in Mekhilta deR. Ishmael we deal with what is in fact a medieval document. Not knowing how to sort out the issues, I have simply bypassed the evidence of that document at this time. Wacholder takes for granted that merely because the names of authorities that occur in the Mishnah also occur in Mekhilta deR. Ishmael, we cannot maintain that that writing derives from the period of the Mishnah. Since everyone has known for a half-century that the Zohar, attributed to Tannaite authority, in fact was made up in the high Middle Ages as a work of pseudo-imitation (there is in fact nothing imitative about it), Wacholder surely expressed a kind of consensus. But that consensus has not yet affected the reading of the documents of late antiquity, all sayings of which are assigned to those to whom they are attributed – pure and simple.

[6]Maccoby further seems not to have read a variety of scholarship. He says that it is absurd to say that "the Mishnah is not much concerned with justice, or with repentance, or with the Messiah." He does not seem to realize the way in which the Messiah-theme is used in the Mishnah, by contrast to its use in other

At stake are not merely literary, but also cultural and religious conceptions. So let us return to this matter of "the Judaism beyond" to explain the connection between a narrowly hermeneutical debate and the much broader issue of culture and the nature of religion. When I speak of "the Judaism beyond," I mean a conception of a very concrete character. To define by example, I invoke the definition of this "Judaism out there" operative in the mind of E. P. Sanders when Sanders describes rabbinic writings. In my debates with Sanders[7] I have complained that his categories seem to me improperly formed, since the rabbinic texts do not conform to the taxonomy Sanders utilizes. They in other words are not talking about the things Sanders wants them to discuss. That complaint is turned against me, as we see, in Maccoby's critique of my picture of how we may describe (not "explain," as Maccoby would have it) the system of the Mishnah in particular.

Commenting on this debate with Sanders, William Scott Green says, Sanders "reads rabbinic texts by peering through them for the ideas (presumably ones Jews or rabbis believed) that lie beneath them." This runs parallel to Maccoby's criticism of my "ignoring" a variety of conceptions I do not find in the Mishnah. Both Maccoby and Sanders, in my view, wish to discuss what *they* think important – that is, presentable

---

documents, as demonstrated in my *Messiah in Context. Israel's History and Destiny in Formative Judaism* (Philadelphia, 1983: Fortress Press). I am genuinely puzzled at who has said that the Mishnah is not much concerned with justice or with repentance. I look in vain for such statements on the part of any scholar, myself included. Mishnah-tractate Yoma on repentance and Mishnah-tractate Sanhedrin on the institutions of justice have not, to my knowledge, been ignored in my account of the Mishnah and its literature and system. It would appear that Maccoby reads somewhat selectively.

[7]These begin in my review of his *Paul and Palestinian Judaism*, in *History of Religion* 1978, 18:177-191. I reprinted the review in my *Ancient Judaism: Debates and Disputes* (Chico, 1984: Scholars Press for Brown Judaic Studies), where I review more than a score of modern and contemporary books in the field in which I work and also present several bibliographic essays and state of the question studies. I also reworked parts of my Sanders review in essays on other problems. To my knowledge he has not reviewed my *Judaism: The Evidence of the Mishnah*, and if he has in print responded to my questions of method addressed to his *Paul and Palestinian Judaism*, I cannot say where he has done so. Quite to the contrary, in his *Paul, The Law, and the Jewish People* (Philadelphia, 1985: Fortress), which I review also in my *Ancient Judaism*, where he claims to reply to critics of the original book, he not only ignores my review, and also that of Anthony J. Saldarini in *Journal of Biblical Literature*, cited in my review of *Paul, The Law, and the Jewish People*, which makes the same point, but he even omits from his list of reviews of the original work Saldarini's review as well as mine. This seems to me to impede scholarly debate.

in terms of contemporary religious disputation[8] – and therefore to ignore what the texts themselves actually talk about, as Green says, "the materials that attracted the attention and interest of the writers."[9] In my original review I pointed out that Sanders's categories ignore what the texts actually say and impose categories the Judaic-rabbinic texts do not know. Sanders, in Green's judgment, introduces a distinct premise:

> For Sanders, the religion of Mishnah lies unspoken beneath its surface; for Neusner it is manifest in Mishnah's own language and preoccupations.[10]

Generalizing on this case, Green further comments in those more general terms that bring us into a debate on the nature of religion and culture, and that larger discourse lends importance to what, in other circumstances, looks to be a mere academic argument. Green writes as follows:

> The basic attitude of mind characteristic of the study of religion holds that religion is certainly in your soul, likely in your heart, perhaps in your mind, but never in your body. That attitude encourages us to construe religion cerebrally and individually, to think in terms of beliefs and the believer, rather than in terms of behavior and community. The lens provided by this prejudice draws our attention to the intense and obsessive belief called "faith," so religion is understood as a state of mind, the object of intellectual or emotional commitment, the result of decisions to believe or to have faith. According to this model, people

---

[8]Maccoby makes this explicit in his contribution to the symposium cited above, "The Mishnah: Methods of Interpretation," *Midstream*, October, 1986, p. 41, "It leads to Neusner's endorsement of 19th-century German anti-Jewish scholarship.... [Neusner] admires the Mishnah for the very things that the New Testament alleges against the Pharisees: for formalism, attention to petty legalistic detail, and for a structuralist patterning of reality in terms of 'holiness' rather than of morality, justice, and love of neighbor." Here Maccoby introduces the bias of Reform Judaism, with its indifference to "petty legalistic detail." But I (among millions of Jews) find intensely meaningful the holy way of life embodied, for one example, in concern for what I eat for breakfast, along with love of neighbor, and the conception that the Judaic way of life leads to a realm of holiness is hardly my invention. It is contained in the formula of the blessing, *...who has sanctified us by the commandments and commanded us to....* I can treat with respect Maccoby's wish to describe as his Judaism some other system than the received one, but the "very things" that the New Testament alleges against the Pharisees are recapitulated by the Reform critique of the way of life of the Judaism of the Dual Torah, today embodied in Orthodoxy and Conservative Judaism, to which I adhere. It follows that not all of the "other side" are Orthodox, although, as to intertextuality, that seems to be the sector from which the principal advocates derive.

[9]Personal letter, January 17, 1985.

[10]William Scott Green in his Introduction, *Approaches to Ancient Judaism* (Chicago, 1980: Scholars Press for Brown Judaic Studies) II, p. xxi.

have religion but they do not do their religion. Thus we tend to devalue behavior and performance, to make it epiphenomenal, and of course to emphasize thinking and reflecting, the practice of theology, as a primary activity of religious people.... The famous slogan that "ritual recapitulates myth" follows this model by assigning priority to the story and to peoples' believing the story, and makes behavior simply an imitation, an aping, a mere acting out.[11]

Now as we reflect on Green's observations, we of course recognize what is at stake. It is the definition of religion, or, rather, what matters in or about religion, emerging from one reading of Protestant theology and Protestant religious experience.

For when we lay heavy emphasis on faith to the exclusion of works, on the individual rather than on society, on conscience instead of culture, and when, as in the language of Maccoby, we treat behavior and performance by groups as less important, and present as more important the matters of thinking, reflecting, theology and belief – not to mention the abstractions of "love of neighbor" and "morality," to which Reform theologians in the pattern of Maccoby adhere, we simply adopt as normative for academic scholarship convictions critical to the Lutheran wing of the Protestant Reformation. And that accounts for the absolutely accurate instinct of Maccoby in introducing into the debate the positions of the Lutheran New Testament scholars who have dominated New Testament scholarship in Germany and the USA (but not Britain or France).

Judaism and the historical, classical forms of historical Christianity, Roman Catholic and Orthodox, as well as important elements of the Protestant Reformation, however, place emphasis on religion as a matter of works and not faith alone, behavior and community as well as belief and conscience. Religion is something that people do, and they do it together. Religion is not something people merely have, as individuals. Since the entire civilization of the West, from the fourth century onward, has carried forward the convictions of Christianity, not about the individual alone but about politics and culture, we may hardly find surprising the Roman Catholic conviction that religion flourishes not alone in heart and mind, but in eternal social forms: the Church, in former times, the state as well.

At stake in the present debate therefore is the fundamental issue of hermeneutics. For claims as to the character of the literature of Judaism entail judgments on the correct hermeneutics, down to the interpretation of words and phrases. We can read everything only in light of everything else, fore and aft. That is how today nearly everyone

---

[11]Personal letter, January 17, 1985.

interested in these writings claims to read them – citing the Bavli as proof for that hermeneutics. Or we can read each item first of all on its own, a document as an autonomous and cogent and utterly rational, syllogistic statement, a unit of discourse as a complete and whole composition, entire unto itself, taking account, to be sure, of how, in the larger context imposed from without, meanings change(d). That is how – and not solely on the basis of the sample we have surveyed – I maintain any writing must be read: in its own context, entirely on its own, not only in the one imposed by the audience and community that preserved it.

For whatever happens to thought, in the mind of the thinker ideas come to birth cogent, whole, complete – and on their own. Extrinsic considerations of context and circumstance play their role, but logic, cogent discourse, rhetoric – these enjoy an existence, an integrity too. If sentences bear meaning on their own, then to insist that sentences bear meaning only in line with friends, companions, partners in meaning contradicts the inner logic of syntax that, on its own, imparts sense to sentences. These are the choices: everything imputed, as against an inner integrity of logic and the syntax of syllogistic thought.[12] But there is no compromise between what I argue is the theologically grounded hermeneutic, taken as a given by diverse believers, and the descriptive and historical, utterly secular hermeneutic which I advocate. As between the philosophical heritage of Athens and any other hermeneutics, I maintain that "our sages of blessed memory" demonstrate the power of the philosophical reading of the one whole Torah of Moses, our rabbi. And, further, I should propose that the reason for our sages' remarkable success in persuading successive generations of Israel of the Torah's ineluctable truth lies not in arguments from tradition, from "Sinai," so much as in appeals to the self-evidence of the well-framed argument, the well-crafted sentence of thought.

If the mythic appeal stands for religion, and the reasoned position for secularity, then I point to what in Judaism we call "our sages of blessed memory," masters of the one whole Torah of Moses, our rabbi, as paragons of practical logic and secular reason. Why at the end introduce the (inflammatory, provocative) category of secularity? The reason is that the literature of Judaism, exemplified by the Bavli, commonly finds representation as wholly continuous, so that everything always testifies to the meaning of everything else, and, moreover, no book demands or

---

[12]No one can maintain that the meanings of words and phrases, the uses of syntax, bear meanings wholly integral to discrete occasions. Syntax works because it joins mind to mind, and no mind invents language. But that begs the question and may be dismissed as impertinent, since the contrary view claims far more than the social foundation of the language.

sustains a reading on its own. As a theological judgment, that (religious) view enjoys self-evidence, since, after all, "Judaism" is "a religion," and it presents its doctrines and dogmas, rules and regulations. So every document contributes to that one and encompassing system, that Judaism. But a system, a religion, makes its judgments at the end, *post facto*, while the authorships at hand worked at the outset, *de novo*. They were philosophers in the deepest and richest sense of the tradition of philosophy. In that sense (but that sense alone) I classify our sages as fundamentally secular. I mean to say that a secular hermeneutics for a theological literature alone can lead us to learn how to read their writing. The upshot of such a hermeneutics can only be a profoundly reasoned, religious view of a rational and well-proportioned world: a world of rules and order and reason and rationality. That constitutes their religion: the affirmation of creation as a work of logic and order and law, to which the human mind, with its sense of logic, order, and rule, conforms, as it was created to conform.

So reading what they wrote – a problem of textual analysis and interpretation – undergoes distortion we impose, to begin with, who form the after-the-fact interpretation of the audience that received the writing. We err if we confuse social and theological with literary and hermeneutical categories, and the religious system at the end constitutes a social and theological, not a literary classification. Hermeneutics begins within the text and cannot sustain definition on the basis of the (later, extrinsic) disposition of the text. Nor should we miss the gross anachronism represented by the view that the way things came out all together at the end imposes its meaning and character upon the way things started out, one by one. Reading the Mishnah, ca. 200, as the framers of the two Talmuds read it two hundred, then four hundred years later, vastly distorts the original document in its own setting and meaning – and that by definition. But the same must be said, we now see, of the Bavli: reading the Bavli as if any other authorship but the Bavli's authorship played a part in making the statement of the Bavli is simply an error.[13] A mark of the primitive character of discourse[14] in the

---

[13]Critics of my translations of the Bavli into English prove the necessity of making this simple point, because they invariably fault me for translating not in accord with the medieval interpreter, Solomon Isaac (1040-1105), "Rashi." They accuse me not of ignoring Rashi, to which I plead guilty, but not understanding Rashi. But I consistently translate the words before me, as best I can, without reference to Rashi's interpretation of them – except – for reason, not for piety – as an interesting possibility. I point to the world of biblical scholarship, which manages to translate the Hebrew Scriptures without consistently accepting the interpretation of the medieval commentators. Why should the Talmuds be treated differently? There are other approaches to the sense and meaning, other

field at hand derives from the need to point to self-evident anachronism in the prevailing hermeneutics.

This formulation of matters brings us to the issues investigated in my *Judaism behind the Texts*, most of which I completed in my research term in Åbo. In asking about not the Judaism beyond, but the Judaism behind, the texts, what I want to know is how the various writings hold together. Can we identify a set of premises that animate all writers, presuppositions that guide every compilation's compositions' authors and compositors' framers? If we can, then we shall have found what makes that Judaism into a single coherent religious system. If we cannot, then we shall have to ask a fresh set of descriptive questions concerning the theology of that religious system – a different set from those that guide the present work. Let me state with heavy emphasis what I want to find out: *At stake is not only the Mishnah and its premises (presumably bringing us back into circles of first-century thinkers) but the presuppositions of numerous representative documents of Rabbinic Judaism throughout its formative period. The second question vastly outweighs the one that animates interest in premises and presuppositions: Is there a Judaism that infuses all texts and forms of each part of a coherent whole? At issue in the quest for presuppositions is not the Judaism that lies beyond the texts (which the texts by definition cannot tell us and indeed do not pretend to tell us), but the Judaism that holds together all of the texts and forms the substrate of conviction and conscience in each one.*

That body of writings is continuous, formed as it is as commentaries on the Written Torah or the Mishnah, and the period in which they took shape for formal and substantive reasons also is continuous and of course not to be truncated at its very starting point, with the Mishnah, as Sanders's formulation proposes. For the Mishnah presents only the first among a long sequence of problems for analysis, and cutting that writing off from its continuators and successors, in both Midrash compilations and Talmuds, represents a gross error, one commonplace, to be sure, among Christian scholars of Judaism, for whom, as in Sanders's case, Judaism ends in the first century or early second and ceases beyond that point to require study at all. But the Judaism of the Dual Torah, viewed in its formative canon, is single and whole, and the premises and presuppositions of any of its writings, treated in isolation from those of all the others, contain nothing of interest for the analysis of that massive

---

criteria, other definitions of the problem. But we cannot expect a hearing from those who know in advance that Rashi has said the last word on the matter.

[14]We note that Shaye Cohen is explicit about indifference to priority or documents.

and complex Judaic system, only for the Judaism of a given piece of writing.

Now to broaden the frame of discussion: at stake in any study of a religion is the definition of that religion and of religion, and what I am trying to do here is to find the correct way to define Judaism in its formative age, which is to say, describe, analyze, and interpret the earliest stage in the formation of the Judaism of the Dual Torah. To that project, which has occupied me for thirty years, the question of premise and presupposition is critical.   No one can imagine that the explicit statements of a generative text, such as the Mishnah or the Talmud of Babylonia, for example, exhaust all that that text conveys – or means to convey – about God's truth. With what Sanders correctly emphasizes no one can argue, and with that obvious premise, none has argued. To the contrary, even in the founding generation of the field that used to be called "Talmudic history," the true founder and greatest mind in the field, Y.I. Halevi, *Dorot harishonim* (Vienna-Berlin, 1923 et seq.), insisted that a statement rested on a prior history of thought, which can and should be investigated, and that premises of available facts yield a pre-history that we can describe. Everybody understands that the definitive documents of a religion expose something, but contain everything. Sanders is in good company.

But it is not enough to posit such premises; we have in detail to identify just what they were. So it is the task of learning to explore the premises, presuppositions, and processes of imagination and of critical thought that yield in the end the statements that we find on the surface of the writings. But the work has to be done systematically and not episodically, in a thorough way and not through episode, anecdote, and example. We address an entire canon with the question: Precisely what are the premises demonstrably present throughout, the generative presuppositions not in general but in all their rich specificity? Here I take up this analytical problem, having completed my descriptive work.

My research in Åbo provided a protracted, systematic and detailed answer to two questions, first, the question set forth in Professor Sanders's quite reasonable proposal to "press behind the contents...to discover what the contents...presuppose." I have already explained why I have taken Sanders's formulation at face value – behind the texts, not beyond the texts, though his writing in general leaves his intention quite blatant. While Sanders speaks of the Mishnah, in fact the commanding question – if I know this, what else do I know about the intellect of the writers of a document or a whole canon? – pertains to the entirety of the Oral part of the Torah. And the second question, as I have explained, is a still more urgent one: Are there premises and presuppositions that engage thought throughout the documents? Or are the documents discrete episodes in a sustained procession of thought that requires description upon some basis other than a documentary one?

The project thus presents an exercise in the further definition of the Judaism of the Dual Torah that encompasses not only what its principal documents make articulate but also what they mean to imply, on the one end, and how what they presuppose coheres (if it does), on the other. Since many of the answers to those questions are either obvious or trivial or beg the question, we have to refine matters with a further critical consideration. It is this: Among the presuppositions, the critical one is, which ones matter? And how can we account for the emergence of the system as a whole out of the presuppositions demonstrably present at the foundations of systemic documents? The program of this project, in three volumes for the Mishnah and further volumes for selected documents thereafter, aims at uncovering the foundations of the Judaism of the Dual Torah.

When I ask the general question about "the Judaism behind the texts," I refer to a variety of quite specific matters. All of them concern the premises or presuppositions of a document and of important statements within said document. I want to know what someone must take for granted as fact in order to make an allegation of some consequence within a legal or theological writing. Taking as our given what is alleged in a document, we ask, in order to take that position, what do I have to have known as fact? What must I have taken for granted as a principle? What set of issues or large-scale questions – fundamental issues that seem to me to pop up everywhere – has to have preoccupied me, so as to lead me to identify a given problem for solution, a given possibility awaiting testing?

These statements left unsaid but ubiquitously assumed may be of three kinds, from the obvious, conventional, unsurprising, unexceptional, uninteresting, routine and systemically inert to the highly suggestive, provocative and systemically generative.

First, a statement in a text may presuppose a religious norm of belief or behavior (*halakhah* or *aggadah*, in the native categories). For one example, if a rule concerns itself with when the Shema is to be recited, the rule presupposes a prayer, the *Shema* – and so throughout. Such a presupposition clearly is to be acknowledged, but ordinarily, the fact that is taken for granted will not stand behind an exegetical initiative or intellectual problem to which a document pays substantial attention.

Second, a statement in a text may presuppose knowledge of a prior, authoritative text. For instance, rules in the Mishnah take for granted uncited texts of Scripture, nearly the whole of tractate Yoma providing a particularly fine instance, since the very order and structure of that tractate prove incomprehensible without a verse-by-verse review of

Leviticus Chapter 16. Knowing that the framers of a document had access to a prior holy book by itself does not help us to understand what the framers of that document learned from the earlier one; they will have selected what they found relevant or important, ignoring what they found routine; we cannot simply assign to the later authorship complete acquiescence in all that a prior set of writers handed on, merely because the later authorship took cognizance of what the earlier one had to say. It is one thing to acknowledge, it is another to make use of, to respond to, a received truth.

Third, a concrete statement in a text may rest upon a prior conception of a more abstract character, much as applied mathematics rests upon theoretical mathematics, or technology upon principles of engineering and physics. And this set of premises and presuppositions does lead us deep into the foundations of thought of a given, important and systematic writing. In the main, what I want to know here concerns the active and generative premises of Rabbinic documents: the things the writers had to know in order to define the problems they wished to solve. I seek the key to the exegesis of the law that the framers of the Mishnah put forth, the exegesis of Scripture that they systematically provided. When we can say not only what they said but also what they took for granted, if we can explain their principles of organization and the bases for their identification of the problems they wished to solve, then, but only then, do we enter into that vast Judaic system and structure that their various writings put forth in bits and pieces and only adumbrated in its entirety.

Accordingly, this project of mine, covering the principal documents of Rabbinic Judaism in its formative age, while paying attention to data of the first two classes, focuses upon the third category of presuppositions, stipulating that the first two require no more than routine inquiry. That is to say, we all know that the sages of the Rabbinic writings deemed the Scriptures of ancient Israel, which they knew as the written part of the Torah, to be authoritative; they took for granted the facticity and authority of every line of that writing, to be sure picking and choosing, among available truths, those that required emphasis and even development. That simple fact permits us to take for granted, without laboring to prove the obvious, that the Judaism not articulated in the Rabbinic literature encompassed the way of life and worldview and conception of Israel that, in broad outlines, Scripture set forth. But that fact standing on its own is trivial. It allows for everything but the main thing: what characterized the specific, distinctive character of the Judaic system set forth in Rabbinic writings, and, it goes without saying, how the particular point of view of those writings dictated the ways in which

Scripture's teachings and rules gained entry into, and a place for themselves in, the structure and system of the Judaism of the Dual Torah.

Prior to a vast number of rulings, generating the problems that require those rulings, a few fundamental conceptions or principles, never articulated, await identification. And, once identified, these several conceptions or principles demand a labor of composition: How does the generative problematic that precipitates the issues of one tractate, or forms the datum of that tractate's inquiry, fit together with the generative problematic of some other tractate and its sustained exegesis of the law? Once we know what stands behind the law, we have to ask, what holds together the several fundamental principles, all of them of enormous weight and vast capacity for specification in numerous detailed cases? Before we know how to define this Judaism, we have to show that a coherent metaphysics underpins the detailed physics, a cogent principle the concrete cases, a proportioned, balanced, harmonious statement the many, derivative and distinct cases of which the law and theology of Judaism are comprised.

What Rabbinic documents tell us that bears consequence for the definition of their Judaism in particular – not merely what was likely to be common to all Judaism, for example, a sacred calendar, a record of generations' encounter with God and the like – then requires specification, and the third of the three types of presuppositions or premises points toward the definition of what is at stake and under study here. That is, specifically, the deeper, implicit affirmations of documents: what they know that stands behind what they say, the metaphysics behind the physics (to resort to the metaphor just now introduced). For a close reading of both law and lore, *halakhah* and *aggadah*, yields a glimpse at a vast structure of implicit conceptions, those to which Sanders makes reference in his correct prescription of what is to be done: "...one must press behind the contents of the Mishnah and attempt to discover what the contents of the Mishnah presuppose."

Some of these implicit conceptions pertain to law, some to questions of philosophy and metaphysics, some to theology. Once we have examined important constitutive documents, we shall see that all of them circulate hither and yon through the law and the theology of the various documents; and only when we identify the various notions that are presupposed and implicit and show how they coalesce shall we understand the details of the Judaic system – law and theology alike – that comes to concrete expression in the Rabbinic writings. I have already set forth a systematic account, treating the Mishnah as a whole, of the document's premises in regard to philosophy, politics, and economics, and these results are summarized in the first three chapters. These are large-scale exercises in answering the question, "If I know this, what else do I know?" My answer is, if I know the specific rulings of the Mishnah on topics relevant to economics and politics, I know that the Mishnah sets forth a philosophical politics and a philosophical economics. If I know how the Mishnah formulates and solves a problem, I know that the framers of the Mishnah think philosophically – but mostly, though not entirely, about questions of a very different order from those that philosophers pursued.

It remains to explain that, when I refer to "generative premises," I mean to exclude a variety of other givens that strike me as demonstrably present but systemically inert. There are many facts our documents know and acknowledge but leave in the background; there are others, that is, premises and presuppositions, that generate numerous specific problems, indeed that turn out, upon close examination of the details of documents, to stand behind numerous concrete inquiries. The former are systemically inert, the latter, systemically provocative and formative. Such premises as the sanctity of Israel and the Land of Israel, the election of Israel, the authority of the Torah (however defined), and the like in these writings prove systemic givens, assumed but rarely made the focus of exegetical thought.

Not only so: a very long list of platitudes and banalities can readily be constructed and every item on the list shown to be present throughout the documents under study here; but those platitudes and banalities make no contribution to the shaping of our documents and the formulation of their system. Therefore, having proven that the sun rises in the east, from those systemically inert givens, we should know no more about matters than we did beforehand. True, to those in search of "Judaism," as distinct from the diverse Judaic systems to which our evidence attests, that finding – God is one, God gave the Torah, Israel is God's chosen people, and the like – bears enormous consequence. But that God is one in no way accounts for the system's specific qualities and concerns, any more than does the fact that the laws of gravity operate.

What makes a Judaic system important is what marks that system as entire and imparts to that system its integrity: what makes it different from other systems, what holds that system together. Defining that single, encompassing "Judaism" into which genus all species, all Judaisms, fit helps us understand nothing at all about the various Judaisms. But all we really have in hand are the artifacts of Judaisms. As the prologue has already argued, efforts to find that one Judaism that holds together all Judaisms yields suffocating banalities and useless platitudes: we do not understand anything in particular any better than we did before we had thought up such generalities. So by "generative premises," I mean, the premises that counted: those that provoked the framers of a document's ideas to do their work, that made urgent the questions they address, that imparted self-evidence to the answers they set forth. This brings us to the documents under study in this part of the work.

In the earliest Midrash compilations, not to mention the Tosefta, premises and presuppositions – "the Judaism behind the texts" – prove rare and episodic. The reason is that the character of the documents under study imposes limitations upon the free exercise of speculation. They undertake the systematic exposition of a prior document. Consequently, most of the task finds its definition in the statements that have been received and now require paraphrase, clarification, extension, and augmentation. The way in which this work is done – the hermeneutics that govern the exegesis of Scripture – yields no premises or presuppositions susceptible of generalization. And the result of the exegesis itself proves from our perspective sparse and anecdotal. Let me commence with a single example of how a sublime text is treated in a manner that, while not trivial, still in no way yields the kind of theological or moral or legal principles that at various points in the Mishnah show the document to rest upon deep foundations of thought. Our example is the exposition of the priestly benediction, and it shows us what to expect in the Midrash compilations that are treated here, therefore explaining, also, why the results of the survey prove frustrating:

XXXIX

I.1   A.   "The Lord said to Moses, 'Say to Aaron and his sons: Thus shall you bless the people of Israel. [You shall say to them: "The Lord bless you and keep you, the Lord make his face to shine upon you and be gracious to you, the Lord lift up his countenance upon you and give you peace." So shall they put my name upon the people of Israel, and I will bless them]' (Num. 6:22-27)":

       B.   Since the deed required in the present passage is to be carried out by Aaron and his sons, the statement that is made is not only to Moses but also to Aaron and his sons.

       C.   For this is the encompassing rule:

       D.   Whenever the statement is made to the priests, then the deed is required only of the priests.

       E.   When the statement is made to Israel, then the entirety of what is required is incumbent on Israel.

       F.   When the statement is made to Israel but the deed is to be done by everyone, then one has to encompass proselytes as well.

II.1   A.   "The Lord said to Moses, 'Say to Aaron and his sons: Thus shall you bless the people of Israel'":

       B.   The blessing is to be said in the Holy Language [Hebrew].

       C.   For any passage in which reference is made to "responding" or "saying" or "thus," the statement is to be made in Hebrew.

III.1   A.   "The Lord said to Moses, 'Say to Aaron and his sons: Thus shall you bless the people of Israel'":

B.   [This must be done when the priests are] standing.

C.   You maintain that this must be done when the priests are standing.

D.   But perhaps it may be done either standing or not standing?

E.   Scripture states, "And these shall *stand* to bless the people" (Deut. 27:42).

F.   The word "blessing" occurs here and the word "blessing" occurs there. Just as the word "blessing" when it occurs at the later passage involves the priests' standing, so here, too, the word blessing indicates that the priests must be standing.

G.   R. Nathan says, "It is not necessary to invoke that analogy. For it is said, 'And the Levitical priests shall draw near, for the Lord has chosen them to serve him and to bestow a blessing in the name of the Lord' (Deut. 21:5). The act of bestowing a blessing is compared to the act of service. Just as service is performed only when standing, so bestowing a blessing is bestowed when standing."

IV.1 A.   "The Lord said to Moses, 'Say to Aaron and his sons: Thus shall you bless the people of Israel'":

B.   It must be done by raising the hands.

C.   You say it must be done by raising the hands.

D.   But perhaps it may be done either by raising the hands or not by raising the hands?

E.   Scripture says, "And Aaron raised his hands toward the people and blessed them" (Lev. 9:22).

F.   Just as Aaron bestowed the blessing by raising his hands, so his sons will bestow the blessing by raising their hands.

G.   R. Jonathan says, "But may one then say that just as that passage occurs in the setting of a blessing bestowed at the new moon, on the occasion of a public offering, and through the medium only of the high priest, so here, too, the blessing may be bestowed only at the new moon, on the occasion of a public offering, and through the medium only of the high priest!

H.   "Scripture states, 'For the Lord your God has chosen him above all your tribes' (Deut. 18:5). The Scripture compares his sons to him: Just as he bestowed the blessing by raising his hands, so his sons will bestow the blessing by raising their hands."

V.1   A.   "The Lord said to Moses, 'Say to Aaron and his sons: Thus shall you bless the people of Israel'":

B.   It is to be done by expressing the fully spelled out Name of God.

C.   You maintain that it is to be done by expressing the fully spelled out Name of God. But perhaps it may be done with a euphemism for the Name of God?

D.   Scripture says, "So shall they put my name upon the people of Israel" (Num. 6:27).

V.2   A.   "In the sanctuary it is to be done by expressing the fully spelled out Name of God. And in the provinces it is to be done by a euphemism," the words of R. Josiah.

B.   R. Jonathan says, "Lo, Scripture states, 'In every place in which I shall cause my name to be remembered' (Ex. 20:20). This verse of Scripture is out of order, and how should it be read? 'In every place in which I appear before you, there should my Name be mentioned.' And where is it that I appear before you? It is in the chosen house [the Temple]. So you should mention my name [as fully spelled out] only in the chosen house.

C.   "On this basis sages have ruled: 'As to the fully spelled out name of God, it is forbidden to express it in the provinces [but only in the sanctuary].'"

VI.1   A.   "The Lord said to Moses, 'Say to Aaron and his sons: Thus shall you bless the people of Israel'":

B.   On this basis I know only that the blessing is directed to Israel.

C.   How do I know that it is directed to women, proselytes, and bondsmen?

D.   Scripture states, "...and I will bless *them*" (Num. 6:27), [encompassing not only Israel, but also women, proselytes, and bondsmen].

VI.2   A.   How do we know that a blessing is bestowed on the priests?

B.   Scripture states, "...and I will bless them" (Num. 6:27).

VII.1   A.   "The Lord said to Moses, 'Say to Aaron and his sons: Thus shall you bless the people of Israel'":

B.   It must be done face to face [with the priests facing the people and the people facing the priests].

C.   You say that it must be done face to face [with the priests facing the people and the people facing the priests]. But may it be back to face?

D.   Scripture says, "You shall say *to* them" (Num. 6:23), [which can only be face to face].

VIII.1   A.   "The Lord said to Moses, 'Say to Aaron and his sons: Thus shall you bless the people of Israel'":

B.   The sense is that the entire congregation should hear what is said.

C.   Or may it be that the priests say the blessing to themselves [and not in audible tones]?

D.   Scripture says, "*Say* to them...," (Num. 6:23), meaning that the entire congregation should hear the blessing.

E.   And how do we know that the leader of the prayers has to say to the priests, "Say..."?

F.   Scripture says, "*You* shall say to them" (Num. 6:23).

Whatever the hermeneutics that is taken for granted, the unarticulated layer of law and theology is scarcely to be discerned; the givens are Scripture and its facts and formulations, on the one side, and a set of principles of exegesis deriving from a transparent hermeneutics, on the other. For our survey, I find nothing in the treatment of a passage of surpassing interest to enrich our grasp of the law or theology behind the text. What we see is what there is – that alone. When I observe that most of the documents surveyed here generate little of interest to an inquiry into the Judaism behind the texts, this passage speaks for me. What we derive is refinement and clarification, but the passage scarcely suggests that taken for granted is a deep layer of theological or moral speculation. What we see is what we get, which is, a text with some minor points of refinement.

Even though these results prove paltry, the issues remain vital, and a negative result itself bears formidable implications. Let me spell out what I conceive to be at stake in this protracted study. In fact, the issue of premises, the question, if I know this, what else do I know? – these form the entry point. But my goal is other. For the task of history of religions always is that of definition of religions: what can we possibly mean by those encompassing categories, "Judaism" or "Buddhism" or "Islam" or "Christianity" that descriptively conform to data. In the case of "Judaism," I want to know whether the construct refers to documents that cohere, or whether the fabricated category is imposed thereon. So I aim at finding out whether, and how, the various documents valued by the Judaism of the Dual Torah relate, not in imputed but in substantive ways. Do I find that the various writings that the Judaism of the Dual Torah produced in late antiquity rest upon a shared and common fundament convictions, that is, this "Judaism behind the texts," or does each piece of writing stand essentially on its own? It is clear that as a matter of theory documents that are held by those who deem them authoritative to cohere relate in three ways. First, they stand each on its own, that is, each is autonomous. Second, in some ways they may intersect, for example, citations or long quotations of one writing appear in some other. They are therefore connected in some specific ways. But, third, do these writings also form a continuous whole? That is what I want to find out in this exercise. Let me spell out these three dimensions of relationship, autonomy, connection, and continuity.

Documents – cogent compositions made up of a number of complete units of thought – by definition exist on their own. That is to say, by invoking as part of our definition the trait of cogency of individual units as well as of the entire composite, we complete a definition of what a document is and is not. A document is a cogent composite of cogent statements. But, also by definition, none of these statements is read all by itself. A document forms an artifact of a social culture, and that in diverse dimensions. Cogency depends on shared rhetoric, logic of intelligible discourse, topic and program – all of these traits of mind, of culture. Someone writes a document, someone buys it, an entire society sustains the labor of literature. But people value more than a single document, so we want to know how several documents may stand in connections with one another.

Each document therefore exists in both a textual and literary context, and also a social dimension of culture and even of politics. As to the former, documents may form a community whose limits are delineated by shared conventions of thought and expression. Those exhibiting distinctive, even definitive traits, fall within the community, those that do not, remain without. These direct the author to one mode of topic, logic, and rhetoric, and not to some other. So much for intrinsic traits. As to the extrinsic ones, readers bring to documents diverse instruments of intelligibility, knowledge of the grammar of not only language but also thought. That is why they can read one document and not some other. So one relationship derives from a literary culture, which forms the authorship of a document, and the other from a social culture. The literary bond links document to document, and the essentially social bond links reader to document – and also document (through the authorship, individual or collective) to reader. The one relationship is exhibited through intrinsic traits of language and style, logic, rhetoric, and topic, and the other through extrinsic traits of curiosity, acceptance and authority. While documents find their place in their own literary world and also in a larger social one, the two aspects have to remain distinct, the one textual, the other contextual.

It follows that relationships between and among documents also matter for two distinct reasons. The intrinsic relationships, which are formal, guide us to traits of intelligibility, teaching us through our encounter with one document how to read some other of its type or class. If we know how to read a document of one type, we may venture to read another of the same type, but not – without instruction – one of some other type altogether. The extrinsic relationships, which derive from context and are relative to community, direct us to how to understand a document as an artifact of culture and society. Traits not of documents but of doctrines affecting a broad range of documents come into play. The document, whatever its contents, therefore becomes an instrument of social culture, for example, theology and politics, a community's public policy. A community then expresses itself through its choice of documents, the community's canon forming a principal mode of such self-definition. So, as I said, through intrinsic traits a document places itself within a larger community of texts. Extrinsic traits, imputed to a document by not its authorship but its audience, select the document as canonical and make of the document a mode of social definition. The community through its mode of defining itself by its canonical choices forms a textual community – a community expressed through the books it reads and values.

So to summarize: the relationships among the documents produced by the sages of Judaism may take three forms: complete dependence, complete autonomy, intersection in diverse manner and measure. That second dimension provokes considerable debate and presents a remarkably unclear perspective. For while the dimensions of autonomy and continuity take the measure of acknowledged traits – books on their own, books standing in imputed, therefore socially verified, relationships – the matter of connection hardly enjoys the same clear definition. On the one side, intrinsic traits permit us to assess theories of connection. On the other, confusing theological and social judgments of continuities and literary and heuristic ones of connection, people present quite remarkable claims as to the relationships between and among documents, alleging, in fact, that the documents all have to be read as a single continuous document: the Torah. As we shall now see, some maintain that the connections between and among documents are such that each has to be read in the light of all others. So the documents assuredly do form a canon, and that is a position adopted not in some distant past or alien society but among contemporary participants to the cultural debate.

While I take up a community of texts and explore those intrinsic traits that link book to book, my inquiry rests on the premise that the books at issue derive from a textual community, one which, without reference to the intrinsic traits of the writings, deems the set of books as a group to constitute a canon. My question is simple but critical:

If in advance I did not know that the community of Judaism treats the writings before us (among others) as a canon, would the traits of the documents have told me that the writings at hand are related?

In this study, these "traits of documents" are the most profound and pervasive: premises and presuppositions. I cannot think of a more penetrating test of the proposition that the documents form a unity and are continuous with one another. The inquiry is inductive, concerns intrinsic traits of not form or proposition but premise, and therefore pursues at the deepest layers of intellect, conviction, attitude, and even emotion the matter of connection between document and document.

What makes the work plausible and necessary? It is a simple fact. All of the writings of Judaism in late antiquity copiously cite Scripture. Some of them serve (or are presented and organized) as commentaries on the former, others as amplifications of the latter. Since Judaism treats all of these writings as a single, seamless Torah, the one whole Torah revealed by God to Moses, our rabbi, at Mount Sinai, the received hermeneutic naturally does the same. All of the writings are read in light of all others, and words and phrases are treated as autonomous units of tradition, rather than as components of particular writings, for example, paragraphs – units of discourse – and books – composite units of sustained and cogent thought. The issue of connection therefore is legitimate to the data. But the issue of continuity is a still more profound and urgent one, and it is that issue that the present project is formulated to address.

With reference to the determinate canon of the Judaism of the Dual Torah, therefore, I ask about what is unstated and presupposed. I want to know the large-scale premises that form the foundations for the detailed statements of those writings. I turn to what is beneath the surface because I have completed my account of what lies right on the surface: the canon's articulated, explicit statements. It is time to look beneath the surface. In my tripartite program for the study of the Judaism of the Dual Torah in its formative age, an enterprise of systematic description, analysis, and interpretation, I have now completed the first stage and proceed to the second. Now that I know what the canonical writings say and have described the whole in the correct, historical manner and setting, I proceed to ask about what they do not say but take for granted. That defines the question on which I worked in Åbo.

These questions bear a more profound implication than has been suggested. What I really want to find out here is not the answer to the question, if I know this, what else do I know? It is, rather, what are the things that all of the documents that make up the writings accorded the status of the Oral Torah know and share? When I ask about the Judaism behind the texts, I mean to find out what convictions unite diverse writings and form of them all a single statement, a cogent religious system? Every document stands on its own; each is autonomous. Many documents furthermore establish points of contact or intersection; they are connected. But, as a matter of fact, the Judaism of the Dual Torah maintains that every writing is continuous with all other writings, forming a whole, a statement of comprehensive integrity. If that is so, then at the premises or presuppositions of writings I ought to be able to identify what is continuous, from one writing to another, and what unites them all at their deepest layers of conviction, attitude, or sentiment. That is what is at stake in this study based at Åbo.

Accordingly, the experimental work of an analytical character that is undertaken here and in the companion volumes forms a natural next step, on the path from description through analysis to interpretation. From my beginning work on the Mishnah, in 1972, I have undertaken a sustained and systematic description of that Judaism. In 1992, twenty years later, that sustained and uninterrupted work reached its conclusion in the two volumes that state the final results of the two programs that I pursued simultaneously: description of the literature, description of the history of the religious ideas set forth in that literature. The results are now fully in print in a variety of books and have now been systematically summarized, for a broad academic audience, in my *Introduction to Rabbinic Literature* and *Rabbinic Judaism: A Historical Introduction* (New York, 1994 and 1995, respectively: Doubleday Anchor Reference Library). These two books state my final results for the description of the literature and the history of Rabbinic Judaism; at this time, I have nothing to add to the descriptive process, and not much to change in the results set forth over this long span of time.

In finding the way into the deeper layers of conviction and consciousness of the Rabbinic documents, I propose to move inward from my description of Rabbinic Judaism, its writings and its historical development, document by document, to the analysis of the inner structure of that Judaism; and this search, in due course, should open the way to an interpretation of the system of that same Judaism. That is what is at stake in the work carried on, in part, in Åbo in 1993.

10

The Context of Research:
The Debate on Judaism beyond or
Judaism behind the Texts

Four Approaches to the Description
of Rabbinic Judaism:
Nominalist, Harmonistic,
Theological, and Historical

Four approaches have defined the modern and contemporary description of Rabbinic Judaism, of which the fourth has been followed in my works, culminating in my *Rabbinic Judaism: An Historical Introduction* (New York, 1995: Doubleday Anchor Reference Library).[1]

NOMINALIST: The first is the radically nominalist view that every Jew defines Judaism. Judaism is the sum of the attitudes and beliefs of all the members of an ethnic group; each member of the group serves equally well to define Judaism, with the result that questions of the social order – for example, which particular group or social entity of persons held this view, which that – are dismissed. All issues of philosophy and intellect then are dismissed, and the work of intellectual description and

---

[1]See William Scott Green, "Ancient Judaism, Contours and Complexity," in the *James Barr Festschrift*, to whom I owe the identification and classification of the first of the four. I have elaborated my account of problems of method in the following books: *The Ecology of Religion: From Writing to Religion in the Study of Judaism* (Nashville, 1989: Abingdon), and *Studying Classical Judaism: A Primer* (Louisville, 1991: Westminster/John Knox Press).

definition is abandoned before it is undertaken. This is the method of S.J.D. Cohen. It yields the opposite of description and forestalls all analysis and interpretation.

HARMONISTIC: if the nominalist description regards "Judaism" as the sum of everybody's personal "Judaism," the harmonistic finds its definition in the common denominator among the sum of all Judaisms. So the second is at the opposite extreme: all Jewish data – writings and other records – together tell us about a single Judaism, which is to be defined by appeal to the lowest common denominator among all the data. That is the view taken by E.P. Sanders in the 1992 version of his opinion. This is an approach that accomplishes description, but produces banality.

THEOLOGICAL JUDAISM: Just as the first two approaches to the description of Judaism, or of Rabbinic Judaism, ignore all questions of context and deem irrelevant the inquiry into the relationship between the ideas people held and the world in which they lived, so the third equally takes its position in the idealist, as against the social, world of interpretation. The third is the method of theological description, followed by George Foot Moore, Joseph Bonsirven, Ephraim E. Urbach, and E.P. Sanders in the 1977 version of his views. This approach provides a well-drafted description, but ignores all questions of context and social relevance. Its "Judaism" came into existence for reasons we cannot say, addressed no issues faced by ordinary people, and constituted a set of disembodied, socially irrelevant ideas, lacking history and consequence. So it can be described and even analyzed, but not interpreted.

The fourth position is the approach to description taken in this book: we work our way through the sources in the order in which, it is generally assumed, they reached closure, so finding the order and sequence in which ideas came to expression. This approach produces not only historical description and systemic analysis, but also hypotheses of interpretation on the interplay of texts and contexts, ideas and the critical issues addressed by the people who put forth those ideas.

HISTORICAL: The results of the fourth approach are laid out in my *Rabbinic Judaism: A Historical Introduction* (New York, 1995: Doubleday Anchor Reference Library). Mine is the sole effort at the historical description, analysis, and interpretation of Rabbinic Judaism.

Our survey therefore will identify three major problems in the approaches typified by Cohen, Sanders (1992), and Moore-Urbach-Sanders (1977). These are conceptual, contextual, and historical.

The conceptual problem is best illustrated by S.J.D. Cohen, who simply defines "Judaism" as the sum of the beliefs of all Jews. Cohen simply evades the issues of the study of religion, to which he scarcely claims to be party. He investigates religious writings without the tools of the academic study of religion.

The contextual problem affects all the others treated here; it is, alas, paralyzing but ubiquitous. To do their work everyone assumes that if a story is told, it really happened; if a saying is assigned to a named authority, he really said it, and his opinion, moreover, is shared by everybody else, so we have not his opinion but "Judaism." The operative question facing anyone who proposes to translate writing into religion – that is, accounts of "Judaism," as George F. Moore claims to give, or "The Sages," that Ephraim E. Urbach imagines he has made, or Sanders's charming, if puerile, "harmony of the sources" – is the historical one. It is this: How you know exactly what was said and done, that is, the history that you claim to report about what happened long ago? Specifically, how do you know he really said it? And if you do not know that he really said it, how can you ask the question that you ask, which has as its premise the claim that you can say what happened or did not happen?

We shall now see how prior scholars have described Rabbinic Judaism, or just "Judaism" including Rabbinic Judaism. My view of the other three approaches to the description of Rabbinic Judaism, or of all Judaisms of antiquity, takes the form of truncated reviews of the books of their principal proponents. In the course of these reviews, I characterize the method, as to description of Judaism(s), of the scholar under discussion and explain what is wrong with that method and its results.

I. Nominalist: The Innumerable Judaisms of S.J.D. Cohen

From the Maccabees to the Mishnah. By Shaye J.D. Cohen. *Library of Early Christianity* (Philadelphia, 1987: Westminster Press).

Cohen's account reminds us of the prophetic description of Israelite religion, with its altars on every hilltop and at every street corner. For him, every Jew tells us about a Judaism, one by one. Cohen presents a textbook for college students on Judaism: "The goal of this book is to interpret ancient Judaism: to identify its major ideas, to describe its salient practices, to trace its unifying patterns, and to assess its relationship to Israelite religion and society. The book is arranged thematically rather than chronologically...." Cohen begins with a general chronology of ancient Judaism and offers definitions thereof. He proceeds to "Jews and Gentiles," covering political matters, gentile domination, in that section: the Maccabean rebellion, the rebellion against the Romans, the wars of 115-117 and 132-135; cultural: Judaism and Hellenism, covering "Hellenism," "Hellenization, and "Hellenistic Judaism and the like; social: Jews and gentiles, anti-Judaism and "Anti-

Semitism" and Philo-Judaism; then the Jewish "religion" (his quotation marks), practices and beliefs, in which he defines "religion" (again, his quotation marks), practices, worship of God, ritual observances, ritual, ethics, and the yoke of the law, legalism, beliefs, kingship of God, reward and punishment, redemption. Then comes "the community and its institutions," dealing with the public institutions of the land of Israel, the Temple and sanhedrin, the public institutions of the diaspora, the synagogue, private organizations, sects, professional guilds, schools. Then he treats "sectarian and normative," with attention to "sect and heresy," "focal points of Jewish sectarianism," "orthodox and "normative," proto-sectarianism in the Persian period, Ezra and Nehemiah, Isaiah 65, Pharisees, Sadducees, and Essenes; other sects and groups, touching "fourth philosophy," Christians, Samaritans, Therapeutae. This is followed by "canonization and its implications," with attention to the history of the biblical canon. At the end is "the emergence of rabbinic Judaism," with the main point "from Second Temple Judaism to Rabbinic Judaism." All of these topics – and many more not catalogued – are covered in 230 pages, with a few pages of notes, and a few more for further reading.

The book exhibits a number of substantial flaws in presentation, conception, and mode of argument. These are three, and each one is so fundamental as to turn the book into a good bit less than meets the eye. The first of the three is the one relevant to the problem of describing Rabbinic (or any other) Judaism, and the others connected to it.

First, Cohen's plan of organization yields pure chaos. Reading this book is like reading a sequence of encyclopedia articles. That is why the first, and the principal minus is the mode of organization, which separates important components of the picture at any given moment. That is to say, in one chapter, Cohen treats "Jews and gentiles," in another, Jewish religion, yet in a quite separate chapter, "sectarianism," and so on. In that way we are denied a sense of the whole and complete picture, at any one time, of the religious worldview and way of life of the Jews in the land of Israel.

Within the chapters, too, we find the same incapacity at forming a cogent and coherent statement of the whole. "Jews and gentiles" covers, separately, matters of political, cultural, and social policy, one by one. But these of course are not separate matters and never were. Within politics we move from Jeremiah to the Persians, the Maccabees, the Romans; then on the cultural agenda, we have Judaism and Hellenism, out of phase with the foregoing. And then we come to "social: Jews and gentiles," and yet a fresh set of issues. So the book is chaotic in character. But that results from a more profound intellectual chaos, Cohen's disciplinary inadequacy.

The second principal failure of the book derives from a simple methodological incapacity. Cohen's knowledge of the study of religion is remarkably shallow, with the result that he operates with crude and unworkable definitions of principal categories and classifications. Though Cohen's prior scholarship lies in history, not in religion, he proposes to speak not of Jews' histories, or "the Jews' history" in some one place or time, but of "Judaism." By his own claim, then, he is to be judged; but he has not done his homework. He simply has not got the training in the field of the history of religion to develop an interpretive framework adequate to his task. As a result he is left to try to present cogently a vast array of diverse materials that are not cogent at all. With this he simply cannot cope, and the result is a series of rather unfortunate "definitions," which define nothing and lead nowhere.

Let me give two probative examples. In both of them he substitutes classical philology for the history of religion. Nominalism takes over when Cohen wishes to define religion. This he does by asking what the word "religio" meant in antiquity. Using the words of Morton Smith, he says, "If a contemplative person in antiquity sought systematic answers to questions about the nature of the gods and their involvement in human affairs, he would have studied philosophy, not 'religion.'" Placing religion in quotation marks does not solve any problems left unsolved by this monumentally irrelevant definition. For when *we* study religion, it is within the definition(s) of religion that we have formed and brought to evidence we have identified as pertinent. That process is in part inductive and in part deductive, but it is never defined wholly within the definitions of another language and another age. There is a vast literature, from the Enlightenment forward, on the definition of religion, a literature in philosophy, history of religions, and a range of other fields. Cohen does not seem to have followed the discussions on the nature and meaning of religion that have illuminated studies in the nineteenth and twentieth centuries, with the result that his discussion is monumentally ignorant. The result is that he does not know how to deal with the data he is trying to sift, organize, and present in a cogent way, and that accounts for the book's wild incoherence.

As to "Judaism," the word occurs on every page and in nearly every paragraph. It starts, "The goal of this book is to interpret ancient Judaism." But I do not know what Cohen means by "Judaism." Cohen recognizes, of course, that various groups of Jews formulated matters, each in its own way, lived each in its own pattern, defined each its own "Judaism." And yet from the opening lines, "Judaism" is an "it," not a "they," and Cohen tells us "its major ideas...its salient practices...its unifying patterns...its relationship to Israelite religion" (which then is another, different "it"). But that is only part of the story. Cohen recognizes that the data that fall into the category, "religion," hence "Judaism," are incoherent and diverse. He says so – but then he is stymied when he tries to justify treating many things as one thing.

Cohen states, "Second temple Judaism was a complex phenomenon. Judaism changed dramatically during the Persian, Hellenistic, Maccabean, Roman, and rabbinic periods. Generalizations that may be true for one period may not be true for another. In addition, at any given moment, Jews practiced their religion in manifold different ways. The Jewish community of Egypt in the first century C.E. was far from uniform in practice and belief...." That then is the question. How is it answered?

Here is the clear statement of that conceptual chaos that I call Cohen's extreme nominalism: one Judaism per Jew. I underline the relevant language:

> What links these diverse phenomena together and allows them all to be called *Judaism*? [Italics his.] <u>The Jews saw (and see) themselves as the heirs and continuators of the people of pre-exilic Israel; the Jews also felt...an affinity for their fellow Jews throughout the world.... This self-perception manifested itself especially in the relations of diaspora Jewry to the land of Israel and the temple....Thus, like the bumblebee which continues to fly, unaware that the laws of aerodynamics declare its flight to be impossible, the Jews of antiquity saw themselves as citizens of one nation and one religion, unaware of, or oblivious to, the fact that they were separated from each other by their diverse languages, practices, ideologies, and political loyalties. In this book I do not minimize the varieties of Jewish religious expression, but my goal is to see the unity within the diversity.</u>

That, sum and substance, is Cohen's solution. What is wrong is that Cohen's "unity" adds up to the sum of all diversities. His is the opposite of Sanders's lowest common denominator Judaism, which we shall examine presently.

As a matter of fact, Cohen's description of "Judaism" simply is wrong, because his data contradict his "method." There were groups of Jews who regarded themselves as the only Jews on earth; everyone else was not "Israel" at all. The Essenes of Qumran saw themselves in that way. But so, too, did the authorship of the Pentateuch, which treated as normative the experience of exile and return and excluded from the normative experience of their particular "Israel" the Samaritans, who had not gone into exile, and the Jews elsewhere, who never went back and who are totally ignored in the pentateuchal statement of 450 B.C.E. So the allegation that Cohen knows what all the Jews thought of themselves is called into question by his rather blithe failure to conduct a survey of opinion, to the degree that we know opinion at all. He seems to me to play somewhat fast and loose with facts – if there are any facts about affinities, public opinion, attitudes, and the like.

As a matter of definition, Cohen does not really answer the question of defining a single Judaism at all. Here again, the vacuity of his theoretical system – of which there is none – accounts for his failure. Historians do not ask the questions that historians of religion do. How people see themselves forms a fundamental fact for the description of their worldview – but not for the world they view. Cohen is correct to claim that the way in which a given group sees itself tells us something about their Judaism. But whether or not their views testify to other Judaisms he does not know. The reason is that he does not explain and unpack the theology within his allegations of a mutually supportive society throughout the world. Cohen claims that "this self-perception manifested itself especially in the relations of diaspora Jewry to the land of Israel and the temple." But diaspora Jews preserved a certain distance; they gave money to the temple, but when the Jews of the land of Israel went to war, diaspora Jews remained at peace, within the same empire – and vice versa. That hardly suggests that the perceived "affinity" made much difference in public policy. What we have is an excuse for not investigating the answers to a well-asked question – but not an answer to that question. Cohen does not have the equipment to answer the question, being a historian, not a historian of religion.

This matter of Cohen's limited knowledge of the study of religion lies at the heart of the book's failure. Lest Cohen's difficulty at conceptualization seem one episode in an otherwise well-crafted work, let me point to yet another example of how Cohen dismisses as trivial a central question of definition. Cohen has, of course, to address the issue of "sects," meaning (in my language) diverse Judaisms. He has to tell us the difference between the sectarian and the normative, and, to his credit, he devotes a whole chapter to the matter. Here, too, Cohen appeals to ancient usage in the solution of a problem of conceptualization – as though anybody any more is bound to word usages of Greek or Latin. He contrasts the negative use of "sect" and "heresy," deriving from theology. "'Sects' and 'heresies' are religious groups and doctrines of which we disapprove." That is true, but only for the uninformed.

A vast literature on the definition of "sect" and "church" has been written. Cohen does not use it. Here is Cohen's definition: "A sect is a small, organized group that separates itself from a larger religious body and asserts that it alone embodies the ideals of the larger group because it alone understands God's will." A sect then seems to me in Cohen's mind to be no different from a religion, except that it is small ("small") and differs from a group that is larger ("a larger religious body"). How the sect relates to the "larger religious body" we do not know. If the "sect" dismisses the "larger group" because the sect claims alone to understand God's will, then why is the sect not a "religious body" on its own? It would seem to me to claim exactly that. Lest I appear to exaggerate the conceptual crudity at hand and to impute to Cohen opinions he does not hold, let me now cite Cohen's own words (including his italics):

> A sect must be *small* enough to be a distinctive part of a *larger religious body*. If a sect grows to the extent that it is a large body in its own right, it is no longer a sect but a "religion" or a "church." The precise definition of "large body" and "church" is debated by sociologists, but that question need not be treated here.

This, I submit, is pure gibberish – and so is Cohen's "Judaism." A small group is a sect. A big one is a "religion" or a "church." What has led Cohen to this impasse is simple. Since there is one "Judaism" we have to figure out some way to deal with all the other Judaisms, and by calling them "little" we can find a suitable pigeonhole for them; then we do not have to ask how "little" is different from "big" except that it is little. So much for his crude definitions and unworkable classifications.

II. Harmonistic: The One Judaism of Sanders (1992)

Judaism. Practice and Belief 63 B.C.E. - 66 C.E. by E.P. Sanders (London, 1992: SCM Press and Philadelphia, 1992: Trinity Press International)

E.P. Sanders has described "Judaism" twice, one intelligently, the other stupidly. The intellectually challenging and perspicacious one appeared in 1977 and is dealt with below, as one of the principal examples of theological volumes; there he distinguishes among Judaisms, with special reference to the Dead Sea Scrolls and Rabbinic Judaism in comparison to Paul's system, and he finds characteristics of a single Judaism – with special reference to what he calls "covenantal nomism" – shared among the carefully distinguished systems. That work presents problems of a historical and hermeneutical character. In the more recent volume, by contrast, Sanders joins all evidences concerning Judaic religious systems into a single, harmonious "Judaism," the equivalent to the New Testament "harmonies of the Gospels" that people used to put together.

Sanders claims to give us an account of one, single, comprehensive Judaism, but underscores the profound misconstruction that emerges from the confusion of history and theology. So far as I know, Sanders must be the first scholar in recent times to imagine that all sources produced by Jews, anywhere, any time, by any sort of person or group, equally tell us about one and the same Judaism. Schürer was far more critical nearly a century ago. The other major "Judaisms" – Bousset-Gressman's or Moore's or Urbach's for instance – select a body of evidence and work on that, not assuming that everything everywhere tells us about one thing, somewhere: Judaism. True, to account for a single Christianity, Christian theologians have also to define a single Judaism, and that explains why Sanders has fabricated a single "Judaism" out of a mass of mutually contradictory sources. But others did the work with greater acumen and discernment, and, when we examine Sanders's results closely, we see that there is less than meets the eye.

Sanders really thinks that any and every source, whoever wrote it, without regard to its time or place or venue, tells us about one and the same Judaism. The only way to see everything all together and all at once, as Sanders wishes to do, is to rise high above the evidence, so high that we no longer see the lines of rivers, the height of mountains, the undulations of plains – any of the details of the earth's true configuration. This conflation of all sources yields his fabricated Judaism. It is a "Judaism" that flourished everywhere but nowhere – Alexandria, Jerusalem, Galilee, Babylonia (to judge from the sources we mixed together); a Judaism that we find all the time but in no one period – represented equally by the historical Moses and the rabbinic one, the pseudepigraph of the third century B.C.E. and the first century C.E., the Dead Sea Scrolls of the second and first centuries B.C.E., and, where Sanders has decided, the Mishnah of the early third century C.E.

Sanders does not identify "the synagogue" where this Judaism offered up its prayers, the community that was shaped by its rules, the functioning social order that saw the world within its vision. And of course, that failure of specificity attests to the good sense of the Jews of antiquity, who cannot have affirmed everything and its opposite: the sacrifices of the Temple are valid (as many sources maintain) and also invalid (as the Dead Sea Scrolls hold); study of the Torah is critical (as the rabbinic sources adduced ad lib. by Sanders) and eschatological visions prevail (as many of the pseudeipgraphic writers conceive). Philo's cool, philosophical mind and the heated imagination of visionaries form for Sanders a single Judaism, but no single corpus of evidence, deriving from a particular place, time, circumstance, and community, concurs for "Judaism." To refer to a single issue, baptism can have been for the eschatological forgiveness of sins, as John the Baptist and Jesus maintained; or it can have been for the achievement of cultic purity in an eternal rhythm of nature and cult, as the Pharisees and the Mishnah held; but not both.

Sanders sees unities where others have seen differences. The result of his Judaic equivalent of a "harmony of the Gospels" is simply a dreary progress through pointless information. Sanders's relentlessly informative discourse persistently leaves open the question, so what? Throughout this long and tedious book, readers will find themselves wondering why Sanders thought the information he set forth important, and the information he omitted unimportant. If we know that his conflationary Judaism prevailed everywhere, then what else do we know about the Judaisms to which each source in turn attests (as well)? Do all the writers subscribe to this one Judaism, so that we are supposed to read into each document what all the documents together supposedly affirm?

He elaborately tells us why he thinks various documents tell, or do not tell, what really happened; he never explains why he maintains these same documents and artifacts of archaeology, commonly so profoundly at variance with one another, all concur on a single Judaism or attest to a single Judaism. Did all these Jews pray together in the same synagogue, did they eat together at the same table, did they give their children in marriage to one another as part of the same social entity? If he thinks that they did, then he contradicts a fair part of the evidence he allegedly reviews. Certainly the members of the Essene community at Qumran, for one example, did not regard the Jerusalem Temple as holy, and the Mishnah is explicit that its faithful are not going to eat supper with other Israelites, a view on which the Gospels concur as well.

Now that capricious conflation of all the sources Sanders thinks fit together and silent omission of all the sources he rejects is something Moore, Schechter, and even Urbach never did. Urbach cited Philo but not the Dead Sea Scrolls, having decided that the one was *kosher*, the other *treif*. Sanders has decided there are no intellectual counterparts to dietary laws at all: he swallows it all and chews it up and spits out a homogenized "Judaism" lacking all specific flavor. Nor can I point to any other scholar of ancient Judaism working today who cites everything from everywhere to tell us about one and the same Judaism. The contrast between the intellectually rigorous thinking of James Dunn on defining "Judaism" in his *Partings of the Ways* and the conceptually slovenly work of Sanders on the same problem – adding up all the sources and not so much finding as inventing through mushy prose what he conceives to be the common denominator – tells the story. Sanders's *Judaism* is a mulligan stew, a four-day-old, over-cooked *tcholent* – for us plain Americans, like *Wonder Bread*, full of air and not very tasty.

This fabrication of a single Judaism is supposed to tell us something that pertains equally to all: the Judaism that forms the basis for all the sources, the common denominator among them all. If we know a book or an artifact is "Jewish," (an ethnic term, Judaic being the religious category) then we are supposed automatically to know various other facts about said book or artifact. But the upshot is either too general to mean much (monotheism) or too abstract to form an intelligible statement. Let me be specific. How Philo will have understood the Dead Sea Scrolls, the authors of apocalyptic writings, those of the Mishnah passages Sanders admits to his account of Judaism from 63 B.C.E. to C.E. 66, we are never told. Each of these distinctive documents gets to speak whenever Sanders wants it to; none is ever brought into relationship – comparison and contrast – with any other. The homogenization of Philo, the Mishnah, the Dead Sea Scrolls, Ben Sira, apocryphal and pseudepigraphic writings, the results of archaeology, and on and on and on turns out to yield generalizations about a religion that none of those responsible for the evidence at hand will have recognized: lifeless, dull, hopelessly abstract, lacking all social relevance. After a while, readers come to realize, it hardly matters, the results reaching so stratospheric a level of generalization that all precise vision of real people practicing a vivid religion is lost.

These remarks, meant to suggest before us is an empty, pointless compilation of this and that and the other thing, will appear harsh and extravagant until we take up a concrete example of the result of Sanders's huge labor of homogenization. To understand what goes into Sanders's picture of Judaism, let me now provide a reasonable sample (pp. 103-104), representative of the whole, the opening paragraphs of his discussion, Chapter Seven, entitled "Sacrifices":

> The Bible does not offer a single, clearly presented list of sacrifices. The legal books (Exodus, Leviticus, Numbers and Deuteronomy), we know now, incorporate various sources from different periods, and priestly practice evidently varied from time to time. There are three principal sources of information about sacrifices in the first century: Josephus, Philo and the Mishnah. On most points they agree among themselves and with Leviticus and Numbers; consequently, the main outline of sacrifices is not in dispute. Josephus, in my judgment, is the best source. He knew what the common practice of the priesthood of his day was: he had learned it in school, as a boy he had watched and assisted, and as an adult he had worked in the temple. It is important for evaluating his evidence to note that his description of the sacrifices sometimes disagrees with Leviticus or goes beyond it. This is not an instance in which he is simply summarizing what is written in the Bible: he is almost certainly depending on what he had learned as a priest.
>
> Though the Mishnah is often right with regard to pre-70 temple practice, many of the discussions are from the second century: the rabbis continued to debate rules of sacrifice long after living memory of how it had been done had vanished. Consequently, in reading the Mishnah one is sometimes reading second-century theory. Occasionally this can be seen clearly. For example, there is a debate about whether or not the priest who sacrificed an animal could keep its hide if for any reason the animal was made invalid (for example by touching something impure) after it was sacrificed but before it was flayed. The mishnah on this topic opens with an anonymous opinion, according to which the priest did not get the hide. R. Hanina the Prefect of the Priests disagreed: "Never have I seen a hide taken out to the place of burning"; that is, the priests always kept the hides. R. Akiba (early second century) accepted

this and was of the view that the priests could keep the hides of invalid sacrifices. "The Sages," however, ruled the other way (*Zevahim* 12.4). R. Hanina the Prefect of the Priests apparently worked in the temple before 70, but survived its destruction and became part of the rabbinic movement. Akiba died c. 135; "the Sages" of this passage are probably his contemporaries or possibly the rabbis of the next generation. Here we see that second century rabbis were quite willing to vote against actual practice in discussing the behavior of the priests and the rules they followed. The problem with using the Mishnah is that there is very seldom this sort of reference to pre-70 practice that allows us to make critical distinctions: not only are we often reading second-century discussions, we may be learning only second century theory.

Philo had visited the temple, and some of his statements about it (for example the guards) seem to be based on personal knowledge. But his discussion of the sacrifices is "bookish," and at some important points it reveals that he is passing on information derived from the Greek translation of the Hebrew Bible (the Septuagint), not from observation. The following description basically follows the Hebrew Bible and Josephus, but it sometimes incorporates details from other sources.

One may make the following distinctions among sacrifices:

> With regard to what was offered: meal, wine, birds (doves or pigeons) and quadrupeds (sheep, goats and cattle).
> With regard to who provided the sacrifice: the community or an individual.
> With regard to the purpose of the sacrifice: worship of and communion with God, glorification of him, thanksgiving, purification, atonement for sin, and feasting.
> With regard to the disposition of the sacrifice: it was either burned or eaten. The priests got most of the food that sacrifices provided, though one of the categories of sacrifice provided food for the person who brought it and his family and friends. The Passover lambs were also eaten by the worshippers.

Sacrifices were conceived as meals, or, better, banquets. The full and ideal sacrificial offering consisted of meat, cereal, oil and wine (Num. 14:1-10, Ant. 3.233f.; the menu was sometimes reduced: see below).

I ask readers to stipulate that I can have cited numerous other, sizable instances of the same sort of discourse.

Now let us ask ourselves, what, exactly, does Sanders wish to tell his readers about the sacrifices in this account of *Judaism. Practice and Belief*? He starts in the middle of things. He assumes we know what he means by "sacrifices," why they are important, what they meant, so all we require is details. He will deal with Josephus, Philo, the Mishnah, and Leviticus and Numbers. Does he then tell us the distinctive viewpoint of each? Not at all. All he wants us to know is the facts common to them all. Hence his problem is not one of description, analysis, and interpretation of documents, but a conflation of the information contained in each that he deems usable. Since that is his principal concern, he discusses "sacrifice" by telling us why the Mishnah's information is useless, except when it is usable. But Sanders never suggests to his readers what the Mishnah's discussion of sacrifice wishes to find out, or how its ideas on the subject may prove religiously engaging. It is just a rule book, so it has no ideas on the subject (so Sanders; that is not my view). Philo is then set forth. Here, too, we are told why he tells us nothing, but not what he tells us. Then there follow the facts, the indented "with regard to" paragraphs.

Sanders did not have to tell us all about how Leviticus, Numbers, Philo and Josephus and the Mishnah concur, then about how we may ignore or must cite the several documents respectively, if his sole intent was to tell us the facts of the "with regard to..." paragraphs. And how he knows that "sacrifices were conceived...," who conceived them in this way, and what sense the words made, "worship of and communion with God, glorification of him, thanksgiving, purification, atonement for sin, and feasting," and to whom they made sense, and how other Judaisms, besides the Judaism portrayed by Philo, Josephus, the Mishnah, and so on and so forth, viewed sacrifices, or the Temple as it was – none of this is set forth. The conflation has its own purpose, which the following outline of the remainder of the chapter reveals: community sacrifices; individual sacrifices ("Neither Josephus, Philo, nor other first-century Jews thought that burnt-offerings provided God with food..."); a family at the Temple, an example; the daily Temple routine. In this mass of information on a subject, one question is lost: what it all meant. Sanders really does suppose that he is telling us how things were, what people did, and, in his stress on common denominator Judaism, he finds it entirely reasonable to bypass all questions of analysis and interpretation and so forgets to tell us what it all meant. His language, "worship of and communion with God, glorification of him, thanksgiving, purification, atonement for sin, and feasting" – that Protestant formulation begs every question and answers none.

But this common denominator Judaism yields little that is more than simply banal, for "common theology," for example, "The history of Israel in general, and of our period in particular, shows that Jews believed that the one God of the universe had given them his law and that they were to obey it" (p. 240). No one, obviously, can disagree, but what applies to everyone equally, in a nation so riven with division and rich in diversity, also cannot make much of a difference. That is to say, knowing that they all were monotheists or valued the Hebrew Scriptures (but which passages he does not identify, how he read them he does not say) does not tell us more than we knew about the religion of those diverse people than before. Sanders knows what people thought, because anything any

Jew wrote tells us what "Jews" or most Jews or people in general thought. What makes Sanders' representation bizarre is that he proceeds to cite as evidence of what "Jews" thought opinions of Philo and Joseph, the Dead Sea Scrolls, Rabbinic Literature, and so on and so forth. The generality of scholarship understands that the Dead Sea Scrolls represent their writers, Philo speaks for Philo, Josephus says what he thinks, and the Mishnah is whatever it is and is not whatever it is not. No one, to my knowledge, until Sanders has come to the facile judgment that anything any Jew thought has to have been in the mind of all the other Jews.

But it is only with that premise that we can understand the connections Sanders makes and the conclusions about large, general topics that he reaches. His juxtapositions are in fact beyond all understanding. Let me skim through his treatment of graven images, which captures the flavor of the whole:

> Comments by Philo and Josephus show how Jews could interpret other objects symbolically and thus make physical depictions acceptable, so that they were not seen as transgressions of one of the Ten Commandments, but as symbols of the glory of the God who gave them.

There follows a reference to War 5:214. Then Sanders proceeds:

> Josephus, as did Philo, found astral and other symbolism in many other things....

Some paragraphs later, in the same context, we have:

> The sun was personified and worshipped.... The most important instance was when Josiah...instituted a reform of worship...[now with reference to II Kings 23:4f]. This is usually regarded as having been a decisive rejection of other deities, but elements derived from sun worship continued. Subsequently Ezekiel attacked those who turned "their backs to the Temple of the Lord..." (Ezek. 8:16). According to the Mishnah, at one point during the feast of Booths priests "turned their faces to the west," recalling that their predecessors had faced east and worshipped the sun and proclaimed that "our eyes are turned toward the Lord" (Sukkah 5:4). Despite this, the practice that Ezekiel condemned was continued by some. Josephs wrote that the Essenes "are particularly reverent towards the divinity...."

This is continued with a citation of the Qumran Temple Scroll and then the Tosefta:

> That the Essenes really offered prayer to the sun is made more probable by a passage in the Qumran Temple Scroll.
> Above we noted the floor of the synagogue at Hammath that had as its main decoration the signs of the zodiac in a circle.... This synagogue floor, with its blatant pagan decoration, was built at the time when rabbinic Judaism was strong in Galilee – after the redaction and publication of the Mishnah, during the years when the material in the

Tosefta and the Palestinian Talmud was being produced and edited. According to the Tosefta, Rabbi Judah, who flourished in the middle of the second century, said that "If anyone says a blessing over the sun – this is a heterodox practice" (T. Berakhot 6[7]). In the light of the floor, it seems he was opposing contemporary practice.

And so on and on he goes, introducing in the paragraph that follows references to Christian symbols (John 1:9, 15:1); the issue of whether "one God" meant there were no other supernatural beings (yielding a citation to Paul who was a Pharisee, with reference to Phil. 3:2-6). And so he runs on, for five hundred tedious pages. This "harmony" yields chaos.

III. Theological: The Dogmatic Judaism of Moore, Urbach, and Sanders (1977)

Among numerous descriptions of Rabbinic Judaism, or of ancient Judaism in general, that organize themselves around theological topics, ordinarily Protestant Christian theological categories, three serve to illustrate the state of the question, the first and most influential, George F. Moore's, the Israeli version, Ephraim E. Urbach's, and the American model, E.P. Sanders in his initial statement of his views. The source of the category formation for all three is uniform. First, it does not derive from the documents of Rabbinic Judaism, which do not focus on the points of main concern to the theological dogmatics of Protestant Christianity that govern. Second, it does raise questions important to Pauline Christianity but hardly critical to Rabbinic or any other Judaism of this time. All three moreover claim to provide a historical description, but read the sources in an uncritical manner, believing all the attributions and treating as fact all the fables of all the Rabbinic documents, without discrimination.

Judaism in the First Centuries of the Christian Era. The Age of the Tannaim. By George Foot Moore (Cambridge, 1927: Harvard University Press) I-III.

Moore's description of "Judaism" invokes standard Protestant categories of dogmatic theology. Moore fails to tell us of whom he wishes to speak. So his repertoire of sources for the description of "Judaism" in the "age of the Tannaim" is awry. He makes use of sources which speak of people assumed to have lived in the early centuries of the Common Era, even when said sources derive from a much later or a much earlier time. What generates this error is the problem of dealing with a category asymmetrical to the evidence. That is, an essentially philosophical theological construct, an -ism, "Judaism," is imposed upon wildly diverse evidence deriving from many kinds of social groups and testifying to the state of mind and way of life of many sorts of Jews, who in their own day would scarcely have understood one another (for instance, Bar Kokhba and Josephus, or the teacher of righteousness and Aqiba).

So for Moore, as for the others who have described "Judaism" solely in terms of theological dogmas, without reference to the time, place, and circumstance of those who framed these dogmas, "Judaism" is a problem of ideas, and the history of Judaism is the history of ideas abstracted from the groups that held them and from the social perspectives of said groups. This seems to me a fundamental error, making the category "Judaism" a construct of a wholly fantastic realm of thought: a fantasy, I mean. What is wrong with the philosophical theological description of "Judaism" is not only the failure to correlate ideas with the world of the people who wrote the books that contain those ideas. There are problems of a historical, and history-of-religions, character.

Moore's work to begin with is not really a work in the history of religions at all – in this instance, the developmental and formative history of a particular brand of Judaism. His research is in theology, and there is no social foundation for the theology he describes. The description of Judaism is organized in theological categories. Moore presents a synthetic account of diverse materials, focused upon a given topic of theological interest. There is nothing even rhetorically historical in the picture of opinions on these topics, no pretense of systematically accounting for development and change. What is constructed is a static exercise in dogmatic theology, not an account of the history of religious ideas and – still more urgent – their unfolding in relationship to the society of the people who held those ideas.

Moore in no way describes and interprets the religious worldview and way of life expressed, in part, through the ideas under study. He does not explore the interplay between that worldview and the historical and political context of the community envisioned by that construction of a world. So far as history attends to the material context of ideas and the class structure expressed by ideas and institutions alike, so far as ideas are deemed part of a larger social system and religious systems are held to be pertinent to the given political, social, and economic framework which contains them, Moore's account of dogmatic theology to begin with has nothing to do with religious history, that is the history of Judaism in the first two centuries of the Common Era.

Moore describes the Judaism his sources set forth as "normative." So far as that represents a descriptive, not an evaluative, judgment, Moore simply does not make the case. A brilliant critique of his view appeared in 1927, in the review of the work by F.C. Porter. Here is what he says:

The Judaism which Professor Moore describes with such wealth of learning is that of the end of the second century of our era, and the sources which he uses are those that embody the interpretations and formulations of the law by the rabbis, chiefly from the fall of Jerusalem, 70 A.D., to the promulgation of the Mishnah of the Patriarch Judah, about 200 A.D. When Moore speaks of the sources which Judaism has always regarded as authentic, he means "always" from the third century A.D. onward. It is a proper and needed task to exhibit the religious conceptions and moral principles, the observances, and the piety of the Judaism of the Tannaim. Perhaps it is the things that most needed to be done of all the many labors that must contribute to our knowledge of that age. But Professor Moore calls this Judaism "normative"; and means by this, not only authoritative for Jews after the work of the Tannaim had reached its completion in the Mishnah, but normal or authentic in the sense that it is the only direct and natural outcome of the Old Testament religion. It seems therefore, that the task here undertaken is not only, as it certainly is, a definite, single, and necessary one, but that other things hardly need doing, and do not signify much for the Judaism of the age of Christian beginnings. The book is not called, as it might have been, "The Judaism of the Tannaim," but Judaism in the First Centuries of the Christian Era: The Age of the Tannaim. Was there then no other type of Judaism in the time of Christ that may claim such names as "normative," "normal," "orthodox"? The time of Deuteronomy was also the time of Jeremiah. The religion of revelation in a divinely given written law stood over against the religion of revelation in the heart and living words of a prophet. The conviction was current after Ezra that the age of prophecy had ended; the Spirit of God had withdrawn itself from Israel (I, 237). But if prophecy should live again, could it not claim to be normal in Judaism? Where, in the centuries after Ezra, are we to look for the lines of development that go back, not to Ezra and Deuteronomy, but to Jeremiah and Isaiah? R.H. Charles claims the genuine succession for his Apocalypses. The Pharisees at least had the prophets in their canon, and it is claimed by many, and by Moore, that the rabbis were not less familiar with the prophets than with the Pentateuch, and even that they had "fully assimilated" the teaching of the prophets as to the value of the cultus (II, 13), and that their conception of revealed religion "resulted no less from the teaching of the prophets than from the possession of the Law" (I, 235). Christians see prophecy coming back to Judaism in John the Baptist and in Jesus, and find in Paul the new experience that revelation is giving in a person, not in a book, and inwardly to each one through the in-dwelling Spirit of God, as Jeremiah had hoped (31:31-34). And now, finally, liberal Judaism claims to be authentic and normal Judaism because it takes up the lines that Jeremiah laid down.

It would require more proof than Professor Moore has given in his section on "History" to justify his claim that the only movements that need to be traced as affecting religion are these that lead from Ezra to Hillel and Johanan ben Zakkai and Akiba and Judah the Prince. Great events happened during the three centuries from Antiochus IV to Hadrian, events which deeply affected Judaism as a religion. But of these events and their influence Moore has little to say. It is of course in connection with these events that the Apocalypses were written.

A proper description, by contrast, should invoke considerations of social circumstance and context, so as to yield a Judaism portrayed within a specific, socially circumscribed corpus of evidence.

Porter's second criticism of Moore seems to me still more telling. He points out that Moore ignores the entire legal corpus, so that his "Judaism" builds upon categories alien, and not native, to the sources at hand. A principal flaw in theological description, affecting not only Moore, but the others who follow, flows from a category formation awry to the sources; the category formation is that of Protestant Christianity, not Rabbinic Judaism. This is how Porter states matters:

> In [Moore's] actual exposition of the normative, orthodox Judaism of the age of the Tannaim comparatively little place is given to Halakah. One of the seven parts of his exposition is on observances; and here cultus, circumcision, Sabbath, festivals, fasts, taxation, and interdictions are summarily dealt with; but the other six parts deal in detail with the religion and ethics, the piety and hopes, of Judaism, matters about which the Haggada supplies most of the material, and for which authority and finality are not claimed. The tannaite (halakic) Midrash (Mechilta, etc.) contains a good deal of Haggada together with its halakic exegesis, and these books Moore values as the most important of his sources (I, 135ff.; II, 80). The principles of religion and morals do indeed control the interpretation of certain laws, so that Halakah is sometimes a source for such teachings, and "is in many instances of the highest value as evidence of the way and measure in which great ethical principles have been tacitly impressed on whole fields of the traditional law" (I, 134). This sounds as if the ethical implications constituted the chief value of the Mishnah for Moore's purposes. But these are not its chief contents. It is made up, as a whole, of opinions or decisions about the minutiae of law observance. It constructs a hedge of definitions and restrictions meant to protect the letter of the law from violation, to make its observance possible and practicable under all circumstances, and to bring all of life under its rule....
>
> The Jewish scholar, Perles, in a pamphlet with which Moore is in sympathy, criticized Bousset, in Die Religion des Judentums, for using only books such as Bacher's, on the Haggada, and for expressing a preference for haggadic sources; whereas the Halakah in its unity, in its definitive and systematic form, and its deeper grasp upon life is much better fitted to supply the basis of the structures of a history of the Jewish religion. Moore agrees with Perles' criticism of Bousset's preference for the later, haggadic, Midrashim; but it is not because they are halakic that he gives the first place to the early Midrash. "It is this religious and moral element by the side of the interpretation of the laws, and pervading it as a principle, that gives these works [Mechilta, etc.] their chief value to us" (I, 135). Perles insists on the primary importance of the Halakah, not only because it shows here and there the influence of prophetic ethics, but because throughout as it stands, it is the principal

work of the rabbis, and the work which alone has the character of authority, and because, concerned as it is with ritual, cultus, and the law (Recht), it has decisive influence upon the whole of life. This applies peculiarly to the religion of the Tannaim. The Haggada neither begins nor ends with them, so that Bousset ought not, Perles thinks, to have used exclusively Bacher's work on the Haggada of the Tannaim, but also his volumes on the Haggada of the Amoraim, as well as the anonymous Haggada which Bacher did not live to publish. It is only in the region of the Halakah that the Tannaim have a distinctive place and epoch-making significance, since the Mishnah, the fundamental text of the Talmud, was their creation.

Would Perles be satisfied, then, with Moore's procedure? Would he think it enough that Halakah proper, observances, should occupy one part in seven in an exposition of the Judaism of the Tannaim, considering that in their classical and distinctive work Halakah practically fills sixty-two out of sixty-three parts? Moore agrees with Perles that there is no essential distinction between earlier and later Haggada (I, 163), and that the teachings of the Tannaim about God and man, morals and piety, sin, repentance, and forgiveness are not only also the teachings of the later Amoraim, but run backward, too, without essential change into the Old Testament itself. There is no point at which freedom and variety of opinion and belief, within the bounds, to be sure, of certain fundamental principles, came to an end, and a proper orthodoxy of dogma was set up. But orthodoxy of conduct, of observance, did reach this stage of finality and authority in the Mishnah; and the tannaite rabbis were those who brought this about. It is in accordance with Moore's chief interests in haggadic teachings that he does not confine himself to sayings of the Tannaim, but also quotes freely from the Amoraim; how freely may be seen by the list that ends Index IV.

Professor Moore's emphasis upon his purpose to present normative Judaism, definitive, authoritative, orthodox, would lead one to expect that he would give the chief place to those "jurisdic definitions and decisions of the Halakah" to which alone, as he himself sometimes says, these adjectives strictly apply. We should look for more about the Mishnah itself, about its systematic arrangement of the laws, its methods of argument and of bringing custom and tradition into connection with the written law, and more of its actual contents and total character, of those actual rules of life, that "uniformity of observance" which constituted the distinction of the Judaism of the rabbis.

It is not possible to improve on Porter's critique. The halakhic materials address the issues of the social order in relationship to the intellectual structure and system of the documents themselves. Neglecting the contents and categories of the legal documents, the Mishnah, Tosefta, Yerushalmi, and Bavli, results in ignoring of the social context of a religious structure and system. For the law deals precisely with that – the construction of society, the formation of a rational, public way of life. The history of a religion should tell how a religion took shape and describe its concern for a relationship to the concrete historical context in which that religion comes to full expression. These simply are not topics which form part of the hermeneutical framework of Moore's book.

The critical issue in my view is the relationship between a religion, i.e., the worldview and way of life of a coherent social group, and history, i.e., the material, economic, and political circumstance of that same social group. This history in Moore simply is not addressed. True, the history of a religion and the dogmatics of that religion are going to relate to one another. But a description of dogmatics of seven centuries or more and an account of the contents thereof simply do not constitute a history of the religion which comes to formal ideological expression in dogmatic theology. So Moore did not do what the title of his book and of his professorship ("professor of the history of religion") promises, even though in his work he discusses numerous matters bearing historical implication. Moore's failure flows from two contradictory facts. First, he believes everything he reads, so his "history" is gullible. Second, he forgets the work of historians, which is to tell us not only exactly how things were, but why. His history is not history, and anyhow, it lacks all historical context.

The Sages. Their Concepts and Beliefs. By Ephraim E. Urbach.
Translated from the Hebrew by Israel Abrahams
(Jerusalem: The Magnes Press, The Hebrew University, 1975).
Two volumes. I. Text II. Notes

Ephraim E. Urbach, professor of Talmud at the Hebrew University and author of numerous articles and books on the Talmud and later rabbinic literature, here presents a compendious work intended "to describe the concepts and beliefs of the Tannaim and Amoraim and to elucidate them against the background of their actual life and environment." The work before us has been accurately described by M.D. Heer (Encyclopaedia Judaica 16:4): "He [Urbach] outlines the views of the rabbis on the important theological issues such as creation, providence, and the nature of man. In this work Urbach synthesizes the voluminous literature on these subjects and presents the views of the talmudic authorities."

The topics are as follows: belief in one God; the presence of God in the world; "nearness and distance – Omnipresent and heaven"; the power of God; magic and miracle; the power of the divine name; the celestial retinue; creation; man; providence; written law and oral law; the commandments; acceptance of the yoke of the kingdom of heaven; sin, reward, punishment, suffering, etc.; the people of Israel and its sages, a chapter which encompasses the election of Israel, the status of the sages in the days of the Hasmoneans, Hillel, the regime of the sages after the destruction of the Temple, and so on; and redemption. The second volume contains footnotes, a fairly brief and highly selective bibliography, and alas, a merely perfunctory index. The several chapters, like the work as a whole, are organized systematically, consisting of sayings and stories relevant to the theme under discussion, together with Urbach's episodic observations and comments on them. It is clear that Urbach has taken over, but improved upon, the description of "Judaism" as dogmatic theology set forth by Moore.

Urbach's categories, like Moore's, come to him from dogmatic theology, not from the sources on which he works. For let us ask, does the worldview of the talmudic sages emerge in a way which the ancient sages themselves would have recognized? From the viewpoint of their organization and description of reality, their worldview, it is certain that the sages would have organized their card files quite differently. We know that is the case because we do not have, among the chapters before us, a single one which focuses upon the theme of one of the orders, let alone tractates, within which the rabbis divided and presented their various statements on reality, for example, Seeds, the material basis of life; Seasons, the organization and differentiation of time; Women, the status of the individual; Damages, the conduct of civil life including government; Holy Things, the material service of God; and Purities, the immaterial base of divine reality in this world. The matter concerns not merely the superficial problem of organizing vast quantities of data. The talmudic rabbis left a large and exceedingly complex, well-integrated legacy of law. Clearly, it is through that legacy that they intended to make their fundamental statements upon the organization and meaning of reality. An account of their concepts and beliefs which ignores nearly the whole of the halakhah surely is slightly awry. How Porter will have reviewed Urbach's book is readily imagined: he would have said of Urbach exactly what he said of Moore, with the further observation that Israeli Orthodox Judaism should produce greater appreciation for the halakhic embodiment of theology than Urbach here shows.

Not only so, but Urbach's "Judaism" is, to say the least, eclectic. And it is not historical in any conventional sense. Urbach's selection of sources for analysis is both narrowly canonical and somewhat confusing. We often hear from Philo, but seldom from the Essene Library of Qumran, still more rarely from the diverse works assembled by R.H. Charles as the apocrypha and pseudepigrapha of the Old Testament, and the like. If we seek to describe the talmudic rabbis, surely we cannot ask Philo to testify to their opinions. If we listen to Philo, surely we ought to hear – at least for the purpose of comparison and contrast – from books written by Palestinian Jews of various kinds. The Targumim are allowed no place at all because they are deemed "late." But documents which came to redaction much later than the several Targumim (by any estimate of the date of the latter) make rich and constant contributions to the discussion.

Within a given chapter, the portrayal of the sources will move rapidly from biblical to Tannaitic to Amoraic sources, as though the line of development were single, unitary, incremental, and harmonious, and as though there were no intervening developments which shaped later conceptions. The contrast between the results set forth here, documents viewed in groups, with attention to how ideas differ, document by document, when they do, or do not evolve from earlier to later writings, when they do not, and Urbach's rather simple-minded repertoire of this, that, and the other thing, is striking. Differentiation among the stages of Tannaitic and Amoraic sayings tends to be episodic. Commonly, slight sustained effort is made to treat them in their several sequences, let alone to differentiate among schools and circles within a given period.

The uniformities are not only temporal. There is no differentiation within or among the sayings Urbach adduces in evidence: all of them speak equally authoritatively for "the sages." Urbach takes with utmost seriousness his title, the sages, their concepts and beliefs, and his "history," topic by topic, reveals remarkably little variation, development, or even movement. Urbach does little more than just publish his card files. That is because his skill at organization and arrangement of materials tends to outrun his interest in differentiation and comparison within and among them, let alone in the larger, sequential history of major ideas and their growth and coherent development over the centuries. One looks in vain for Urbach's effort to justify treating "the sages" as essentially a coherent and timeless group.

Readers will hardly find surprising the judgment that Urbach's "history" is simply uncritical. He never deals with the question, how do we know that what is attributed in a given document, often redacted centuries after the events of which it speaks, to a named authority really was said by him? Yet we must ask, if a saying is assigned to an ancient authority, how do we know that he really said it? If a story is told, how do we know that the events the story purports to describe actually took place? And if not, just what are we to make of said story and saying for historical purposes? Further, if we have a saying attributed to a first-century authority in a document generally believed to have been redacted five hundred or a thousand years later, how do we know that the attribution of the saying is valid, and that the saying informs us of the state of opinion in the first century, not only in the sixth or eleventh in which it was written down and obviously believed true and authoritative? Do we still hold, as an axiom of historical scholarship, ein muqdam umeuhar ["temporal considerations do not apply"] – in the

Talmud?! And again, do not the sayings assigned to a first-century authority, redacted in documents deriving from the early third century, possess greater credibility than those first appearing in documents redacted in the fifth, tenth, or even fifteenth centuries? Should we not, on the face of it, distinguish between more and less reliable materials? The well-known tendency of medieval writers to put their opinions into the mouths of the ancients, as in the case of the Zohar, surely warns us to be cautious about using documents redacted, even formulated, five hundred or a thousand or more years after the events of which they speak. Urbach ignores all of these questions and the work of those who ask them. The result is a reprise of Moore: not history but dogmatic theology.

Paul and Palestinian Judaism. A Comparison of Patterns of Religion.
By E.P. Sanders (London: SCM Press, 1977).

So far as Sanders's earlier book has a polemical charge, it is to demonstrate (pp. 420-21) that "the fundamental nature of the covenant conception... largely accounts for the relative scarcity of appearances of the term 'covenant' in Rabbinic literature. The covenant was presupposed, and the Rabbinic discussions were largely directed toward the question of how to fulfill the covenantal obligations." This proposition is then meant to disprove the conviction ("all but universally held") that Judaism is a degeneration of the Old Testament view: "The once noble idea of covenant as offered by God's grace and obedience as the consequence of that gracious gift degenerated into the idea of petty legalism, according to which one had to earn the mercy of God by minute observance of irrelevant ordinances." Once more issues of Protestant theological concern govern the category formation for a book on Judaisms.

Still, what Sanders did wrong in his 1992 work, he did right in his 1977 book. That is, he differentiated carefully among the evidence for diverse Judaisms and described each in its own terms. Thus his "Palestinian Judaism" is described through three bodies of evidence, described, quite properly and intelligently, one by one: Tannaitic literature, the Dead Sea Scrolls, and Apocrypha and Pseudepigrapha, in that order. The excellence of Sanders's earlier work lies in its explicit recognition that we may describe "Judaisms," each Judaic system attested by its own canonical writings. Here is no single, unitary, incremental, harmonious, lowest common denominator "Judaism," such as Sanders in 1992 has given us.

But as we saw at the outset, the work in the model of Moore and Urbach still is organized around Protestant Christian theological categories. To each set of sources, Sanders addresses questions of systematic theology: election and covenant, obedience and disobedience, reward and punishment and the world to come, salvation by membership in the covenant and atonement, proper religious behavior (so for Tannaitic sources); covenant and the covenant people, election and predestination, the commandments, fulfillment and transgression, atonement (Dead Sea Scrolls); election and covenant, the fate of the individual Israelite, atonement, commandments, the basis of salvation, the gentiles, repentance and atonement, the righteousness of God (Apocrypha and Pseudepigrapha, meaning, specifically: Ben Sira, I Enoch, Jubilees, Psalms of Solomon, IV Ezra).

This is not to suggest Sanders's covenanal nomism is a fabrication of his own; to the contrary, the datum he proposes can certainly be shown to accord with sayings here and there. At issue is whether he has formed a judgment of proportion and consequences. Is this issue the generative concern, the governing consideration, in the Judaic systems the documents of which Sanders reads? Sanders' search for patterns yields a common pattern in "covenantal nomism," which, in general, emerges as follows (p. 422):

> The "pattern" or "structure" of covenantal nomism is this: (1) God has chosen Israel and (2) given the law. The law implies both (3) God's promise to maintain the election and (4) the requirement to obey. (5) God rewards obedience and punishes transgression. (6) The law provides for means of atonement, and atonement results in (7) maintenance or re-establishment of the covenantal relationship. (8) All those who are maintained in the covenant by obedience, atonement, and God's mercy belong to the group which will be saved. An important interpretation of the first and last points is that election and ultimately salvation are considered to be by God's mercy rather than human achievement.

Anyone familiar with Jewish liturgy will be at home in that statement. Even though the evidence on the character of Palestinian Judaism derives from diverse groups and reaches us through various means, Sanders argues that covenantal nomism was "the basic type of religion known by Jesus and presumably by Paul...." And again, "covenantal nomism must have been the general type of religion prevalent in Palestine before the destruction of the Temple." But whether the various Judaisms of the time and place will have found in these ideas the center of their statement, whether this common denominator really formed the paramount agenda of thought and of piety, is a different question.

My account of Rabbinic Judaism answers that question in the negative; Rabbinic Judaism had other concerns than those of Protestant Christianity; it solved other problems; its theology and law made a statement that attended to different issues altogether, even though, on the issue important to Sanders, the writers can have concurred, casually and tangentially, with what he thought they should think on the questions critical to his polemic. That is how Sanders imposes on his evidence a Liberal Protestant theological agendum, defending his particular Judaism from Protestant condemnation. Accordingly, he simply does not come to Rabbinic Judaism to uncover the issues of Rabbinic Judaism, about which he cares very little and knows less.

He brings to the Rabbinic sources the issues of Pauline scholarship and Paul. This blatant trait of his work, which begins, after all, with a long account of Christian anti-Judaism ("The persistence of the view of Rabbinic religion as one of legalistic works-righteousness," pp. 33-58), hardly requires amplification. In fact, Sanders does not really undertake the systemic description of earlier Rabbinic Judaism in terms of its critical tension. True, he isolates those documents he thinks may testify to the state of opinion in the late first and second centuries. But Sanders does not describe Rabbinic Judaism through the systemic categories yielded by its principal documents.

While I think he is wholly correct in maintaining the importance of the conceptions of covenant and of grace, the polemic in behalf of Rabbinic legalism as covenantal does not bring to the fore what Rabbinic sources themselves wish to take as their principal theme and generative problem. For them, as he says, covenantal nomism is a datum. So far as Sanders proposes to demonstrate the importance to all the kinds of ancient Judaism of covenantal nomism, election, atonement, and the like, his work must be pronounced a success but trivial. So far as he claims to effect systemic description of Rabbinic Judaism ("a comparison of patterns of religion"), we have to evaluate that claim in its own terms.

The Mishnah certainly is the first document of Rabbinic Judaism. Formally, it stands at the center of the system, since the principal subsequent Rabbinic documents, the Talmuds, lay themselves out as if they were exegeses of Mishnah (or, more accurately, of Mishnah-Tosefta). It follows that an account of what Mishnah is about, of the system expressed by Mishnah and of the worldview created and sustained therein, should be required for systemic comparison such as Sanders proposes. Now if we come to Mishnah with questions of Pauline-Lutheran theology, important to Sanders and New Testament scholarship, we find ourselves on the peripheries of Mishnaic literature and its chief foci. True, the Mishnah contains a very few relevant, accessible sayings, for example, on election and covenant. But on our hands is a huge document which does not wish to tell us much about election and covenant and which does wish to speak about other things. Sanders's earlier work is profoundly flawed by the category formation that he imposes on his sources; that distorts and misrepresents the Judaic system of those sources. To show that Sanders's agendum has not been shaped out of the issues of Rabbinic theology, I shall now adduce negative evidence on whether Sanders with equal care analyzes the inner structure of a document of Rabbinic Judaism.

Throughout his "constructive" discussions of Rabbinic ideas about theology, Sanders quotes all documents equally with no effort at differentiation among them. He seems to have culled sayings from the diverse sources he has chosen and written them down on cards, which he proceeded to organize around his critical categories. Then he has constructed his paragraphs and sections by flipping through those cards and commenting on this and that. So there is no context in which a given saying is important in its own setting, in its own document. This is Billerbeck scholarship.

The diverse Rabbinic documents require study in their own terms. The systems of each – so far as there are systems – have now been thoroughly uncovered and described, as an examination of the companion volume to this one, *Introduction to Rabbinic Literature,* shows for more than a score of them. The way the several systems relate and the values common to all of them have now been spelled out. The work now completed simply closes off the notion that we may cite promiscuously everything in every document (within the defined canon of "permitted" documents) and then claim to have presented an account of "the Rabbis" and their opinions is not demonstrated and not even very well argued. We hardly need dwell on the still more telling fact that Sanders has not shown how systemic comparison is possible when, in point of fact, the issues of one document, or of one system of which a document is a part, are simply not the same as the issues of some other document or system; he is oblivious to all documentary variations and differences of viewpoint. That is, while he has succeeded in finding Rabbinic sayings on topics of central importance to Paul (or Pauline theology), he has ignored the context and authentic character of the setting in which he has found these sayings. He lacks all sense of proportion and coherence, because he has not even asked whether these sayings form the center and core of the Rabbinic system or even of a given Rabbinic document. To state matters simply, How do we know that "the Rabbis" and Paul are talking about the same thing, so that we may compare what they have to say? And if it should turn out that "the Rabbis" and Paul are not talking about the same thing, then what is it that we have to compare? I think, nothing at all.

IV. Historical: The Documentary Description of Rabbinic Judaism

Clearly, all prior descriptions of Rabbinic Judaism are characterized by one or more of these flaws:

1. Earlier scholars ignore the task of describing the sources, that is to say, the documents, their traits and perspectives. Documentary analysis is commonplace in Tanakh scholarship, J, E, P, and D rarely being invited to testify in common to a unitary account of the historical unity of the Torah, for example. No picture of Pentateuchal religion comprised of a harmony of the sources, or the lowest common denominator among the sources, or a sum of all sources, is apt to gain a solemn hearing in biblical studies. In New Testament scholarship it is routine to recognize that Matthew, Mark, Luke, and John formulate distinctive statements, and nobody harmonies sayings from this, that, and the other gospel into a harmonious account of what Jesus really said. I doubt that a "Christianity" written the way Sanders has written his two "Judaisms" will exercise much influence.

2. They take for granted the historicity of stories and sayings. The critical-historical program of the nineteenth century has made no impact at all. I challenge Cohen and Sanders to point to a single work in ancient Israelite history that uses scriptural sources the way they use Rabbinic ones. In New Testament scholarship people routinely call into question the historicity of sayings and stories and devise methods for distinguishing the authentic from the fabricated.

3. But they all ignore the historical setting and context in which the ideas of a given "Judaism" took place. The social-historical program of the twentieth century humanities, with its interest in the relationship between text and context, idea and the circumstance of those who held that idea, has contributed nothing. So ideas exist disembodied, out of all relationship to the lives of those who held them or later on preserved the documents that present them.

4. And they all invoke for their category formations classifications alien to the sources, instead of allowing the documents to dictate their own generative and definitive categories of thought and inquiry. Categories, the sense of proportion and of structure and order, are lifted from one world and parachuted down upon the data of another. The

recognition that one category formation cannot be imposed upon the data of a different culture – surely commonplace among historians of all periods, aware as they are of anachronism – has yet to register. The program of cultural anthropology has not made a mark. That is why we can insist the rabbis of the Mishnah tell us their views concerning propositions important to Paul, even though they may have said nothing on the topics to which Paul accorded critical importance.

Now to turn to the approach worked out in my *Rabbinic Judaism. An Historical Introduction,* and the many prior monographs summarized in that final statement of mine. The documentary approach provides a solution to these problems.

1. The documentary approach asks about the circumstances, traits, and generative problematic of the several writings, from the Mishnah through the Talmud of Babylonia. In that way, each document is read in its own terms and setting.

2. The same method simply dismisses as not subject to falsification or verification attributions of sayings to named masters.

3. But, treating the document as irrefutable evidence of the viewpoint of those who compiled the document and how they saw matters, the documentary method asks about the context in which a given document's contents found consequence.

4. And the documentary method formulates issues as these are defined by the respective documents: their concerns, their problematic, their categorical structure and system. It further proceeds to the question of how several documents relate to one another, in the aspects of autonomy, connection, and continuity, as I shall explain.

In the picture of Rabbinic Judaism given there and in the monographs and books drawn together in that book, I have provided a history of ideas based on the sequence of documents and their intellectual relationships. I have examined a structure that rests upon the native categories of these same documents. And by paying attention to the (for Israel) world-historical events prior to, and surrounding, the formulation of these documents, I have reviewed the functioning of the system of Rabbinic Judaism in response to the circumstances and contexts of those who wrote the documents at hand. It goes without saying that I have relied for facts concerning a given time and its issues upon the character of the documents, not on the attributions of sayings or the narratives of stories alleged to have been said or to have taken place at a given time prior to the closure of the document itself. The result is a theory of the description of Rabbinic Judaism that pays close attention to the formulation of distinct sets of ideas at determinate times and in specific contexts, that is, in response to important events: the Mishnah read in response to the crisis of the later second century, in which it was written; the Yerushalmi read in response to the crisis of the later fourth and early fifth centuries, in which it was written; and so with the Midrash compilations.[2]

The documentary method followed there responds to the failures of the prior descriptions of "Judaism" as portrayed by Rabbinic, and other writings.

1. What if we recognize that documentary formulations play a role in the representation of compositions, so that the compositors' formulation of matters takes a critical place in the making of the documentary evidence?

2. And what if, further, we no longer assume the inerrancy of the Oral Torah's writings, so that attributions are no longer taken at face value, stories no longer believed unless there are grounds for disbelief (as the Jerusalem canard has it)?

Then the fundamental presuppositions of the received method of studying the history of Judaism prove null. And that fact bears in its wake the further problem: Since we cannot take their answers at face value, can we pursue their questions any more? In my judgment, the answer is negative. All work in the history of the formative age of the

---

[2]The one significant lacuna in this reading, of course, is formed by my sustained treatment of the Bavli as only an intellectual, not a social statement – a problem of hermeneutics and theology, not of social description. I have not set the Talmud of Babylonia into the context in the historical circumstance of those who produced it, but only in the setting of the intellectual problem addressed by them. My sense is that the solution to that problem will be found in the intellectual challenges of the earliest phases of Islam, that is, the seventh and eighth centuries. In that case, the Bavli will come to appear as parallel to the Yerushalmi. Just as the latter presented a religious-doctrinal response to Christianity's triumph, the former will then emerge as a response to the advent of Islamic philosophy. The power of the Bavli to recapitulate religious beliefs in the rigorous disciplines of philosophy to produce a theological statement then will find its source in the eighth-century setting. No external evidence requires us to locate the Bavli prior to the eighth century. It remains for scholars of Judaism in earliest Islam to take up this possibility.

Judaism of the Dual Torah that treats documentary lines as null and attributions as invariably valid must be dismissed as a mere curiosity; a collection and arrangement of this and that, bearing no compelling argument or proposition to be dealt with by the new generation.

The question that demands a response before any historical issues can be formulate is this: How are we to determine the particular time and circumstance in which a writing took shape, and how shall we identify the generative problems, the urgent and critical questions, that informed the intellect of an authorship and framed the social world that nurtured that same authorship? Lacking answers to these questions, we find our work partial, and, if truth be told, stained by sterile academicism. Accordingly, the documentary method requires us to situate the contents of writings into particular circumstances, so that we may read the contents in the context of a real time and place. How to do so? I maintain that it is by reference to the time and circumstance of the closure of a document, that is to say, the conventional assignment of a piece of writing to a particular time and place, that we proceed outward from context to matrix.

I have defined the work as the movement from text to context to matrix. I have proposed that the relationships among documents run from autonomy through connection to continuity. That is, a text stands on its own; an author or set of writers have made decisions concerning the rhetoric, logic, topical and propositional program, that the document embodies. The context of one text is defined by the other texts to which, on demonstrable, formal bases, it clearly relates. A text also relates to other documents, being connected with them in some specific ways (the Talmuds to the Mishnah, the Midrash compilations to Scripture, for two self-evident examples). And, finally, all documents identified as authoritative or canonical in Rabbinic Judaism by definition form a continuity. A text thus finds its ultimate position within that larger matrix of a single religious system and structure that accounts for its preservation and imparts its ultimate significance. We have, then, a complex grid of three dimensions, the one to take the measure of documents and their ideas, the other to assess the historical unfolding of the Judaism – the unfolding Judaic religious system – to which those documents attest:

	LITERATURE	HISTORY	RELIGION
[1]	text	autonomy	description
[2]	context	connection	analysis
[3]	matrix	continuity	interpretation

1. The work proceeds from document to system. Systemic description begins in the form analysis of documents: their rhetorical traits, principles of cogent discourse or logic, topical program and even (in most documents) propositional plan. The counterpart is systemic analysis of a document in its own terms. This work has been done for more than a score of documents and is spelled out and summarized in the companion volume to this one.

2. Systemic analysis proceeds to investigate the connection between and among groups of documents, for example, the Mishnah and its associated Midrash compilations, the Yerushalmi and its companions, and the like; it asks how these documents relate, and answers the question by an analysis of the category formation, and the system that formation adumbrates. The matter spells over, at the historical side, into an inquiry into the connection between and among documents, on the one side, and the circumstances in which an entire set of documents was produced, on the other.

3. The problem of the matrix of writings, on the one side, and the continuity of all the documents viewed whole, carries us into the work of theological description, to which I now turn. Descriptions of how an entire corpus of literature holds together as a coherent, proportioned, and cogent statement – a theological system – and analyses of how the system viewed whole and complete (if open-ended to the history that would follow) require a different set of methods from those literary-analytical and social-historical inquiries that come to fruition in this book. The earliest exercises even now are underway, but I cannot yet see where they shall lead, for the entire labor on which this book rests, twenty years as a matter of fact, has required analysis, and I have now to turn to descriptive synthesis.

When we follow this procedure at its first two stages, as we have done in this book, we discover how, within the formation of the rabbinical canon of writings, the idea at hand came to literary expression and how it was then shaped to serve the larger purposes of the nascent canonical system as a whole. These purposes find their definition in the setting in which the documents took shape, group by group: the late second and third centuries, then the late fourth and fifth centuries. That is the basis of the picture of the formative history of Rabbinic Judaism set forth here. Since that history continued to unfold, and in our own day still presents surprises as the system of Rabbinic Judaism exhibits renewed vitality, it goes without saying that the picture given here is partial; but, so far as it goes, I should claim it also is definitive for the formative age of this, the normative Judaism.

11

From Text to Historical Context:

If Our Sages of Blessed Memory Had Written History, of What Would Their History Have Consisted?

The governing episteme in the study of ancient Judaism a century and a half ago found its governing definition in Hegelian historicism. If we know what happened, we can explain why things are one way, rather than some other, and we also can settle the question of how things should now be or evolve. Things changed; change is legitimate. Facts then dictate answers to questions of faith, and historical study bears formidable theological consequence. Any reconsideration of the uses of history in the Judaism of the Dual Torah – more really, the conception of time past, time present, and time future – begins in a clear statement of the present state of the question.

My intent really is to shift into a different direction altogether the entire inquiry concerning history. People want to know what historical facts, if any, Rabbinic literature yields. I want to know what historical conviction – covering time and eternity – animates the literature. Mine is a search for the religious character of the writings, not their historical evidences for an essentially secular (and I think, irrelevant) program. The search for historical fact – "exactly how things were" – gained urgency in the premise that, if we know how things were, we can determine how things now should be done as well. And the first corollary has long been, the texts of Rabbinic Judaism present exact, reliable facts; once we have established the text and its meaning, through text-criticism and philology, then we know facts, not of text and philology, but of history. Hence understanding the question that is raised here – precisely what claim to historical knowledge and insight do our sages of blessed memory set forth for themselves – requires that we briefly review the now-abandoned conceptions that explain the formation of earlier research programs, on the one side, and the presuppositions concerning the historical character and advocacy of the contents of Rabbinic writings, on the other.

The two principal theories that in the parochial setting define the Jews, both religious and nationalist scholarship on Judaism for different reasons concurs on the primacy of historical knowledge in the study of the writings of formative Judaism. Child of post-Hegelian theology, Reform Judaism commenced with the claim that historical knowledge ("history") forms a reliable tool for the reformation of Judaism. Proposing to control and manipulate the corpus of precedents for change that would legitimate future reform as well, the Reformers maintained that change was all right because historical precedent proved that change was all right. It pays to dwell on this point, since only when we grasp why historical fact carried heavy theological weight shall we understand the character of Jewish learning in parochial auspices.

What provided the justification for the changes was the theory of the incremental history of a single, linear Judaism played a powerful role in the creative age of Reform Judaism. The ones who made changes (it is too soon to call them Reformers, or the changes Reforms) to begin with rested their case on an appeal to the authoritative texts. Change is legitimate, and these changes in particular wholly consonant with the law, or the tradition, or the inner dynamics of the faith, or the dictates of history, or whatever out of the past worked that day. The justification of change always invoked precedent. People who made changes had to show that the principle that guided what they did was not new, even though the specific things they did were. So to lay down a bridge between themselves and their past they laid out beams resting on deep-set piles. The foundation of change was formed of the bedrock of precedent. And more still: change restores, reverts to an unchanging ideal. So the Reformers claimed not to change at all, but only to regain the correct state of affairs, one that others, in the interval, themselves have changed. That forms the fundamental attitude of mind of the people who make changes and call the changes Reform. The appeal to history, a common mode of justification in the politics and theology of the nineteenth century, therefore defined the principal justification for the new Judaism: it was new because it renewed the old and enduring, the golden Judaism of a mythic age of perfection. Arguments on precedent drew the Reformers to the work of critical scholarship, as we shall see, as they settled all questions by appeal to the facts of history.

We cannot find surprising, therefore, the theory that Reform Judaism stood in a direct line with the prior history of Judaism. What we observed in considering the dogma of a single, unitary Judaism has now to register once more. Judaism is one. Judaism has a history, that history is single and unitary, and it was always leading to its present outcome: Reform Judaism. Others later on would challenge these convictions. Orthodox Judaism would deny that Judaism has a history at all. Conservative, or positive Historical Judaism, would discover a different goal for history from that embodied by Reform Judaism. But the mode of argument, appealing to issues of an historical and factual character, and the premises of argument, insisting that history proved, or disproved, matters of theological conviction, characterized all the Judaisms of the nineteenth century and therefore shaped the intellectual life of all Judaisms of the synagogue in the twentieth century as well.

The Judaisms of the age took shape in the intellectual world of Germany, with its profoundly philosophical and historical mode of thought and argument. So the challenge of political change carried with it its own modes of intellectual response: in the academic, scholarly framework. The method of the Judaism aborning as Reform exhibited a certain congruence to the locale. Whether Luther demanding reversion to the pure and primitive faith of the Gospels or the earliest generation of Reform leaders appealing to the Talmud as justification for rejecting what others thought the contemporary embodiment of the Talmud's requirements, the principle remains the same. Reform renews, recovers the true condition of the faith, selects, out of a diverse past, that age and that moment at which the faith attained its perfect definition and embodiment. Not change but restoration and renewal of the true modes, the recovery of the way things were in that perfect, paradigmatic time, that age that formed the model for all time – these deeply mythic modes of appeal formed the justification for change, transforming mere modification of this and that into Reform. And since all intellectual currents in Judaism in the West began with Reform Judaism, the powerful paradigm of historical research would deeply root itself in every place where, under Jewish auspices, the study of ancient Judaism flourished.

When the subject shifted into the academy, the one discipline that actively accorded it a welcome was the academic study of religion. History departments found slight interest in "Jewish history," not concurring with the Zionist and Judaic conviction that a single, unitary history written by the Jews everywhere and anywhere formed a historical episteme. Few history departments made appointments in "Jewish history" unless Jewish community funds paid for them; many Religion departments made appointments in Judaism without any outside support at all. As to the social sciences, they rarely make ethnic appointments, for example, Jewish economics, though area studies accommodated the study of the State of Israel within the Middle East. In the humanities, where Religion departments flourished, there the academic study of Judaism found its home; where not, Jewish Studies as a disciplinary potpourri defined the field. In Religion departments, the secular historical program attracted slight interest, but the study of Judaism as a religion fit well into the study, along systematic lines, of a variety of other religions and, especially, their classical writings.

In place of the reforming program, using philology and exegesis as instruments of change, which had treated as secular – a matter of positive historical fact – writings with another focus altogether, the academic study of Religion asked a different set of questions. These questions sidestepped and treated as null issues of whether a given rabbi said or did not say, did or did not do, what is attributed to him. The study of religion required reading the received writings as the canon, the coherent statement of a religious system, a Judaism comprising a worldview, way of life, and theory of the social entity, Israel. To the description of Judaisms as statements of a social order grounded in a supernatural conviction, questions of historical fact, while not irrelevant, scarcely prove urgent. For what really happened on a given day and how a group of people formulated their shared life in response to, for example, the vocation of forming the Kingdom of God – these matters scarcely intersect.

History gave way to religion because of the recognition, a given in the study of religion, that the canonical writings of Judaism are fundamentally religious books, framing an account of a Judaic religious system. A further factor in the decline of interest in history as the study of what really happened lay in the fact that the study of religion encompassed history within a different definition. The academy's insistence that a religious system deals in a fundamental way with an urgent and ineluctable question that faces a social entity, and that that system provides an answer deemed self-evidently valid to the question people confront – these redefined the study of history. The Judaisms of late antiquity then have come to form a laboratory case for the examination of religion and society: religion as something people do together to solve their problems.

In these books as the academy reads them, authors speaking for communities (no document bears the name of an individual writer) have made statements about how they have worked out answers to critical and urgent problems that faced them. Read properly, the canonical writings tell us history of a different sort from the account of persons and events that earlier was thought to emerge. In more general terms, conceiving that religion is the work of real people working together to solve pressing problems, the academy has worked out, for Judaisms as for other bodies of religious writings, a particular way of addressing the canonical writings. It read them within the hermeneutics serviceable for religious writings that set forth the (to their authors) self-evidently valid answers that they have founded to these problems. Read each on its own and then all together, the canonical writings form an account of the worldview, way of life, and theory of the social entity, the "Israel," that realizes the worldview in its everyday life, that we may call a Judaism. So the problem of the right reading of the canon is to discern the religion that the authors of documents meant to set forth for us. That is the framing of the matter that I claim to have innovated.

The movement from history to religion as the focus of interest in the documents of formative Judaism took away the urgency of the question, did it really happen? That is not to suggest that historians of the Jews, including historians of Judaisms, adopted the critical program of historical study well-established in the academy in its study of Scripture. In the Jewish seminaries and Israeli universities people still write articles on the personality of this rabbi and the events of such and such a time and place, using the Rabbinic writings as though they come to us from court reporters, accurately recording what was said; or from first-hand observers; or from journalists with a keen eye for accurate detail.

The questions people think these sources reliably answer attests to the premises of gullibility and credulity in the veracity of the Judaic writings that, in biblical studies, are classified as "fundamentalist" and certainly as uncritical. But outside of sectarian institutions here and overseas, it is now a settled question that premises deemed unfounded in the study of Scripture (Old and New Testament, for instance) have to be discarded also in the study of other Judaic writings. There is no longer any serious debate on why we should believe "our holy rabbis would not lie," and arguments for the historicity of attributions of sayings attract no considerable hearing and, where heard, are dismissed.

So the movement in the academy from history to religion also marks the end of the narrowly historical reading of religious writings. In the academy in North America and Europe, the old-style "history of the Jews in the time of the Mishnah and the Talmud," with its promiscuous citation, without analysis, of the line and page of a document as adequate evidence for what really was said and done, hardly registers any longer. Most of that kind of history, moreover, is now published only in Hebrew, a mark of the disinterest of the writers in a hearing outside of their setting and of their concession that outsiders to that setting will not likely take to heart the conclusions that are set forth. Talmudic history finds slight acceptance in the academy; the study of the Rabbinic literature for the description, analysis, and interpretation of a principal Judaic system occupies the center of public discourse and debate.

Having maintained that the academy addresses religion, not history, I have now concretely to spell out what I mean. History asks about matters of origin and development, claiming to explain things when it can account for the order in which they took place and the connections among them. But by the time religions produce the documents that permit us to study them in historical context, they have long passed their point of origin. We describe systems mainly from their end products, the writings. But we have then to work our way back from canon to system, not to imagine either that the canon is the system, or that the canon creates the system. The canonical writings speak, in particular, to those who can hear, that is, to the members of the community, who, on account of that perspicacity of hearing, constitute the social entity or systemic community.

The community then comprises that social group the system of which is recapitulated by the selected canon. The group's exegesis of the canon in terms of the everyday imparts to the system the power to sustain the community in a reciprocal and self-nourishing process. The community through its exegesis then imposes continuity and unity on whatever is in its canon. The writings then yield a different kind of information from that that conventional historians require. Most of the questions of origin and development that historians claim to answer cannot find answers in the evidence canonical writings provide, as historians of Christianity have found in their work on the Gospels and Church traditions. But the canonical evidence answers other, and in the view of many, more urgent and formidable questions of religious persistence: Why this, not that?

While, therefore, we cannot account for the origin of a successful religious-social system, we can explain its power to persist. It is a symbolic transaction in which social change comes to expression in symbol change. That symbolic transaction, specifically, takes place in its exegesis of the systemic canon, which, in literary terms, constitutes the social entity's statement of itself So, once more, the texts recapitulate the system. The system does not recapitulate the texts. The system comes before the texts and defines the canon. The exegesis of the canon then forms that ongoing social action that sustains the whole. A system does not recapitulate its texts, it selects and orders them. A religious system imputes to them as a whole cogency, one to the next, that their original authorships have not expressed in and through the parts, and through them a religious system expresses its deepest logic, *and it also frames that just fit that joins system to circumstance.*

The whole works its way out through exegesis, and the history of any religious system – that is to say, the history of religion writ small – is the exegesis of its exegesis. And the first rule of the exegesis of systems is the simplest, and the one with which I conclude: *The system does not recapitulate the canon. The canon recapitulates the system.* The system forms a statement of a social entity, specifying its worldview and way of life in such a way that, to the participants in the system, the whole makes sound sense, beyond argument. So in the beginning are not words of inner and intrinsic affinity, but (as Philo would want us to say) the Word: the transitive logic, the system, all together, all at once, complete, whole, finished – the word awaiting only that labor of exposition and articulation that the faithful, for centuries to come, will lavish at the altar of the faith. A religious system therefore presents a fact not of history but of immediacy, of the social present.

The issue of why a system originates and survives, if it does, or fails, if it does, by itself proves impertinent to the analysis of a system but of course necessary to our interpretation of it. A system on its own is like a language. A language forms an example of language if it produces communication through rules of syntax and verbal arrangement. That paradigm serves full well however many people speak the language, or however long the language serves. Two people who understand each other form a language community, even, or especially, if no one understands them. So, too, by definition religions address the living, constitute societies, frame and compose cultures. For however long, at whatever moment in historic time, a religious system always grows up in the perpetual present, an artifact of its day, whether today or a long ago time. The only appropriate tense for a religious system is the present. A religious system always *is*, whatever it was, whatever it will be. Why so? Because its traits address a condition of humanity in society, a circumstance of an hour – however brief or protracted the hour and the circumstance. To the historians working on the writings of Rabbinic Judaism in its formative age, these considerations prove baffling; to scholars of religion, they recapitulate the banalities and truisms of an active scholarly inquiry. We should look in vain for writing on religion, not theology, coming from the rabbinical seminaries, not one of which in offers courses in the study of religion (just as Yeshiva University and Brandeis University have no departments of religious studies); and as to the Israeli universities, scholarship on Judaism as a religion has yet to get underway.

This brings us to the work at hand: an assessment of the historical claim set forth by the texts of the Judaism of the Dual Torah. Precisely what do the framers of the documents and the authors of the compositions and composites of which they are comprised claim to tell us about the past, both the long ago past before their day, and the past that, in their writing, they transmit into the future? We begin with a passage representative of most of the Mishnah, which is commonly taken to tell us precisely the way things were:

5:8   A.   In accord with the rite as conducted on an ordinary day, so was the conduct of the rite on the Sabbath.
       B.   And the priests mopped up the courtyard [on the Sabbath, just as on a weekday],
       C.   contrary to sages' wishes.
       D.   R. Judah says, "A cup was filled with the mingled blood [which had been spilled]. One tossed it with a single act of tossing on the altar."
       E.   And sages did not concur with him.
5:9   A.   How do they hang up [the carcasses] and flay them?
       B.   Iron hooks were set into the walls and pillars, on which they would hang up and flay the carcasses [M. Mid. 3:5].
       C.   And for whoever did not have space for hanging and flaying his carcass,
       D.   there were thin smooth poles, and one would put one end on his shoulder and one on the shoulder of his fellow,
       E.   and [thereon] hang and flay the carcass.
       F.   R. Eliezer says, "On the fourteenth of Nisan which coincided with the Sabbath, he would put his hand on the shoulder of his fellow, and the hand of his fellow on his shoulder, and thereon suspend and flay the carcass."
5:10   A.   He slit open the carcass and removed its sacrificial portions, put them on a tray and [a priest] burned them on the altar.
       B.   [When the fourteenth of Nisan coincided with the Sabbath], the first group went out and took seats on the Temple mount, the second on the Rampart, and the third remained in its place.
       C.   Once it got dark, they went out and roasted their Passover lambs.

M. Pesahim 5:8-10

This passage – in both its tone and its program – with its innumerable counterparts throughout the Mishnah introduces the way in which our sages of blessed memory, represented by the documents of the Dual Torah brought to closure in late antiquity, viewed the past and made use of it. The use of the past tense here carries the clear claim that this is how things were done at a determinate point in the past, and, further, that the rule governing prior conduct of the rite continued to dictate contemporary practice. Saying how things were done accurately portrays how they are supposed to be done. In that sense, therefore, the entire corpus of Rabbinic literature, beginning to end, sets forth a systematic history of Israel. If, then, we ask about the presence of the past in the present as our sages contemplate matters, we come up with a simple answer: the past flows across an unmarked boundary into today's affairs. A single example of a specific, determinate incident shows the state of the writings:

K.   M^cSH B: An old shepherd came before Rabbi [Judah the Patriarch] and said to him, "I recall that the townsfolk of Migdal Geder would go down to Hammata, up to the outermost courtyard near the bridge."

L.   And Rabbi permitted the townsfolk of Migdal to go down to Hammata, up to the outermost courtyard, by the bridge.

M.   And Rabbi further permitted the townsfolk of Geder to go down to Hammata and to go up to Geder.

N.   But the townsfolk of Hammata did not go up to Geder.

T. Erubin 4:16K-N

The past and the present form a single continuum, and, it must follow, if we were to ask our sages to point out the historically consequential writings within their canon, they would direct our attention to virtually every line of every document of their authorship. It is the simple fact that for our sages of blessed memory, as for the sages of the Written Torah, the writers of much of the New Testament literature, and their continuators for many centuries, the historical question that for some proves urgent and decisive lay beyond all comprehension. The notion that the past and the present divide, the conception that what happened the day before yesterday remains to be discovered, the further notion that events of the past possess an authority over the present by reason of their pastness (the idea of a "classical" or "golden age" that historians uncover) – these principles of the historical reading of the human condition, should our sages and their counterparts have known them, would have proved puzzling.

To set forth the problem of this project, it hardly suffices, however, to take note of the fact that the entirety of the corpus of the Torah, oral and written, formed a compilation of entirely accurate facts. Anyone who imagines that prior to Hegel and the founders of historicism, people wrote chronicles or other records of their own time and past time by reason of an autonomous interest in precisely what happened, or that, before that influential moment in intellectual history, the conception of history as we now know it even existed, simply has fallen out of touch with learning. Everybody knows that all of our documents and their Christian counterparts took shape in a world in which few conceived the pastness of the past, and most understood events to form a theological paradigm, not a free-standing source of authority or even an autonomous body of principles meant to explain, in this-worldly terms, how things now are. The broad acceptance of these facts, however, does not prevent people from bringing to religious documents a set of quite secular, narrowly historical questions. And it is to that ongoing, and in my view intellectually dubious, enterprise that I turn in formulating the problem of this monograph and its planned sequels. What I wish to know is how to define the category, history, in the language and terms native to the intellect of our sages of blessed memory. That is to say, I investigate in acute detail the uses of the past that these sages found sound and illuminating – the uses of the past, not their conception of history, for – as I show in these volumes – it is the simple fact that they had none.

If that were the sole fact – the absence of materials of a historical character – then the study before us would hardly demand attention. In fact, we find in Rabbinic literature the three categories of writing characteristic of history writing then and now: accounts of events, stories of great and important lives, and sustained, explanatory accounts of how events connect and form patterns that explain how things are. These three kinds of writing were characteristic of the one Judaic figure who did produce history in the conventional sense, Josephus. His History of the Jewish War forms portrays events and their connections; his Vita defines as its organizing category a Life (biography); and his Jewish Antiquities sets forth an encompassing, connected, intelligible history of Israel. So the categories, event, chapters in biography, and sustained, connected accounts of history, derive from how history was then written, as much as how, in other times and circumstances, history is ordinarily written.

Accordingly, this catalogue and repertoire of mine invokes historical categories: events, biography, the pattern and direction of history. What I now portray is how our sages identified events, produced chapters of biography, set forth accounts of the direction of history, both in times past and in their own day. Precisely how, in other words, do they respond to that same set of questions that animate historical study in accord with modern (though not contemporary) conventions of historical research? In simple terms, deriving from prior research of mine,[1] my enterprise is the formation of a counterpart category for the category of history as we now understand it.

To explain what is at stake, I ask a simple question. History ordinarily maintains the claim that we cannot understand the present without knowing the past, and historical study commonly has maintained that lessons drawn from the past illumiante the present in some compelling manner. History therefore yields events and patterns – events recaptured out of the detritus of data critically examined, patterns induced through the objective study of well-considered events. Historical categories as conventionally defined speak of lives

---

[1]The conception of counterpart category is carefully spelled out in *The Transformation of Judaism. From Philosophy to Religion* (Champaign, 1992: University of Illinois Press).

(biography), events, and patterns of history that account for how things now are. Now in addressing a literature that designs the entire worldly structure of the holy people, Israel, without once requiring the compilation of a history of any kind, we have to address the simple question: What forms the counterpart to historical study (chronicle, biography) and to historical knowledge (sustained narrative history) in this encompassing corpus of writing?

The answer is, our sages of blessed memory had their own ideas about all of the problems solved by history and all of the uses to which historians put the data of the past. They formulated categories covering the data organized by historical research in its way, for example, events, lives, sustained narratives, and there was a category corresponding to history's "events," to its "lives," and to its organizing and encompassing narrative. These conventionally historical categories, therefore, are the ones that I employ here in order to identify the counterpart categories that served our sages so well in their formation of a viable account of events, lives, and trends or patterns. Their account interpreted in its own way the pastness of the past, utilized the data of the day before yesterday in a quite distinctive way, and set forth answers to precisely the same questions historians then answered within a different set of premises and presuppositions. Our inquiry here is to move from the identification of pertinent data to an account of the counterpart category that served this Judaism in its confrontation with issues framed by facts concerning what came first, and what happened then. The inductive work begins here.

Having explained what I wish to accomplish, let me hasten to identify what is not at stake here. What I set forth here is not what really happened in to the Jews of the Land of Israel in the time of the writings surveyed, but what those writings set forth as an account that, in our setting and terms, forms history. What I explain in acute detail is where and how what was happening in the world at large, the principal and formative events, the patterns and movements of events that make history consequential – how these documents portray the intellectual counterpart to what we should expect as history. The issue is not one of historical fact, such as I have addressed in works noted in the Preface, but historical perception. The upshot, in due course, will be an answer to the question: Did our sages of blessed memory see reality in terms that qualify in any way whatsoever as historical? I spend these several volumes to refute the notion that the category, "history," as we define that category in the aftermath of Hegel, applies or even pertains to Rabbinic Judaism. What I show in laborious detail is that no conception of history that we should recognize as historical animated the minds of our sages, that, so far as the founders of Judaism were concerned, reality in the form of events and patterns of events (the simplest sense of "history" I can propose) bore an altogether different meaning and mode of construction and explanation. It must follow that to ask the historical question of the definitive writings of this Judaism – in the way in which one might ask the historical question to Heroditus, Thucydides, Josephus or Eusebius, for instance – defies the categorical structure of those writings and therefore is inappropriate and irrelevant. That, and not the "historical usefulness" of the writings of the Oral Torah in late antiquity, forms the object of concern.

The research I conducted in Åbo, yielding *From Text to Historical Context*, presents a systematic answer to a simple question: In important documents of Rabbinic Judaism, what materials do we find that claim to give us historical facts, and what kind of history pertaining to the time of the documents themselves do those writings purport to contain? To answer that question, I survey some principal writings and identify their statements that clearly allege facts about the time and place of the writers, or the near-past about which they may fairly claim to have precise factual knowledge. This study will give us perspective upon the historical facts that systemic writings purportedly transmit to us, as well as a fairly comprehensive catalogue of those facts themselves.

"Systemic documents" are writings that set forth the law, theology, or scriptural exegesis that, all together, comprise the canon of Rabbinic Judaism. They are "systemic" because each of them participates in the formulation of a complete theory of the social order of eternal Israel, the holy, supernatural people of God, providing an account of its way of life, its worldview, and its status as a social entity. What I want to know is whether, and how, these theological, legal, and exegetical writings composed to state a vast and encompassing religious system along the way also provide us with historical information, and in what manner we may make of such information as the writings do give us into a coherent historical statement.

There are two distinct problems to address. First, precisely where do the writings allege that they provide historical facts concerning the time in which those documents took shape? What claims do the compilations themselves make to transmit historical data about not ancient Israelite days but their own times? Since our inquiry concerns conventional historical materials and not stories told to carry out the documentary purpose, for example, to illustrate a point of law, or to enrich the exegesis of a Scriptural passage, respectively, I omit from this catalogue legal precedents in narrative form, which are introduced as legal precedents and not as historical tales of things that really happened on some singular occasion, as well as fables concerning Scriptural times, persons and events.

These latter need not detain us, since all they tell us is about the theological program, expressed in exegetical language, for the writers of such stories. True, the theologians may be assumed to have taken for granted events in ancient Israelite times took place as they imagined; but we do not have to pretend to honor as a claim to present historical facts by contemporary criteria of facticity what obviously conveys fabrication and invention. Narrative language served as one important medium for theological expression; it conveys no claim to the historicity of tales that we, for our part, must entertain even for a single minute.

Second, if we compile such information as the writings contain, seeing it all together and all at once, precisely what historical data do we have, and what sort of history can we conceive on that foundation?

The work begins in the silence of the canon of the Dual Torah concerning history and historical narrative; there is no connected narrative of Israel's life and history, no sustained and continuous account of sequences of events over a long period of time, nothing remotely comparable to the kinds of history done at the time that the writings of that canon were being worked up. Whether Joseph in the first century, or Eusebius in the fourth, whether the authors of the Gospels, Matthew, Mark, Luke, and John with their biographies, or the writers of lives of the saints later on – none of these find a counterpart in the Rabbinic literature, which contains no history worthy of the name or biography of any ambitious order whatsoever. But the documents do refer to incidents, and they do tell stories about sages and even outsiders. I propose to survey such history and biography as we do find, so as to characterize in a thorough and systematic way the historical facts provided by the systemic documents. Such a characterization will afford an interesting perspective on the Judaism of those documents, and it also will identify such facts about the world beyond the writings that the writings supply.

To be sure, Rabbinic Judaism includes in its canon no document devoted to historical narrative. Drawing on Scriptures, with their extensive appeal to historical writing as a medium for theological discourse in the Pentateuch, Joshua, Judges, Samuel, and Kings, sages recognized no requirement to imitate the scriptural historians. True, in most Rabbinic documents we find brief tales, rarely requiring more than two hundred words from start to finish. But many of these tales in fact provide a narrative setting for what is no more than a dialogue of one kind or another, and few of them lead us very far beyond the limits of those issues of law or theology to which the fables pertain. It follows that, when we ask ahistorical writings, documents of law, exegesis, theological disquisition, and the like, to answer narrow and specific historical questions, we should expect only episodic and occasional answers.

But that expectation does not relieve us of the duty to raise such questions, and that is for three reasons. First, since Rabbinic writings reach us out of a determinate point in the past, by definition they constitute historical evidence, monuments to what someone or group was thinking. Each document by itself constitutes a fact of history, that is, something people made in times past and handed on to the indeterminate future as a record of their time, place, and circumstance. Hence failure to read the ancient writings for historical information would mark a failure to do our duty to the writers, neglect of their own aspiration. But, second and more to the point, documents not only tell us what their writers mean to convey, most of which has no bearing on the conventional issues of history but only on the history of law or theology – history of ideas, broadly construed. They also bear information that to the writers may have meant little, being beside the point they wished to make, but to us may mean much. And, third, the documents' writers themselves allege in so many words that from time to time they convey facts on precisely how things were in the time of the writers or in the near-past about which they allege they have exact information. So let us see what they themselves propose to tell us about history, conventionally defined.

The intellectual program of this project presents no formidable complications. I wish to reread the Rabbinic canon with special attention to identifying, within the writings, historical information the writers convey either explicitly – by their own word – en passant and by indirection. Specifically, I wish systematically to ask what the documents indicate about the world of their writers, not the intellectual world, to which I have devoted so much work, but the material world of politics and culture beyond the Rabbinic circles themselves. So far as the documents contain allegations about how things really were, I here catalogue those allegations and examine their character. A single set of questions guides the reading of each document examined in this project and of the subdivisions of those documents. In my research in Åbo, I systematically identify these kinds of materials:

1. EVENTS THAT ALLEGEDLY TOOK PLACE OTHER THAN LEGAL PRECEDENTS: Where the document presents a story about something that actually happened in the time of the writer of the document or shortly prior to that time, I take note of that claim to provide a historical fact about a one-time, singular event that took place. I do not catalogue legal precedents, since, by nature, these tell us not about one time,

singular events, such as history comprises, but the very opposite: exemplary and authoritative events. True, precedents may actually have taken place, but they are meant to illustrate how things are and should be, and not what actually happened on some one, unique occasion. So far as I am able, I catalogue everything else.

2. CHAPTERS IN THE LIVES OF PERSONS: Where a tale is told that can have found its way into a biography of a person in the time of the compilation of the document, for example, a sage or other near-contemporary, I include that in our survey. I pay no attention to pseudo-narratives, meaning, narrative settings for what are in fact wise sayings, for example, "One day he was walking along and said...," or "He saw such and so happen and commented...." These do not qualify as raw materials for history, but only as settings for wise sayings or authoritative rulings.

3. FRAGMENTS SERVICEABLE IN CONVENTIONALLY HISTORICAL NARRATIVES: A story may be told out of all legal context, about a one-time and unique happening, an event in conventional, historical context; that is the kind of story I include in this survey. In this way we take account of the fact that, even though rabbinic documents never take shape around a clearcut narrative-historical intent, nonetheless we find in them well-crafted stories that can have served in history books of the kind that Josephus or Eusebius put together.

Let me give an example of what I shall not catalogue. The first item is, the legal precedent. This is presented not as a one-time event, but as exemplary (even though the precedent may have taken place only one). One, very familiar instance, suffices:

G. Ma'aseh s: His [Gamaliel's] sons returned from a banquet hall [after midnight].
H. They said to him, "We did not [yet] recite the Shema."
I. He said to them, "If the dawn has not yet risen, you are obligated to recite [the Shema].
J. "And [this applies] not only [in] this [case]. Rather, [as regards] all [commandments] which sages said [may be performed] 'Until midnight' the obligation [to perform them persists] until the rise of dawn."
K. "[For example,] the offering of the fats and entrails – their obligation [persists] until the rise of dawn [see Lev. 1:9, 3:3-5].
L. "And all [sacrifices] which must be eaten within one day, the obligation [to eat them persists] until the rise of dawn.

M.   "If so why did sages say [that these actions may be performed only]
       until midnight?
N.   "In order to protect man from sin."

M. Berakhot 1:1

Such an story conveys not an event, meaning, a one-time, unique,
consequential moment, but the very opposite: the prevailing rule in the
form of a narrative. But merely because a teaching is given narrative
form, that represents no claim to provide the kind of materials for
conventional, narrative history that we seek.

The second item involves what I call "pseudo-narratives." Here we
are given a story that can have served a biography ("gospel"), but really
provides a flesh-and-blood illustration of a rule:

A.   A bridegroom is exempt from the recitation of the Shema on the
       first night [after the wedding] until after the Sabbath [following the
       wedding],
B.   if he did not consummate [the marriage].
C.   Ma'aseh b: Rabban Gamaliel recited [the Shema] on the first night of
       his marriage.
D.   Said to him [his students], "Did our master not teach us that a
       bridegroom is exempt from the recitation of the Shema on the first
       night?"
E.   He said to them, "I cannot heed you to suspend from myself the
       kingdom of heaven [even] for one hour."

M. Berakhot 2:5

A.   [Gamaliel] washed on the first night after the death of his wife.
B.   Said to him [his students], "Did not [our master] teach us that it is
       forbidden for a mourner to wash?"
C.   He said to them, "I am not like other men, I am frail."

M. Berakhot 2:6

A.   And when Tabi, his servant, died, [Gamaliel] received condolences
       on his account.
B.   Said to him [his students], "Did not [our master] teach us that one
       does not receive condolences for [the loss of] slaves?"
C.   He said to them, "Tabi my slave was not like other slaves. He was
       exacting."

M. Berakhot 2:7

D.   They said concerning R. Haninah b. Dosa, "When he would pray
       for the sick he would say 'This one shall live' or 'This one shall
       die.'"
E.   They said to him, "How do you know?"
F.   He said to them, "If my prayer is fluent, then I know that it is
       accepted [and the person will live].
G.   "But if not, I know that it is rejected [and the person will die]."

M. Berakhot 5:5

Here again, we scarcely find the raw materials for biography; these are episodic incidents, not preserved because of an interest in telling the life of the man, but for a different interest altogether. It is a story told to illustrate how the law may make exceptions, or a sage may make an exception of himself; or a story that illustrates a point about praying. For lives of the saints, such episodic stories can have served, but only if they can have been strung together along some kind of story-line. It is the simple fact that for no figure in all of Rabbinic literature can we put together stories of a sufficient volume and requisite character as to assemble anything resembling a life of a saint, let alone a gospel.

A third type of writing that I do not catalogue involves a story told about an incident of purely legal or polemical character, bearing no rich implications for large historical questions, for example, the history of the nation or the community. Here is an example of something that bears weighty polemical importance but no historical interest:

> G. Said R. Tarfon, "I was coming along the road [in the evening] and reclined to recite the Shema as required by the House of Shammai. And [in doing so] I placed myself in danger of [being attacked by] bandits."
>
> H. They said to him, "You are yourself responsible [for what might have befallen you], for you violated the words of the House of Hillel."
>
> M. Berkahot 1:3

Now from this story, if it could be shown actually to have taken place, we might draw the conclusion that, in Tarfon's time, travel by night was dangerous. That may well have been so, but such a historical fact strikes me as ineffably commonplace; it does not tell us something unusual and important about Tarfon's time and place, such as to warrant inclusion in a catalogue of data of clear, historical consequence, or at least, data that the author and compiler thought should bear consequence.

This classification of the data to be identified and listed omits kinds of compositions and even composites that others would by definition encompass in any historical account of the literature. The examples now given suffice to illustrate the principle that governs here. It is that I do not treat as a claim to narrate a historical fact the attribution of a saying to an authority, on the one side, or the tale of what a given authority said or did on some one day, in connection with a legal ruling, a theological teaching, or a moral instruction. These of course convey facts about what storytellers thought was true. But they serve not to tell us how things really were, only how storytellers imagined things to be or thought they should take place. Not only so, but stories that clearly fall into the program of a legal, theological, or exegetical document by definition do not form conventional data for history; to the contrary, they serve the purposes of law, theology, and exegesis, and these purposes are different from those of conventional historical narrative.

The research having been described, let me now explain the intellectual context in which I conducted it. What I wanted to find out in this part of my research in Åbo is how our sages of blessed memory conceived past, present, and future; time and eternity; the raw materials of history and their product. The issue is not whether or not these documents contain historical facts in the conventional definition of historical facts; each document on its own constitutes a formidable fact of history and society. What I want to know is how, in the aggregate, these writings conceived of, and utilized, the facts as they defined them: What kind of history did they contemplate, fabricate, and postulate? To answer that question, I systematically reread most of the documents of Rabbinic Judaism in its formative age, cataloguing what I find in accord with three simple rubrics, defined presently.

Not a few of those familiar with these writings take for granted every word in them is historical. The documents attribute sayings to named authorities. Many then assume the named authorities really said what is assigned to them. The documents contain stories about what various people did. Many take for granted that these stories portray actual events, not only imagined ones. So we have a great many historical books that paraphrase these documents and collect other information from writings of the same time and place, as well as archaeological data, and put the whole together into history. Such history being abundantly available, how then can I come to the writings deemed precise records of things really said and done and ask, what historical claims are here? What kind of history do people actually allege they transmit to us? And what are we to make of that (conception of) history? While much has been written about the concept of history in "Judaism," and still more has been made of the allegation that Jews by nature or by race or by ethnic affiliation or by culture possess innate traits of historical memory and response, I know of no systematic account of what the documents actually claim to tell us about such matters, let alone the basis – theological, based on revelation, not ethnic or racial, based on innate traits of blood or alleged collective memory – for them.

So I realize that, for most of those who work on the same documents, the question I raise here must present a puzzle (if not an offense). Most, without much sustained and systematic study, already know the answers. And many believe as historical fact, not theological construction, pretty much everything the documents allege. For people who believe that everything the canonical writings say was and is so, every story is a historical fact, every saying the raw material for biography; the documents are history books, in a somewhat ahistorical idiom to be sure, because everything in them is as historical as counterpart statements in Josephus or Herodotus or Eusebius. For a variety of historians in Israeli universities and American seminaries and yeshivot open the Rabbinic writings and find a vast number of historical facts, which they paraphrase and turn into narrative, or upon which they ruminate and pass their opinions. History, including narrative history, still is written as though the Rabbinic literature were composed by historians in the tradition of Josephus or Herodotus for that matter. Not only so, but these same scholars regard it as established fact that stories that are told really happened, and happened in the manner in which the storyteller says; sayings assigned to named authorities really were said by them; and whatever we find in the Rabbinic literature stands for not normative law and theology but historical fact.

No one likely to read this essay requires a review of why the position still held and fiercely defended by Israeli and Rabbinical school historians scarcely requires serious attention any longer. The believers believe, and the others go about their work. That the result of the contrary premise concerning historical research is uncritical, gullible and credulous, is self-evident; that that is not how people work anymore, or how they have worked for nearly two hundred years, is obvious. Certainly, I need not repeat my arguments, set forth in *Reading and Believing: Ancient Judaism and Contemporary Gullibility* (Atlanta, 1986: Scholars Press for Brown Judaic Studies) and *What We Cannot Show, We Do Not Know: Rabbinic Literature and the New Testament* (Philadelphia, 1993: Trinity Press International), among many other places. People who choose to utilize Rabbinic evidence for purposes for which it self-evidently proves unsuited – for which it does not even claim to be suited – are not likely to find persuasive the arguments set forth in those works, in which not a few of those same people, dead and living, are criticized in acute and accurate detail. People who do not choose to do so already have defined for themselves a critical agendum and hardly require a reprise of what I have already said. They have been persuaded and now proceed to define the historical task in a correct and critical manner. It is for the vast critical academy that I do this work, meant as a public service of an elementary character.

Part Four

OTHER CURRENT WRITINGS

12

The Christian Half of the Judaeo-Christian Dialogue through History

For the purposes of their own theological discourse, Christians first invented Judaism, then fabricated a dialogue with this Judaism, an imagined conversation with a made-up protagonist. Why, from the beginnings, Christian writers wrote about outsiders, including Jews, requires no explanation. Every group defines itself by designating the other. Numerous writers in antiquity knew, when they referred to "Judaism" just what they meant: in practice, circumcision, the Sabbath, dietary laws; in belief, one God, Messiah yet to come, chosen people. While, as I said, we have no reason to doubt most Judaisms will have affirmed all these practices and beliefs, I wonder whether they will have grasped them as the point of cogency, the generative problematic, of their Judaisms. That is to say, while all Judaisms presumably believed in one God and refrained from eating pork, defining those Judaisms in these terms surely misses what was important to the believers of those Judaisms in their Judaisms. Why Christianity found it urgent to define Judaism for itself hardly presents a mystery.

Whether in ancient or medieval or modern times, the issue remained constant and entirely comprehensible, in the language of F.C. Bauer:

> How Christianity, instead of remaining a mere form of Judaism...asserted itself as a separate, independent principle, broke loose from it, and took its stand as a new enfranchised form of religious thought and life, essentially different from all the national peculiarities

of Judaism, is the ultimate, most important point of the primitive history of Christianity.[1]

What Judaism did Christianity invent for itself? The conversation partner fabricated by Christianity hardly presented a worthy opponent for dialogue, or even debate and disputation. On the contrary, once invented, "Judaism" served Christianity as a foil, that alone. Invented for the purpose of polemic and apologetic, "Judaism" was so defined as to form a caricature, a mere anti-Christianity, the opposite, the other, the worst possible choice, by contrast to the best possible choice. So this "it" was "a narrow, legalistic religion. Pharisees taught a religion of 'works-righteousness,' of salvation earned by merit...thus providing a stark foil for the gospel of Jesus and of Paul, who, in contrast, brought a religion of forgiveness and grace."[2] Dunn comments in the very next sentence: "The traditional Protestant view of Paul's gospel was derived more from the Lutheran interpretation of Paul than from Paul itself." It would be difficult to show in a more graphic way how critical to the study of the theology of Christianity is the concept of an -ism, in this case, a Judaism: a theological category, defined in theological terms. But the discourse goes awry as soon as we invoke some other category than the theological one to speak of the entire composite of beliefs and practices that characterized all the faithful of (a particular) Israel.

Here is Dunn's language: "A Jesus or Paul who seemed to ignore or deny these characteristic emphases of Judaism they could not understand." Translated into the native categories of the Judaic writings in Hebrew and Aramaic: "A Jesus or Paul who seemed to ignore or deny these characteristic emphases of the Torah they could not understand." The entire frame of reference shifts, the entire argument evaporates; we are now talking about other things in other terms, and the initial formulation, shifted into the native category, loses all coherent meaning.[3]

---

[1]Cited by Dunn, *The Partings of the Ways between Christianity and Judaism and their Significance for the Character of Christianity* (Philadelphia, 1992: Trinity Press International), p. 1.

[2]Dunn, p. 14. Dunn rightly points to important Christian protests against this particular "Judaism," e.g., naming Moore, Herford, Parkes, and Sanders.

[3]Indeed, when we speak of "Torah" and "Christ," or "Israel" and "Christ," the entire discourse changes in character, and its fixed lines of order and structure blur. If and when a true dialogue gets under way, along lines I shall suggest presently, I should think it will be quite natural to tell the story of Jesus Christ, on the one side, and to tell the story of Israel, God's first love, on the other, abandoning these categories that are not native to Judaism, on the one side, and, I should claim, also not required for Christianity, on the other – Judaism, Christianity, respectively. But we are a long way from that moment at which the category-formation will proceed along new lines.

At issue is not merely the defamation of "Judaism" or "Pharisaic Judaism" as "a joyless, narrowly legalistic religion."[4] It is the mode of thinking that yields that whole, that "Judaism," of such a character that, if we know that "it" is present in a part, we know that "it" is present throughout. When Dunn states, "...a fresh reassessment of earliest Christianity's relationship with Judaism...must be one of our highest priorities," he provides a fine example of the conceptual difficulty at hand, so, too, his language, "What was the Judaism within which Jesus grew up and from which earliest Christianity emerged? And why did it break away from that Judaism and become distinct and separate?" This is one way of thinking about religion, therefore about the relationships between religions, and it is the way taken by Christian writers from ancient times to the present, hence, in their language, "by Christianity."

Now that we realize how particular to its own mode of thought is the Christian invention of Judaism, we turn to the Judaism that Christianity invented. As I said, in its outlines, that "Judaism" is easy enough to discern, and it is an entirely valid outline: monotheism, Torah, chosenness of Israel, Sabbath, circumcision, pork – whatever. Givens, denominators that serve at the foundations of all Judaisms, these serve as well as any other equally valid entries, or all of them put together; and, it goes without saying what characterizes every Judaism can have proved systemically urgent to none of them. But what has Christianity made of this -ism that it has invented, what is the Juda- part of the -ism, "Juda-ism"? A convenient survey, easy to summarize, comes to us from the great scholar of history of religions, George Foot Moore.

In his "Christian Writers on Judaism,"[5] George F. Moore identifies the apologetic and polemic, rather than historical character of Christian interest in Jewish literature. But apologetics takes the form of dialogue, for example, a Jew and a Christian, because "it enabled the writers to combat Jewish objections as well as to develop their own argument in the way best adapted to their purpose."[6] The Jewish disputant on the Christian side is always "a man of straw, who raises his difficulties and makes objections only to give the Christian opportunity to show how easily they are resolved or refuted, while in the end the Jew is made to admit himself vanished. This...shows that the authors did not write to convert Jews but to deify Christians, possibly also to convince gentiles wavering between the rival propaganda of the synagogue and the

---

[4]Dunn, p. 14.
[5]*Harvard Theological Review* 1921, 14:197-254. See also Haim Hillel Ben Sasson, "Disputations and Polemics, *Encyclopaedia Judaica* (Jerusalem, 1971) 6:100ff.
[6]Moore, p. 198.

church."[7] In Medieval times, Christians dealt "not with fictitious opponents, but with real antagonists, who stoutly defended themselves and struck back hard."[8] But, over time, the "dialogue" with "Judaism" took on the character of not an argue to persuade, but rather, an exercise in the vilification of Judaism. The title of one of these tells the story (Eisenmenger's Judaism Revealed): "A thorough and truthful account of the way in which the hardened Jews horribly blaspheme and dishonor the most holy Trinity, Father, Son, and Holy Ghost, defame the holy Mother of Christ, jeer and scoff at the New Testament, the Evangelists and Apostles, the Christian religion, and utterly despise and curse all Christian people." Eisenmenger's Judaism involved "murder of children to use their blood in unholy rites."[9]

Modern writers described "Judaism" as "legalism," "the sum and substance of religion...in Jewish apprehension, the only form of religion for all ages." Judaism is then a religion in which "religion is the right behavior of man before God," while Christianity says, "Religion is communion with God; God will admit man to his communion because he is not only holiness but love. In Judaism...where his holiness is exclusively emphasized, God remains absolutely exalted above the world and man, separated from them, abiding unchangeable in himself."[10] The Jewish idea of God is "abstract monotheism and abstract transcendentism," an inaccessible God.[11] Moore is straightforward in characterizing this "Judaism" as an invention for the purpose of dialogue with Jews, and dialogue with Jews as a medium for their conversion. When Schmidt told Buber the only basis on which Jews could live in Germany was their conversion to Christianity, he defined the "Judaeo-Christian dialogue" in terms entirely authentic to the historic reality. Here is how Moore characterizes Weber:

> It is equally important to remark that the "fundamental conception" of an inaccessible God, whom, without perceiving the difference, he converts in the next breath into an Absolute God, is derived from the principle that legalism is the essence of religion, from which, according to Weber, it follows by logical necessity. About this he deceives himself; the necessity is purely apologetic. The motive and method of the volume are in fact apologetic throughout; the author, like so may of his predecessors, sets himself to prove the superiority of Christianity to Judaism.... It may perhaps without injustice be described more

---

[7]Moore, p. 198.
[8]Moore, p. 201.
[9]Moore, p. 214.
[10]Moore citing Weber, p. 229.
[11]Moore, p. 230.

specifically as missionary apologetic: he would convince Jews how much better Christianity is than Judaism.[12]

Weber's influence, to be sure, never matched that of his successor, Emil Schürer, whose History of the Jewish People in the Times of Jesus Christ formed the most influential account of Judaism in the German language, and in its English translation, for the larger part of the Christian world.[13]

Schürer's "Judaism" consists of the Law (meaning, the Torah) and the Messianic expectation. In his account of "life under the law," Schürer treated the motive for religion as "essential external, the result was an incredible externalizing of the religious and moral life, the whole of which is drawn down into the juristic sphere."[14] Schürer states, "And all this trivial and perverted zeal professes to be the true and right religion. The more pains men took, the more they believed that they gained the favor of God." Schürer substantiates his picture by showing how heavy a burden the Torah laid on Israel, describing in detail a variety of regulations. Here Moore judges the matter once more as an apologetic:

> "Life under the Law" was conceived not as a chapter in the history of Judaism but as a topic of Christian apologetic; it was written to prove by the highest Jewish authority that the strictures on Judaism in the Gospels and the Pauline Epistles are fully justified.[15]

The upshot was that, so far as dialogue with Judaism was concerned, the Christian party found itself well-armed for the fray: no dialogue but a war of extermination. Judaism really was no religion at all. Schürer's successor, Bousset, had this to say, in Moore's words:

> The God of Judaism in that age was withdrawn from the world, supramundane, extramundane, transcendent. "The prophetic preaching

---

[12]Moore, p. 231. Moore conducts his own dispute with Weber (p. 233): "Weber's antithesis between the transcendent god of Jewish theology and the contrary in Christian theology shows how little he knew about either the history or the content of Christian dogma."

[13]Moore's *Judaism* (Cambridge, 1927) was intended as a systematic refutation, and Jews vastly appreciated the work. But its influence on Christian thinking about Judaism can be described as merely marginal. Judaism would be described from Schürer onward in pretty much the terms Schürer, standing in mid-flood of a great river, set forth.

[14]Moore, p. 239.

[15]Moore, p. 240. Moore does not suggest that much of the Lutheran Evangelic attack on "Judaism" served the second purpose of discrediting any other "legalistic" religion, of which the leading candidate must be Roman Catholicism. On the mode of Protestant scholarship in religion serving as a medium for anti-Catholic polemic, see now Jonathan Z. Smith, *Divine Drudgery* (Chicago, 1991: University of Chicago Press), who shows that much of the comparative study of Greco-Roman pagan and Christian religions yields a sustained polemic on how the pure faith was corrupted by its Catholicization.

of the exaltation and uniqueness of Jehovah became the dogma of an abstract, transcendent monotheism." "God is no more in the world, the world no more in God." "What is most completely original and truly creative in the preaching of Jesus comes out most strongly and purely when he proclaims God the heavenly Father." "The later Judaism had neither in name nor in fact the faith of the Father-God; it could not possibly rise to it. And as the whole 'Gesetzesfrömmigkeit' of Judaism is based upon its increasingly transcendent conception of God, so the new conception introduced by Jesus is the ground of a wholly new type of piety."[16]

Moore observes that the sources on the strength of which Bousset describes "Judaism" were documents to which Judaism "never conceded any authority," namely, apocryphal and pseudepigraphic writings, "while he discredits and largely ignores those which it has always regarded as normative." In so stating, of course, Moore in 1922 pointed toward the work he would bring to successful publication five years later in his Judaism.

Moore might well have observed, also, that the caricature framed by this invention of "Judaism" served the Protestant polemic against Roman Catholic Christianity. The invented Judaism presented to humanity

> an arid wasteland of legalistic works-righteousness, with an emphasis on merit and achievement, so that one's good works oughtweigh the bad works in the final eschatological evaluation of behavior. In short, Judaism was thought to be a religion of scoreboard mathematics. Easy parallels were then drawn between the formalism and bankruptcy of...Judaism and similar characterizations of sixteenth-century Christianity, against which Luther...reacted.[17]

More than a single purpose was served, therefore, in the invention of Judaism, but, among the many, dialogue was not one of them. In fact, if Christians really supposed their Judaic conversation partners were robots of the law, who added up the commandments they did and subtracted their transgressions, so coming up with a salvation via arithmetic, I cannot understand why in the world they would have found such people worthy of more than a civil good morning. But why a dialogue with such folk?

We find ourselves confronted with only one possible judgment: there has never been a Judaeo-Christian dialogue so far as Christians claimed to be party to a dialogue. From earliest times to the present Christians have invented a Judaism with which they proposed to conduct not a

---

[16]Moore, p. 242.

[17]Bruce W. Longenecker, *Eschatology and the Covenant. A Comparison of 4 Ezra and Romans 1-11* (Sheffield, 1991: Journal for the Study of the New Testament Supplement Series 57), pp. 14-15.

dialogue but a monologue. So far as people made up dialogues, for example, Justin with Trypho, or so far as theologians or scholars imagined that they were arguing one side of a debate with a real opponent, we have to classify them as either misguided or hypocritical. Moore's characterization of the entire history of Christian writing on Judaism points toward the latter conclusion: "In all this time no attempt had been made by Christian scholars to present Judaism in the age which concerned them most...as a whole and as it was in and for itself.... When in the nineteenth century the study of Judaism was in some measure revived, the actuating motive was to find in it the milieu of early Christianity."[18] In this regard the modern period proves capable of the greatest inventions, as Moore says, "...nowhere is a suggestion made that in this respect [abstract monotheism, or a transcendent idea of God as the Absolute] the Jewish idea of God differed from the Christian. So it is also with the 'legalism' which for the last fifty years have become the very definition and the all-sufficient condemnation of Judaism. It is not a topic of the older polemic; indeed, I do not recall a place where it is even mentioned...legalism as a system of religion, not to say as the essence of Judaism, no one [before modern times] seems to have discovered."

Why then should Christians have imagined that they conducted a dialogue with Judaism? And why, given their sustained and governing concern with the refutation of "Judaism" and the conversion of the Jews, why imagine that what they were writing fell into the category of "dialogue" at all? An early convention, theological apologetics in the form of dialogue, turned out to define an entire genre of writing and mode of thinking about "Judaism." First invented as a category, then given categorical definition, this "Judaism" bore no relationship to any Judaic religious system, its Torah and its piety alike. The Judaeo-Christian dialogue on the Christian side aimed from antiquity to its moral disgrace in the person of Karl Ludwig Schmidt in Nazi Germany at only one goal: the conversion of the Jews. So far as Christianity was concerned, "Judaism" once invented served, much as did "Pharisees" for Jesus, as an ever-to-be-humiliated debate partner: the perpetual loser, the example of what not to say, be, or do. Under such conditions, the last thing Christianity wanted was to conduct a dialogue with not its fabricated "Judaism," but "the Torah of Moses, our rabbi," and any comparison or contrast between "Christianity" and "the whole Torah: what is hateful to yourself do not do to your neighbor, all the rest is commentary, now go study" – any such contrast hardly serves an apologetic polemic in behalf of Christianity.

---

[18]Moore, p. 252.

Through time, no one imagined a dialogue between Jesus and Hillel, or between Paul and Yohanan ben Zakkai; but there one can imagine dialogue. In the fabricated category and the invented dialogue, by contrast, the conditions of dialogue are not only not met, they are not even admitted. The Christian party never proposed to take seriously the position of even the "Judaism" it invented; from antiquity to modern times, the Christian party violently denied the integrity of the Judaic; and the Christian party most certainly did not propose to accept responsibility for the outcome of discussion. In the first two thousand years of the Judaeo-Christian dialogue, Christianity never, never once contemplated conceding the legitimacy of the other's viewpoint. But in the world today, much has changed, and, for the first time, we are now seeing a serious exchange between faithful Christians and practicing Judaists – Jews who keep Judaism. Each party is learning to take the other's religion seriously. For neither is it easy. This brief account of the shape of scholarship in the century that is now closing explains why.

13

Niehoff's Joseph

The Figure of Joseph in Post-Biblical Jewish Literature. By Maren Niehoff. *Arbeiten zur Geschichte des Antiken Judentums und des Urchristentums* XVI (Leiden-New York-Köln, 1992: E.J. Brill).

A revised doctoral thesis in Comparative Midrash written with Geza Vermes at Oxford University, the study deals with "the hermeneutics of the ancient interpretations of the biblical story...to explore the new features and the diverse hermeneutic functions which are attributed to Joseph in these early interpretations." The author examines prior studies of Joseph in post-biblical writings, dismissing each in turn (Kugel's *In Potiphar's House. The Interpretative Life of Biblical Texts*, 1990, is casually shunted aside for having "paid less attention to the hermeneutic function of the figure," rather tracing "select motifs" and detecting their exegetical origin!). There follow some brief allusions to hermeneutics, yielding,

> Interpreting an interpretation means to unravel the complex interrelation between the authority of the text and the thought world of the interpreter. Primarily, the exegete's choice of key passages on which he will base his interpretation requires explanation. Subsequently, the exegesis of each biblical item needs to be analyzed also in the context of the interpreter's general views. Proceeding in this fashion, it is possible to shed light on the way in which each reading...of the text is generated by the specific concerns of the exegete. Conversely, the function of the biblical figure of Joseph in different Jewish contexts will emerge.

That is the program of the work. After an account of the biblical Joseph (narrative rhythm and the central points of the story, the narrative rhythm of the interpretations, the characterization of Joseph, sparks of late biblical and early post-biblical exegesis), three readings are then presented: Philo's Figures of Joseph, Josephus's Joseph, and the figure of Joseph in Genesis Rabbah. The book ends with three pages of summary and conclusion.

Philo's Joseph sets forth the biography of a statesman, so we are given an account of Philo's theoretical remarks on "lives" and his own political background, with some thoughts on "how this might influence his biography of a politician." There is a substantial paraphrase of Philo's treatment of chapters in the life of Joseph, with various observations and remarks on this and that. The author concludes,

> Philo reshapes the biblical figure in accordance with his concepts of both the "allegorical" and the "political" biography.... Those passages which Philo himself introduces as allegorical incorporate diverse philosophical material on the role of the politician. The biblical story consequently recedes into the background and the function of the politician also receives more ambivalent notices. On the whole, Philo presents an idealized image of Joseph and accommodates the biblical material to his preconceived ideals of political personalities.

The treatment of Josephus's Joseph reviews various chapters in Josephus's corpus in which Joseph makes an appearance: Joseph and his father, Joseph and his brothers, Joseph and women, Joseph and the Egyptians. Josephus's treatment of these four relationships are surveyed item by item. Joseph's youth is treated sympathetically. As to relations with the brothers, "Because of the numerous parallels to his own life, Josephus has paraphrased them in distinctly autobiographical terms. The exegetical impetus is here astonishingly similar to that of his Vita; he is concerned in both works with the character of the protagonist and defends his impeccable behavior by reference to divinely inspired dreams." As to women, Josephus treats Joseph with Potiphar's wife in a "pietistic image." "It has typically Palestinian features and should not be overlooked besides the more overt Hellenistic motifs." The author concludes that Josephus's interpretation "often reflects the narrator's own concerns."

The figure of Joseph in Genesis Rabbah reviews a variety of topics. The author does not find coherence or program in Genesis Rabbah: "Among the sources discussed here, GR is the most heterogeneous and associative interpretation of the Joseph story. It thus lacks overall coherence, even more than Philo's literal and allegorical account. Most obviously, the exegetical elaborations here on the figure of Joseph are not presented as part of an overall story but rather as direct interpretations of small units of biblical text." The author then reviews "scattered, yet not wanton references. The question of how exegesis and Weltanschauung are interwoven also becomes a dominant concern." There follows a survey of the numerous passages in Genesis Rabbah that deal with Josephus, with footnotes on various items throughout. The author concludes that Joseph is not idealized "but some of his shortcomings are highlighted instead." The encounter with Potiphar's wife is the climax of the story. "Like Philo and Josephus, GR's description of Joseph's administration in Egypt also discloses some perceptions about the Hebrew in the Diaspora."

As to the method of characterization, "GR varies significantly from earlier presentations of the biblical story. These differences partly derive from the exegetical nature of this midrash, which limits the use of authorial remarks or explanatory insertions of thoughts and feelings in the flow of the narrative" but substitutes dialogue instead. "The most frequent literary figure is God who on numerous occasions intervenes with the human agents. In this way, most ethical issues receive a religious dimension. In contrast to later midrash...the theological concerns of GR are expressed with charming directness and thus further serve educational purposes." The conclusion of the book summarizes the foregoing, in a perfunctory reprise.

Comparative Midrash, here as in other tiresome exercises of the method, yields a collection of observations about this and that, but industrious hunting and gathering, paraphrase and arranging things in some sort of suitable order, produces nothing of intellectual interest. The author ends with the banality, "We have seen how the figure of Joseph functions in the different intellectual environments and how it is employed for the individual purposes of each exegete." True – but self-evident. Who ever claimed otherwise? The dissertation recapitulates a method that has commonly yielded massive collections and arrangements of things, along with footnotes on one thing and another, but no insight of any weight or substance. Whether or not the author knows the scholarly traditions of Philo and Josephus, I cannot say, but of Genesis Rabbah she is ignorant. Her characterization of the document as "atomistic, heterogeneous, and merely a set of ad hoc exegetical elaborations" is simply false. It has been amply demonstrated that the document is coherent, cogent, and systematic in its pursuit of its framers' goals. If Niehoff sees Genesis Rabbah as "atomistic," it is because she is alarmingly ignorant of the character of the document and scholarship on it. That is what comes of collecting and arranging whatever a document says about a given topic, then moving on to the next, and the next – till the degree has been gained. Enough has been quoted to justify the judgment, also, that the author writes lifeless, clumsy prose. This superficial, incoherent, and disappointing dissertation serves no important scholarly purpose.

14

Stern's *Parables*

Parables in Midrash. Narrative and Exegesis in Rabbinic Literature.
By David Stern (Cambridge, 1991: Harvard University Press).
ISBN No. 0-674-65447-1.

The intimidating title, promising to cover four enormous subjects, "parables," "midrash," "narrative," and "exegesis," the work in fact is a revised dissertation, with the strengths and weaknesses of the genre. It is compendious and very well researched; it contains a large number of interesting observations of detail. But it is more of a collection of information and opinions on a number of topics than a well-argued, thoughtfully crafted statement of a particular proposition on the general theme at hand. The bridge from the detail to the main point proves shaky. The result is an occasionally interesting but rather prolix and unfocused work, a bit pretentiously claiming to accomplish more than is actually achieved, but, still, valuable for what in fact is given.

Dealing with the mashal as it occurs in two dozen passages in Lamentations Rabbah, which are given in an appendix in the Hebrew texts in two recensions and in translation as well, the monograph, on the strength of which its author gained a tenured professorship at the University of Pennsylvania, deals with these topics: composition and exegesis, rhetoric, poetics, thematics, the mashal in context, and the mashal in Hebrew literature. The mashal, though represented by a remarkably tiny sample, is treated as uniform, the representations of the form in various, diverse documents not being differentiated; so, too, "midrash" is treated as everywhere the same thing, being defined as "the study and interpretation of Scripture by the Rabbis in Late Antiquity." Consequently, the contemporary tools of form analysis and criticism, on the one side, and of the systematic differentiation of documents by their indicative traits of rhetoric, topic, and logic of coherence, on the other, are denied the author. The result is a rather general and unanalytical treatment of the subject. But that does not deny the book a hearing, since the author provides a full, though somewhat repetitious, account of the scholarly literature and problems, and his treatment of the texts he discusses, if a bit prolix, contains interesting ad hoc observations. A brief survey of the main points yields sound reason to value the book.

COMPOSITION AND EXEGESIS: The mashal or parable is to be distinguished from a fable: "A fable utilizes anthropomorphic animals or plants to portray the particularly theriomorphic or phytomorphic features of human behavior. A parable suggests a sort of parallel between an imagined fictional event and an immediate, 'real' situation confronting the parable's author and his audience." Parables in Rabbinic literature are "preserved not in narrative contexts but in exegetical ones, as part of midrash....There is no important formal or functional difference between meshalim recorded as parts of narratives and those presented as exegeses of midrashim of verses." Parables are to be distinguished from allegories, on the one side, and the ma'aseh, or precedent ("example or exemplum, an anecdote told to exemplify or illustrate a lesson") on the other. While Stern concedes that the explanation that accompanies the narrative of the mashal, called the nimshal, first occurs only in Medieval documents, he includes in his discussion a full account of that quite distinct development. Indeed, much of the chapter on poetics invokes the nimshal, so we are asked to understand Rabbinic literature of late antiquity only by appeal to literary forms not found in the writings of late antiquity, a rather confusing mode of analysis.

RHETORIC: The occasions of the mashal are spelled out. The mashal serves for three purposes: illustration, "secret speech," and "rhetorical narrative." Stern sees the mashal as "a story that turns allusiveness to effect in order to persuade its audience of the value of a certain idea or approach or feeling." The key word here is "allusiveness," which Stern does not define with clarity.

POETICS: The center of the book is the interest in "the relationship between exegesis and narrative. The Rabbinic mashal can be defined as a parabolic narrative that claims to be exegesis and serves the purposes of ideology." That definition would prove more compelling if it did not serve equally well a variety of other forms in the rabbinic literature. Much of the rest of the discussion concerns the nimshal, as I said, leaving open a variety of questions concerning the mashal in late antiquity. But the results are not wholly without interest. Stern's most interesting point is this: "among the most distinctive characteristics of the mashal's poetics is the strategically placed point of discontinuity, technically called a gap." Much of the exposition, alas, proceeds to "disparities between narrative and nimshal," leaving us once more somewhat puzzled as to

Stern's program. Lamentations Rabbah is not a medieval document, but much of the exposition of the data spills over into the consideration of kinds of mashal writing that came to the surface much later than that document; that presents a considerable puzzle, if we want to grasp precisely what Stern wishes to say, indeed, even to define that about which he is writing; sometimes late antique writing, sometimes medieval; sometimes, indeed, the mashal in particular, other times Midrash in general.

Indeed, the confusion is intensified by recurring efforts to define the mashal, each fabricated for its context, thus, later in the same chapter, "the mashal is essentially mimetic narrative. It is about events and characters, and particularly one character – the king, or God. Beyond all else, the mashal represents the greatest effort to imagine God in all Rabbinic literature." That definition bears more enthusiasm than enlightenment, since the conception that the "king" in the Mashal means "God" in particular relies upon the particular cases at hand; the point is not so much demonstrated as alleged with gusto.

THEMATICS: "The midrashic mashal is a type of ideological narrative, which seeks to impress the truth and validity of a worldview...upon its audience. In any particular mashal, that worldview is refracted within the mashal's specific message, its theme or thesis." This new definition would prove more useful if it did not define equally well every other type of writing in Rabbinic literature. Thus the chapter treats, further, "apologetics, polemics, eulogy and consolation, complaint, regret and warning," and on and on; that is, various mashals are classified in various ways. None of the classifications encompasses only the mashal, so the results are indeterminate and again somewhat puzzling.

THE MASHAL IN CONTEXT: "In their seemingly haphazard positions in these collections [Talmud, Midrash], the meshalim are no different from the rest of the contents. The structure and composition of these documents are famously difficult to identify. Despite a few recent attempts to demonstrate the 'integrity' – the formal and thematic coherence – of the various midrashic collections, they remain to all appearances more like anthologies of traditional Rabbinic interpretations that an anonymous editor has selected and recorded than like self-contained, logically structured books in their own right." Stern does not then see any differences of a general character between, for example, Sifra and Leviticus Rabbah, both on Leviticus; or the Tosefta and the Talmud of the Land of Israel, both on the Mishnah. This awry view makes difficult for him the determination of the context in which the mashal does, or does not, occur, why here, not there, being questions that, by definition, he finds he cannot answer. That further accounts for his difficulty in seeing formal differences in the mashal as it occurs in the several distinct documents. So he concedes at the outset, "the 'contextual' interpretation of midrash – reading a midrashic passage in its literary, documentary context – is a very problematic venture. The larger literary units that we most comfortably use in reading and interpreting the meaning of literary works – the document as a whole, chapters, even subsections in chapters or discrete narrative or legal sections in a work like the Bible – do not constitute significant units of meaning for midrash."

That explains why Stern sees the units as "fragmentary, miscellaneous, and atomistic." Other views of the documentary character of the Rabbinic corpus are not examined, and the remainder of the chapter replicates in detail the deeply confused character of Stern's reading of the whole. That makes all the more regrettable Stern's failure to understand his own results. After a systematic study, he concludes,

> The passages just discussed all show how midrashic discourse is organized: in recognizable units of discourse, in literary forms like the petihta, the mashal, the enumeration, the series. These forms comprise the genres or subgenres of midrash. They constitute its language, and they maintain themselves in midrashic literature formally and rhetorically, even when they combine with one another. The combinatory pattern of these units is essentially additive. The petihta form provides a frame for the mashal, which in turn is made to serve the special rhetoric of the petihta; but neither form is required to surrender its distinctive structure or formal identity when it joins with the other. Similarly, a mashal can be constructed in the image of an aggadic narrative or ma'aseh, with its own lesson or homily, but it can simultaneously be employed so as to exploit its own parabolic strengths as a paradigmatic, representational narrative.

Quite what Stern means to say is not entirely clear, but the main point is precisely that of form analysis: there are fixed forms, they do govern, and they characterize one kind of writing, rather than some other. Having produced exactly the results that form analysis of documents has yielded, Stern is left unable to explain his own data. That is because he has not come to grips with the position he rejects without discussion, quite out of hand, that documents make a difference. Once he has declared the literature chaotic, he cannot recognize the points of order he himself identifies. The concluding chapter, "The Mashal in Hebrew Literature," need not detain us, since it is tacked on, dissertation style, to cover whatever might have been left out in the substantive chapters.

The strengths of Stern's dissertation are his own. They lie in his ad hoc observations about this and that. In his rambling, sometimes unfocused discussions of the specific passages in Lamentations Rabbah he has chosen to discuss in detail, he makes numerous interesting observations. Though this is not a work of mature scholarship, it is more than a mere collection and arrangement of information, and we may hope for better things to come from its author. The weaknesses of the dissertation are those of the genre; Stern proves a good graduate student, thorough in compiling opinions on various topics, but embarrassingly selective in dealing with published results that the author does not wish to address at all. He covers a broad range of subjects, but has not got a well-crafted thesis to present to make the topical program cohere and form an important proposition and thesis upon a well-crafted problem. So the work is at the same time too general and rambling and altogether too specific, not bridging the gap between the detail and the main point. As a dissertation it certainly is above average; as an account of the parable, this overweight book is more encyclopaedic than interesting.

Part Five

OBSERVING SCANDINAVIAN JUDAISM,
LIVING AND DYING

15

Watching Judaism Die in Åbo

I went to shul the first Shabbat of my term as Visiting Research Professor at Åbo Akademi's Research Institute, just after Pessah. The Jewish community in Åbo, Finland's second largest city, numbers about 150; perhaps 20 came to shul despite snow that morning (a shock to a Floridian), a good turnout, I thought. In this bilingual city, which Finns call Turku and Swedes Åbo, the Jews are Finnish (Suomi) speakers, but, having heard I'd been studying Swedish, they found me a Swedish language siddur. No one offered me a Humash, nor did anyone else have one.

After Shaharit, I found out why. Here, in a shul with separate seating (the one woman present was a mute gentile who found herself attracted to Judaism, Jewish women knew better than to come to shul, a men's club where they were not wanted), with a completely Orthodox davening, they had instituted only a single reform in an otherwise unimpeccable Orthodoxy. They skipped the Torah reading.

No one explained why, the davening was so intense that there was no talking from start to finish – a span of perhaps 45 minutes; I had been placed in the position of honor, facing, and six inches from, the front wall, so I could not ask many questions. They just went from the qaddish after Shaharit to Yequm purqan, Ashre, Qaddish, and on into Mussaf. I was supposed to understand what was not going to happen. On the wall, the announcement of Parashat Hashavua announced that it was Shabbat Mevorekhim, and that Shemini was the sidrah. Maybe so, but not that week. They repeated Mussaf and said Alenu, and a mourner said qaddish. The ark was never opened, Anim Zmirot was not sung.

Readers at home in the Judaic liturgy will require no explanation; others will find it sufficient to know that here, in a synagogue of Orthodox Jews, most of them of Polish or Russian origin, native Finns, three or four generations in Turku, men come to the synagogue on the

247

Sabbath out of a deep sense of Jewish loyalty, but omit from their worship the reason that Judaism specifies for coming to the synagogue at all. I maintain that, on the Sabbath following Passover, the only synagogue in the world, from Reconstructionist to Orthodox, Reform to Hasidic, that omitted to open the Torah and declaim its contents to assembled Israel, was the one I had stumbled upon in Turku.

The Talmud is explicit that people may say their prayers at home, not in a quorum, except for the requirement of hearing the Torah declaimed; for that, they must come to the synagogue (or form a quorum of their own, which is the same thing). When we say our prayers, we speak to God; when the Torah is read, as everyone knows, God speaks to us, holy Israel, that is, Jews made holy by the sanctifying act of accepting the Torah – in that place, at that time.

The synagogue in Turku has had three rabbis; their pictures were on the wall. All are now deceased, and I felt sorry for them; they had left nothing. Today there is no rabbi, except for the High Holy Days. For some seventy-five years, yeshiva trained rabbis had lived and worked here.

The people today maintain the tradition of those three rabbis who had served them for some three generations, from before the beginning of this century, through the time when a sizable building had been constructed in the expectation of a large and lasting Jewish community in the town, to a while ago, when the last rabbi concluded his service. So what tradition had taken root through the ministry of these rabbis, staunchly Orthodox, bearded, yeshiva products all? They clearly had done a fine job of teaching people how to daven, and we may assume the people understood some of what they were saying at a rapid clip. So the forms had taken root. But the substance – the tradition of not only learning in the Torah but also reverence for the declamation of the Torah in the holy community of Israel – that proved another matter. The forms of Orthodox endured; the substance – Torah study – did not.

After services there was a qiddush, some stale cake and kichel, over which the presiding laymen said a motzi (much to my surprise, the kichel not qualifying as bread!). I was introduced, in Swedish as a gesture of courtesy to me. There was no point in speaking in Hebrew; the only Hebrew-speaking person present was an Israeli married to a Finnish gentile (who told me he was unemployed and living with his Finnish in-laws). So I spoke in English, very slowly. What I said was simple. To people without a rabbi, I decided to speak as a rabbi who'd never served a congregation.

I told them, as a rabbi, that I'd visited synagogues throughout the world, and learned something new in every one of them. But here I learned what I did not know was there to be learned. It is that there is in this world an Orthodox synagogue that assembles for Shabbat worship and leaves the Torah orphaned in its ark. Not having a rabbi, lay people could think that wrong was right. But the simple fact is, we are Israel, holy Israel, by reason of the Torah, and without the Torah, we have no reason to come into being at all. If the community's two Torah readers were fatigued because Pessah had just ended, as I was told, then it was time for others to learn what it takes to do the work properly. A Jewish community without pride and self-respect, I concluded, sustained itself over time, even while giving Judaism – the Torah – an indecent burial indeed. The least we owe ourselves is to honor our reason for being.

I sat down after perhaps three minutes – I do not give long speeches. This had made its mark. Several people ran for the door, scowling. Alone I found my coat, and alone I walked out into the snow and gloom of a Finnish April. Only then did I remember, they also had not counted the omer. No one told them to.

The qiddush was over. So, in Turku/Åbo, is the life of Judaism. Before the prayers began, the head of the community had told me that with an aging community and no children, he saw no future, unless Russian Jews chose to settle in Turku and repopulate the synagogue.

Walking home through the snow and the gloom, I could think of no reason to care. Judaism does not die for demographic reasons; whether there are more Jews or less Jews hardly matters, since in the end we cannot compete with the Chinese. I was present for the death of Judaism in Åbo, but, in the nature of things, I also was the only mourner. To mourn, you have to know a death has taken place.

Yes, that but one other thought. Rabbis really do matter. In most communities, and all synagogues outside of Orthodoxy, they are the only Jews who, so far as Judaism is concerned, know right from wrong. And some of them will even tell the people when they're wrong. Without rabbis, Jews can "survive," one year forgetting the omer, the next year deciding it is too much trouble to learn to read the Torah, and on into the gloomy future. And then, when they do survive, I wondered, does it matter – to them, to other Jews, to God? Well, I hoped, at least to God.

But then, I think for the first time since my ordination as a rabbi by Jewish Theological Seminary in 1960, I felt proud to be a rabbi. That calling really does make a difference – and not only to God, but also to the Torah, and sometimes, even, to Israel, the Jewish people. That night, I wrote to Rabbi Joel Meyers, executive secretary of the Rabbinical Assembly, accepting his invitation to honorary membership in that organization – as a gesture of respect to the rabbinate. For on that one day, I had been a rabbi, too, along with the three who, looking down from Heaven, must have wondered what they had accomplished with their lives – a synagogue where people daven beautifully, forgetting only the Torah.

16

Thinking about Judaism in Stockholm: The Choices, the Future

Speaking to you in Stockholm in the Swedish language, or to the Jews in Sao Paulo in Portuguese, or to those in Paris in French, and so on through Italian, German, Spanish, not to mention Hebrew in Tel Aviv and American throughout my own country, I mean to make a statement not through what I say but through what I do. That statement does not concern myself. It is the statement that it is right and proper for us Jews to swim in the mainstream of world civilization. We form a principal part of the cultural lives of the many countries where we live. We take part in the politics of those countries. I do not mean merely that we vote, but that we take a very active role in politics; for instance, 10 percent of the United States Senators are Jewish, and 7 percent of the members of the House of Representatives, though we are scarcely 2 percent of the population. In the Senate of my own state, Florida, upwards of eight of the forty members are Jewish, though the Jews are only 5 percent of the population of the state. Books Jews write in the western languages flow into the literature of those languages and help shape writing.

In higher education, though excluded a generation ago, Jews now take on the presidencies of the ancient universities of America. And the pattern repeats itself, in politics, culture, education, the components of the mainstream of national life, throughout the west. The State of Israel was meant to normalize the Jews, turn them into a political, empowered entity like other nations or peoples of the world, and so it did. But so did the United States and Canada, Australia and France, Britain and Mexico, and most of the other countries of the Golah. Even Russia, of all places, now has its Jewish martyr to Russian democracy, buried with national honors by a rabbi in Moscow.

A hundred years ago, if I wanted to identify with Jews I might meet throughout the world, I should not have had to know eight or ten languages, but only one, Yiddish. And I should not have traveled to every continent, as I have, from Latin America to Scandinavia, Sao Paolo to Stockholm. One trip would have sufficed, because approximately 90 percent of the Jews of the world spoke Yiddish and lived in Poland, Ukraine, White Russia, and the other lands of eastern Europe. And if we now can use English as the international Jewish language, with Hebrew the language of education and culture, then, at that time, with Hebrew yet to accomplish its renaissance, I should have used German as the medium of culture. A hundred years ago, the Jews did not form part of the mainstream of life and culture. Our grandparents' grandparents spoke a Jewish language, Yiddish. They dressed in clothing that was regarded as distinctively Jewish. They ate food that they deemed Jewish and they would not eat the food that gentiles ate. They lived in large Jewish settlements, towns that were a third or half or three-quarters Jewish in population. They practiced Jewish trades. They read Jewish books, sang Jewish music, danced Jewish dances, fought among themselves about the issues of Jewish existence. They were Jews and only Jews. The politics of the democracies excluded Jews or treated them as exotic, defining them as a problem. Cultural life received Jews on condition that they relinquished all marks of difference: English but not Jewish.

And when it came to religion, of course, the Jews' religion, Judaism, scarcely communicated with the world, or the world with it. Jews regarded Christianity in a wholly negative light. Christianity reciprocated. At home, rabbis were not clergymen like other clergymen but defined their work in categories into which priests or ministers scarcely fit. The religion, Judaism, defined the Jews in a way that entirely fit the cultural and social and political circumstances of Judaic existence. That is to say, just as the Jews were only Jewish, were always Jewish, and never conceived of themselves in any other framework but the Jewish and Judaic one, so the religion, Judaism, answered the question, who is this Israel, the people that dwells apart? And what is the meaning of the life of this unique people, absolutely separate and distinct from all the nations of the world? So if I had come to you, I would have spoken to you in Yiddish. You would have perceived me as one of yourselves, like you in all ways but the circumstance of residence somewhere else. But where I lived would make slight difference; how I lived in my place of residence would have corresponded to how you lived in yours, whether in Johannesburg of 1893 or New York of 1893 or London of 1893 or Warsaw, Cracow, Kiev, or the other metropolitan centers of holy Israel, the Jewish people.

The measure of change is easy to define; the reasons hardly require specification at all. Let us concentrate on the facts of change. Now if we have a common language, it is English, not Hebrew, not Yiddish. So we speak the international language of humanity. If we have common clothing, no one can tell from what we wear that we are Jews; our clothes are those of the world at large. Not many of us walk around with covered heads. If we read the same books, they are the international best sellers, and if we talk about the same subjects, they concern pretty much the same subjects we should talk about with gentiles of the same age group or class in society or educational and professional level. Jews play a major role in the formation of education and culture, leading the universities and staffing them, even in the humanities, whence values flow. Not only so, but our rabbis are comparable to the clergy of other religions. Our worship services include the use of the languages of the countries where we live; I have sung Adon Olam in Portuguese and at my seder have had Jews from Mexico read their parts in Spanish, from Brazil in Portuguese, and from Paris in French.

The contrast between the way we were and the way we are may be summed up in a simple way. As an athlete of sorts, a swimmer under the Florida sun pretty much every day, I prefer the metaphors of my own metier, so I state very simply, we Jews now swim in the mainstream. Whether we think that is good or not good, whether we should change things or want to keep them as they are, we have made the decision to be like everybody else, except in the ways in which we are not like everybody else. That swimming in the mainstream represents a decision should not be taken for granted. Many Jews object, and the present social policy of Jews throughout the world, including the State of Israel, provokes considerable debate. It is obviously with a sense of surprise but also pleasure that I speak of the integration of the Jews into world civilization, politics, and culture. But in North America, Western Europe, and the State of Israel tens of thousands of Jews do not want to swim in the mainstream. In the State of Israel they distinguish themselves by their clothing, their schooling, their way of life and their profession. In America they speak Yiddish. In Western Europe they form tight little communities, apart from the rest of Jewry, rejecting the mainstream Orthodoxy that predominates. In fact, a great debate rages through Jewry between integrationists and segregationists. The integrationist position is clear – we are speaking in Swedish together.

The segregationist position takes the view that the Jews cannot and should not swim in the mainstream. Some argue that the Jews in the mainstream will assimilate not only in the ways that they want, in language and culture, but in the ways that they do not want, in religion and in family, so that in the end, the powerful currents of the mainstream will sweep the Jews away into that vast ocean of undifferentiated humanity that in all languages listens to the same loud music, in all cuisines eats the same fast food, in all cultures lives and dies for pretty much the same worldly goods. Others in the segregationist camp take the view that even if the Jews can sustain themselves in the mainstream, they should not do so. We Jews are "holy Israel," the people whom God has called into being at Sinai, and our task is not to be like the gentiles but to be unlike the gentiles; to live a holy way of life; to study the Torah; to pray; to live out the eternal rhythms of the week with its climax at the Sabbath; of the year with its holy seasons of sanctification; of nature, with its new moons; and of eternity in the here and now. And, the segregationists hold, we live in God's dominion, we have no place and should want none in the nations of the world. As you know, that position is taken not only in the Golah, but in the State of Israel by the nonZionist political parties, and they represent more than a negligible proportion of the population of the country.

Now we err if we imagine that segregationist Judaism speaks out of some dim past to people who do not know the world that we know. And we are wrong if we suppose that, if those people knew what we know, they would do what we do. Segregationist Jews read the same newspapers, watch the same television if they wish, read the same history, know the same science, that we do. They know what we call "the modern world" because they live in the same time and place that we do. They choose segregation, they do not merely inherit it, and they do so because they want to. They have seen the world into which we have flowed, and they want no part of it. They actively seek sanctification, they define their lives around the Torah, and they regard Torah study and not science as the highest form of knowledge, culture, and science. This is not by default but by choice, and the choice for many, the generation of return, is one of rejection of the one in favor of acceptance of the other. When you go among the Lubovitch Judaic groups in the United States, while you hear Yiddish, their chosen language, it is spoken by people with an American accent, who speak good old American English just the same way the rest of the Jews do.

The debate in Jewry between integration and segregation forms the counterpart to equally vivid struggles in Islam and Christianity. What we stupidly call "Islamic fundamentalism" represents a movement to build the theological Nation of Islam in the here and now, and what we call the Muslim moderates – equally religious but in a different way – turn out to form an ideal of culture and politics in the context of Islam that is remarkably similar in its outlines and structure to the ideal of culture and politics of the Zionist religious parties in the State of Israel, or of integrationist Orthodoxy in Western Europe and of Reform,

Conservative, and so-called Modern Orthodoxy in the United States. So, too, the battle between Muslim "fundamentalism" and "moderation" or between integrationist and segregationist Judaisms forms the counterpart to the struggle between Christian fundamentalism and what we call in the United States the mainstream denominations. The Christian fundamentalists hear God's word in Scripture, define their lives, and their childrens' education, around direct encounter with God or the holy spirit, and form their own judgments, in light of the Bible, about the claims of science and even technology. They, too, read the same newspapers as the mainstream Christians, vote in the same elections, work in the same economy. Indeed, they are in the aggregate better educated than the American population in general, and they certainly are more articulate about the things that they profess.

What is at stake, therefore, vastly transcends the Jewish condition. The issue of swimming in the mainstream as we Jews have chosen to formulate matters – Jewish survival on terms other than complete segregation – turns out to confront Islam and Christianity, and the formulation of the issue in Islam and in Christianity differs in detail but not in character. For in fact, what divides Islam, Christianity, and Judaism is not segregation versus integration, as I put matters for Judaism, or fundamentalism versus modernism, as Christianity will have it (whether Protestant or Roman Catholic), or Muslim fundamentalism versus democratic secular states, as we in the West wrongly formulate matters. The issue is not particular to the various religious groups; it addresses all of them. And in this international debate within the great transnational religious communities, Judaism, Islam, Christianity, the stakes are high, the outcome still in doubt. Right now it seems that the fundamentalists in Christianity, the Muslims out to build the Nation of Islam, and the Judaic integrationists, hold all the high cards. They exhibit the enthusiasm that the integrationists call fanaticism, they fill the media with their violence, whether demonstrations against archaeology in Jerusalem, or against abortion in the United States, or against tourism in Egypt. Their numbers appear to grow, the integrationists to diminish. So people suppose that the wave of the future flows toward the past. But that is because they wrongly imagine that, in the case of Judaism, the more Orthodox, the more antiquated but authentic; in the case of Christianity, the more fundamentalist, the more devoted to Jesus Christ; in the case of Islam, the more devoted to Islam, the closer to the message of the prophet.

I leave it to the theologians (including myself in a different guise, and I do my theology in American English) to evaluate claims of authenticity, devotion, true faith. I leave to sociologists and political scientists the estimation of whether, indeed, the future will see Christian, Muslim, and

Judaic segregationism take over the world. Social science may tell us what is going to happen, and theology, what ought to happen. I want to say only what I hope happens and why I hope so.

Despite all that has happened in this dreadful century of ours, I hope that the path of integration shows the way forward for us all. I understand, I think, the aspirations of the Christian, Judaic, and Muslim segregationists, those who reject what they regard as the modern world while in fact forming an indicator of modernity. They read books that bear clear and present messages and want to realize those messages: the sanctification of holy Israel, for example, leaves no space for negotiation between integration and segregation. The segregationists have taken the measure of modern science and seen the triumph of the industrialization of murder in the death camps of Germany in World War II. They have taken the measure of modern values and have seen the triumph of the devaluation of human life in abortion upon demand. They have witnessed the disruption of the social order, of established patterns of human relationships and modes of raising children, and they have seen the result in the destruction of the family, so that more than half of all children in the United States and elsewhere now are raised without fathers, or even without parents at all, with catastrophic results for the psychological strength of the coming generation. Talk with the Muslim "fundamentalist," the Christian evangelicals, the Judaic segregationists in Yeshivas, and you will hear not ignorance of the world as it is but a reasoned, vigorous rejection of it. And that is not irrational but well reasoned and rigorously argued. For the segregationists, that complex of values and ideals, political attitudes and public policy for the family, education, culture, even sexuality, that we call "modernity" represents a world that they reject. They do not seek integration with that world but exclusion of it, isolation from it.

What have we integrationists to say in response? Our answer cannot take the path of a disingenuous response: modernity may be bad enough, but the age of faith was worse. The segregationists, after all, do accept the outcomes of modernity, contemporary medicine, for example; most of them fly in airplanes, drive cars, use computers, communicate by fax. So it is not modernity that the segregationists reject, but the condition of humanity in modernity. They choose segregation because they have had enough of the human condition of integration. To take the Judaic case once more, the Judaic segregationists find the study of the Torah more sanctifying, more ennobling, more fitting to the human condition of holy Israel, than any other study. Then the integrationists' task, in the Judaic setting, is to respond to that ideal. Again, the Judaic segregationists see nothing of value in gentile life, nothing of consequence in shared cultural or social or political enterprise with gentiles. Let them have theirs, and we keep ours. Then the integrationists' task in the Judaic setting is to explain what good there is in working with, and living among, gentiles. And if the matters of cultural and social policy be resolved, there still is the segregationist insistence that their vision of the human condition, and not the integrationists', matches the vision of God: this is how God wants things, our way, not your way. At stake, after all, is the language of faith, because the issues in the end take shape around the deepest concerns and commitments of human beings concerning what it means to be "in our image, after our likeness." If we cannot respond to Judaic segregationism in religious terms, then there is no response to be set forth. For Judaic segregationism does not represent merely a continuation of a dead past, as I have argued, nor a response to a problem of sociology or demography. At stake is what it means to be human in God's image: the language of segregationist and the language of integrationist Judaism comes from the same Torah and appeals to the same God. Here we conduct a religious debate about issues of religion.

But can we make the case for the integration of humanity that this is how God wants things, when the Quran, the Torah, and the Bible, all are set forth by obviously knowledgeable people who maintain otherwise? Does the human condition demand that we live not only among, but with, other people, different from ourselves? And is it the highest value that sanctification mean, holier than though, or can God have in mind something other when we contemplate the diversity of created humanity, all in God's image and after God's likeness? Those of you who follow American things will understand that in my own country, the issues of integration and segregation burn hot, not because anyone wishes to push blacks back into their corner any more, but because many people, of various races, religious, and ethnic origin, seek preference and privilege by reason of ethnic or racial origin. But Europeans face precisely the same issue of integration versus segregation, Germans with Turkish Germans, French with African French, Italians with Somali Italians, to name three examples among many. The theological issues of integration versus segregation turn out to frame, in language of revelation, God, and God's will for humanity, the very crisis of public policy in culture and politics that all of the Western nations face in the matter of immigration, nationalism, and the determination of language, culture, and citizenship.

So what do we really conceive to nurture the human condition at its most authentic? Since I introduced the problem by reference to the discipline I have imposed upon myself of trying to speak to Jews in the natural sounds of the Jewish condition, whether Swedish or Spanish or Hebrew or American, let me turn once more to language. Here the issue is not one language or many, but whether we speak more than one language; we do not have the choice, the segregationists do not have the choice, of imposing one language upon all, any more than they can impose one religion upon all. Segregationism takes the view that connections to the other yield nothing of value, and that the outsider has nothing to say to us. Integrationism takes the view that the other has something to say, and that we have to learn to hear; we have to overcome the barriers of language and thought, because something on the other side of the wall is of value. Phrasing matters in these terms, of course, we are led directly to a discussion of this very matter in the Torah, where, in the tale of the tower of Babel, we find an explicit and profound reflection on the unity of humanity. You recall that when everybody spoke one language, then humanity formed the ambition to build a tower to reach heaven. But God laughed at the plan, thinking it arrogant, and confused their languages, so people spread out to all the ends of the world and no longer spoke the same words at all.

Speaking in the language of the Torah, then, we may say that God has not so formed us as to speak only one language, that is, our own. It is not good for humanity to want to be all alike – and to keep the outsider outside – because, the Torah says, that leads to arrogance, to building towers to heaven. In our framework, that means, the arrogance to think we can make a Holy Nation of Islam, making all things into one thing; a Holy People of Israel, dismissing the rest of humanity as faceless and lacking differentiation; or a single, uniform Christianity, in the name of that Christ that other Christians have found it possible to portray in all the colors, shapes, and sizes, of humanity.

Speaking in the language of ordinary affairs, we may say yet one more thing. It is that we are many things, not only Jews or Christians or Muslims, but fathers and sons, or mothers and daughters, athletes and artists, young and old and much else, including, I think above all, neighbors and friends. There is more to life than being Jewish or Christian or Muslim, and when we are only among Jews or Christians or Muslims, then we are conscious of many other things and no longer define ourselves by the Jewish or the Christian or the Muslim point of difference. And that is the human condition as we know it, and I should think, as much of humanity through much of history has known it. The fantasy of uniformity that makes possible segregationist Christianity, Judaism, or Islam, defies the everyday and the here and now of difference. And the difference is not by reason of religion exclusively or even mainly, because we differ from other people in a vast range of possible points of difference.

That is because we are many things, besides Jews or Christians or Muslims: we are human in all the ways in which life calls upon our humanity. The world calls upon us for many things, and if we respond in only one way, solely by reference to the Torah, Quran, or the Bible, we turn out to deny that humanity of ours that has given us hearts and minds and souls of our own, defined in our personhood. We are not only Jews, we are ourselves. Not only so, but learning comes to us not only in revelation but also in the use of our own reason, which the Torah frames as what we have in common with God, how in particular we are in God's image, after God's likeness. And, moreover, we experience the social world in diverse and complex settings, and the segregationist setting proves the least determinative. We do see the other as a person; we do live out a life of politics that defines the other not in terms of religion but of interest or right action. We do sustain a life of culture that defines what is interesting or puzzling or engaging not in terms of us and them, but the here and now of a fragile civilization and an impermanent social order. So my argument for integration appeals not to what is inevitable or merely serviceable, but to what is natural to the human condition. And I appeal not to secular but to religious, revealed truth: this is how God has made us, and it is, further, how, in the Torah, God has told us we have been made. If God had wanted us to segregate ourselves from the rest of humanity, God would not have formed within us that natural sympathy for the other that overcomes our sense of self. And if God had thought it best that in the here and now of the present age, we live wholly by ourselves, God would not have endowed us with the gift of grace to see ourselves in the other, and the other in ourselves. Swimming in the mainstream requires greater effort than paddling in the shallows. But it is natural to the human condition to make that effort. And that is why I have asked you to listen for so long to that Finlandssvenska that I so highly value and work so hard to try to learn.

Index

South Florida Studies in the History of Judaism

DATE DUE

DEMCO 38-297